D1345758

AT THE MASTER'S SIDE

AT THE MASTER'S SIDE

365 MEDITATIONS
FOR DOG-LOVERS

STEPHEN POXON

MONARCH
BOOKS

Text copyright © 2017 Stephen Poxon
This edition copyright © 2017 Lion Hudson

The right of Stephen Poxon to be identified as the author of this work has been asserted by him in accordance with the Copyright, Designs and Patents Act 1988.

Published by Monarch Books
an imprint of
Lion Hudson IP Ltd
Wilkinson House, Jordan Hill Road,
Oxford OX2 8DR, England
Email: monarch@lionhudson.com
www.lionhudson.com/monarch

ISBN 978 0 85721 745 5 (hardback)
ISBN 978 0 85721 907 7 (paperback)
e-ISBN 978 0 85721 746 2

First edition 2017

Acknowledgments
Every effort has been made to trace and contact copyright holders for material used in this book. We apologize for any inadvertent omissions or errors.
Scripture quotations taken from the Holy Bible, New International Version Anglicised. Copyright © 1979, 1984, 2011 Biblica, formerly International Bible Society. Used by permission of Hodder & Stoughton Ltd, an Hachette UK company. All rights reserved. "NIV" is a registered trademark of Biblica. UK trademark number 1448790.
Scripture taken from the New American Standard Bible®, Copyright © 1960, 1962, 1963, 1968, 1971, 1972, 1973, 1975, 1977, 1995 by The Lockman Foundation. Used by permission.
Extracts from The Authorized (King James) Version. Rights in the Authorized Version are vested in the Crown. Reproduced by permission of the Crown's patentee, Cambridge University Press.

Scripture quotations taken from The Holy Bible, English Standard Version® (ESV®) copyright © 2001 by Crossway, a publishing ministry of Good News Publishers. All rights reserved.
Scripture quotations taken from the Holy Bible, New Living Translation, copyright © 1996, 2004, 2007 by Tyndale House Foundation. Used by permission of Tyndale House Publishers, Inc., Carol Stream, Illinois 60188. All rights reserved.
New English Bible © Oxford University Press and Cambridge University Press 1961, 1970.
Scripture taken from the New King James Version. Copyright © 1982 by Thomas Nelson, Inc. Used by permission. All right reserved.
Scriptures quotations are from the Good News Bible © 1994 published by the Bible Societies/HarperCollins Publishers Ltd UK, Good News Bible© American Bible Society 1966, 1971, 1976, 1992. Used with permission.
Scripture quoted by permission. Quotations designated (NET) are from the NET Bible® copyright ©1996-2006 by Biblical Studies Press, L.L.C. http://bible.org All rights reserved.
p. 158: Lyrics from "What Can I say to Cheer a World Full of Sorrow?" by Miriam M. Richards taken from The Song Book of The Salvation Army © 2015, The General of the Salvation Army. Reprinted by permission.
p. 167–69: Extracts taken from Doctor Sangster by Paul E Sangster originally published by Epworth Press, 1962.
p. 256: Lyrics from "By the Love that Never Ceased to Hold Me" by Will J. Brand taken from The Song Book of The Salvation Army © 2015, The General of the Salvation Army. Reprinted by permission.
p. 337: Lyrics from "Take Thou My Life, Lord" by Colonel Brindley Boon taken from The Song Book of The Salvation Army © 2015, The General of the Salvation Army. Reprinted by permission.

A catalogue record for this book is available from the British Library

To human beings everywhere who love dogs, appreciate their company, and realize their worth.

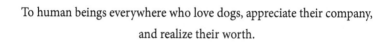

Abraham Lincoln

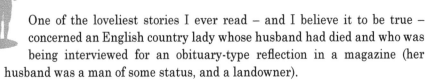

ACKNOWLEDGMENTS

One of the loveliest stories I ever read – and I believe it to be true – concerned an English country lady whose husband had died and who was being interviewed for an obituary-type reflection in a magazine (her husband was a man of some status, and a landowner).

Addressing various aspects of her bereavement, the lady then said, "Well, I never did care for the smell of wet dogs." Her husband had owned several dogs – mainly gun dogs – and was in the habit of allowing them to traipse through their house still wet from the fields or from time outside in the rain. Quite charmingly, the lady's love for her husband had always precluded her mentioning her dislike of that unique odour given off by wet dogs.

I mention that anecdote because it alludes well to some of the aspects of my own personal dog-owning. I am not a man of status or a landowner, but I am as guilty as the husband in the story of inflicting wet dogs, smelly dogs, perpetually hungry dogs, disobedient dogs and other recruits upon my wife and loved ones, with all the experiences that accompany my habit of adopting canines.

Suffice to say, I am truly and permanently indebted to my human life partners for their marvellously kind and endlessly patient approach towards my chaotic adventures with four-legged friends. Thank you, Heather, Jasmine and Alistair, for understanding my need of a dog around the house and for putting up with muddy floors, hairy furniture, cans of dog food in the fridge, and vet's bills. I am most grateful to you, too, for helping out with walks, especially when I can't be at home and it's raining or cold. Likewise, I am grateful to have had grandparents and parents whose hearts were soft and warm towards strays and mutts of all shapes, sizes, and abilities.

Our latest acquisition is Whisky, who features in these pages and who came to live with us when her owner died unexpectedly and the funeral director emailed me with news of her plight. In the words of my mum, "They must have seen you coming!" She (Whisky, not my mum) has settled in superbly, and keeps me company when I am working. Blind, deaf, and ancient she may be, but she is ours to shelter, feed, and enjoy. (She is of Irish stock, so perhaps we should be spelling her name as Whiskey with an "e", but as a teetotal Salvationist, I claim no expertise in such matters.)

What a happy and funny day it must have been, in the Courts of Heaven, when God gathered the angels around to show them his original blueprint for his invention of dogs! I suspect he never once regretted that decision.

My indebtedness also extends towards the equally patient team at Lion Hudson/Monarch.

Granted, I only ever trouble them with ideas, emails, and manuscripts in need of improvement, as opposed to dogs, but their kindness towards my endeavours in consistently impressive.

I am only too aware of the fact that my efforts are greatly enhanced because of their professional expertise.

INTRODUCTION

Which breed of dog is (or was) yours? A pedigree, perhaps? A mongrel, maybe? A rescued ratter, or a retired racer?

If you are perusing these pages, chances are, you are a dog lover. From the Queen of England with her collection of Corgis and Dorgis (a Dachshund/Corgi cross) to the homeless person with a faithful mongrel nestled in a blanket on the High Street, doggie fans have one thing in common; a shared concern for "man's best friend".

What, though, might dogs and God have in common? Can dogs teach us anything about God, or am I barking up the wrong tree? Within these pages, 365 dog stories are homed with Scripture verses to encourage, inform, and possibly even amuse. Use them as a dog might treat a puddle – to gaze upon with curiosity, to dip into, or to have a splash around. It might be that a line from a reflection will lead you towards a deeper concept. Maybe a thought will provide a timely, relevant contemplation for your day. I pray these readings will introduce reminders of his love into the lives of any who read them. As the year unfolds and the seasons change, and our experiences vary between good, bad, and indifferent, may our relationship with a loving Heavenly Father who delights in a multitude of mercies remain a rewarding constant.

NEW YEAR – OLD LOVE

God is love

(I JOHN 4:8 *NIV*)

Border Collies, beloved of shepherds and farmers, thrive when completely but kindly dominated by their owners. Linguists disagree on the origin of the name "Collie", some suggesting it comes from "collied" as in coal/coaled/black (Shakespeare described an event in *A Midsummer Night's Dream* as "Brief as the lightning in the collied night" – Act 1, Scene 1), with others pointing towards ancient Gaelic where "collie" is a derivative of the Irish for "useful". Whichever is correct, Borders live up to their Gaelic billing, responding as intelligently to instructions as Shakespearean thespians to their cues. Alsatians, though, can be more aloof, tending not to welcome strangers until formalities have been completed (try befriending one before it has deigned to like you and you'll discover that overfamiliarity may result in blood at first bite); neither are members of this dignified strain inclined to become immediate friends with visitors; secure in effortless superiority. Our dog, Meg (now departed), was hybrid – not as in half-electric and beneficial to the planet (her excessive production of methane marked her out as distinctly eco-unfriendly), but a Collie/Alsatian cross; appreciative of rules but still her own girl. More about Meg later, but, suffice to say, that old lady's personality was, like each of ours, unique.

The year ahead is as unspotted as a Dalmatian pup. God's grace, though, is ever old, yet ever new. There was never an hour when he failed to love; there wasn't last year, there won't be this year. Whatever John the Evangelist may or may not have known about dogs, he knew that God is love. God loves, generally, and God loves us, specifically, whatever our character traits; those that are pleasing, baffling, frustrating, or even frightening. He may not like everything we do, but he loves us too much to leave us as we are, and even our idiosyncrasies fall within his unrelenting plan to make us Christ-like (Romans 8:29). God's love is always at its zenith. It cannot dilute. Regardless of background, we are loved. If our bloodline is boast-worthy, we are loved. If our history is as chequered as that of Elvis Presley's "hound dog", we are loved.

BIRTHDAY BONE-US

This is the day which the Lord has made; Let us rejoice and be glad in it
(PSALM 118:24 **NASB**)

Today is my wife's birthday! We shall celebrate with gifts, cards, an off-tune rendition of "Happy Birthday to You", and cake. I'm a sentimental sort, and anniversaries cause me to nostalgically reflect upon life; I have even been known to ponder my preferred funeral arrangements – maudlin, apparently. Should my wife go Home before I do, then our offspring have instructions to install me somewhere in Northumberland, then find me a Rottweiler or a German Shepherd who is, like me, in need of companionship. The plan is for my children not to have to worry about Dad if his wife inhabits the Kingdom of Heaven while he remains in the Kingdom of Northumbria, alone, for they may live in the knowledge that I am safe, Rotties and GSDs being superbly loyal to their masters; willing even to put their own lives on the line if needs be. A Rottweiler approached me one day, in London's Battersea Park, placing her gigantic head on my lap as I sat on a bench. She was being walked by a staff member from Battersea Dogs' Home, where she lodged instead of wandering homeless, but was in need of a breather and somewhere to lay a very heavy head. We got on fine; she was the gentlest creature God ever invented, and I stroked her geriatric bonce as we chatted. I regret not adopting her, but Meg would certainly not have welcomed her as a rival for my/our affections.

Strong, yet gentle; the God who created earth, yet had nowhere to lay his head, relying upon friends for hospitality, and even having to borrow a tomb; paraded as a conman, beaten, and "treated worse than a dog". Yet, this battered, bullied, and bleeding God is unequalled in might; the Supreme Governor of the universe who embraced vulnerable weakness for our sakes; the all-powerful aligned with the powerless. St Anselm put it well: "I do not seek to understand so that I can believe, but I believe so that I may understand." Psalm 147 is testament to God's beautifully multi-dimensional nature. Lord God Almighty; truly, the God of the stars but, also, the God of our scars.

TERMS OF SURRENDER

Comfort ye, comfort ye my people, saith your God. Speak ye comfortably to Jerusalem, and cry unto her, that her warfare is accomplished, that her iniquity is pardoned

(ISAIAH 40:1–2 *KJV*)

Isaiah's glorious penmanship eloquently represents a God longing for reconciliation with wayward human beings. J. R. Ackerley, erstwhile editor of *The Listener*, was an opinionated man; a sparky personality who regarded life as a battle. Likewise, an Alsatian Ackerley stole/adopted from his neighbours was a dog who shared a combative approach to living. Ackerley wrote in *My Dog Tulip:*

It was upon Tulip's first home that I blamed her unsociable conduct. She had originally belonged to some working-class people who, though fond of her in their way, seldom took her out ... For nearly a year she scarcely left their house, but spent her time, mostly alone, for they were at work all day, in a tiny backyard ... the only "training" she ever received was an occasional thrashing for the destruction which her owners discovered when they returned home. Alsatians in particular do not take kindly to beatings; they are too intelligent and too nervous. It was from this life, when she was eighteen months old, that I rescued her.[1]

Tulip became the love of his life, he the love of hers. Two creatures at war with the world taught each other how to give and receive love; great friends who came to know and trust one another.

Perhaps the most amazing quality of grace is that God is willing to enter into dialogue with those who withstand his prerequisites of armistice. We are, by nature, at odds with God. Our rebel emotions resist surrender. The Prince of Peace, though, stands, arms outstretched, holding the contract offering pardon. It bears a crimson royal hallmark. Yet, we resist his approach, and sometimes even snap and snarl, strangely preferring the confines of our own imprisonment to life in all its fullness. Even when a rescue is proposed, we hesitate. The leash that constrains us, though it accounts for our disquiet, is preferred to the everlasting embrace of a loving Master. So too, the walls behind which we try to find security. Our missing peace depends upon us signing that contract, bringing to an end a feud that is then silenced by forgiveness and bathed in mercy. Furthermore, God is magnanimous in victory, not lauding it over us when we lay our crowns before him.

---

1   J. R. Ackerley, *My Dog Tulip* (New York: New York Review Books, 1965)

LOVE CHANGES EVERYTHING

You did not choose me, but I chose you
(JOHN 15:16 **NIV**)

Before we assumed ownership, Meg belonged to another pack, the senior member of which was George. Chatting with George's friends after his passing, I was aware of some kind of spell being cast by Meg. She and I had hardly met, previously; she had half-heartedly barked at me once or twice, but I had never been worth the courtesy of a genuine growl. Yet, here she was, staring, listening, and tilting her head with every intonation. (Why, incidentally, do dogs do that head tilting thing? Are they listening to us?) Jerome K. Jerome, whose famous book *Three Men in a Boat* was less famously subtitled *To Say Nothing of the Dog*, wrote:

[Dogs] never talk about themselves but listen to you while you talk about yourself, and keep up an appearance of being interested in the conversation.[1]

Meg did just that, understanding every word. She had figured I might be the one come to adopt her, and wasn't about to let the moment slip. I once read about someone "applying the gimlet eye" and was intrigued by this little phrase, discovering that a "gimlet" is "a tool for drilling small holes". I cannot better "the gimlet eye" as a way of describing the glare of which I was the recipient/victim. Far from me being there to choose Meg, she had chosen me!

Is it incredulous that God should take any interest in us? Maybe, but he does! Psalm 8 confirms that. Our text tells us we are chosen by Jesus for his service, much as we might be tempted to look around in search of some cosmic mistake. Jesus has chosen us as his friends! This selection process is known as the *dotation spirituelle* or "spiritual endowment". Financial advisors deal in endowment policies, the idea of which is that if someone invests, say, £1, it might one day become £2. Jesus has invested in us; a colossal investment that cost him his all, with no guaranteed returns. We are chosen people.

---

1   J. K. Jerome, *Three Men in a Boat* (Ware: Wordsworth Editions Limited, 1993)

THE CALL OF CHRIST

While he was still a long way off, his father saw him and was filled with
compassion for him; he ran to his son, threw his arms round him and kissed him
(LUKE 15:20 **NIV**. SEE ALSO LUKE 15:11–32)

On this day in 1943, Elizabeth Taylor appeared in *Lassie Come Home*. The film was a box-office success, attracting profits of $2,249,000, with a plot involving the Carraclough family, struggling to make ends meet in Yorkshire, who are forced to sell their Rough Collie, Lassie, to the Duke of Rudling, in Scotland. Cue Lassie looking back with a pitiful gaze to camera as the Carracloughs wring flat caps, weep into aprons, and wave goodbye. Fast forward to the day when Lassie is so homesick, she makes a break for freedom; climbing mountains, swimming lochs, surviving assassination attempts from gamekeepers, scaling fences, and living on scraps, all so she can follow the scent back to Yorkshire and look once again to camera while the youngest Carraclough (Elizabeth Taylor's little brother) clasps her (Lassie, not his sister) to his bosom. The film was adapted from a novel written by Eric Oswald Mowbray Knight; son of a diamond merchant, and a novelist, soldier, artist, reporter, Hollywood screenwriter, and (in his spare time) breeder of Collies. Knight the novelist demonstrated an empathy with "the human condition", entering into the emotional lot of working-class people; their aspirations, frustrations, hopes and dreams, giving voice to those whose stories were otherwise unnoticed. Lassie made it home. MGM made their money, Elizabeth Taylor set out for stardom, Lassie probably received a juicy bone for her contribution, Knight collected his royalties, and filmgoers sobbed their way to a happy ending.

Lassie's parting from a loving family was brought about by financial necessity. We read today, though, of the son who left home because he thought having a bit of spare cash would solve his problems, whose motivation was selfish greed. How reassuring it is to know that whenever we drift away from a close relationship with our Heavenly Father, he never ceases to agitate for our return, whether we are "away from home" for days, weeks, months or decades. Whatever the reason for our departure, God the Father does all he can to woo us back to his embrace. If and when we come home, he celebrates, for ours is not a distant God, but a God who, in Christ, proved himself to be at empathy with our dire straits and weaknesses. He is not only the Divine Empathiser, but is uniquely capable of helping us through, out, and up again, watching for our return a thousand times more keenly than even young Master Carraclough ever longed to set eyes upon Lassie again.

HOLY ORDERS

You are a chosen people, a royal priesthood
(I PETER 2:9 **NIV**)

Another novelist, Georges Bernanos, mentioned a "big dog" in his novel *The Diary of a Country Priest*.

The priest in question, unwell, visits his doctor, Dr Delbende, a rural GP with a reluctance to wash his hands before examinations:

"While he was examining me his big dog, lying across the threshold, followed each of his movements with extraordinary eyes, full of adoration. 'You're not up to much,' he said. 'Take a look at that' (he seemed to be calling his dog to witness)."

Post-examination, priest and doctor are chatting, when the medic professes a fatherly interest in the father:

"When you're feeling too fed up for words, you come round and see me. I wouldn't say that to anybody. But the Curé de Torcy has talked to me about you, and you've got the kind of eyes I like. Faithful eyes, dog's eyes. I've got dog's eyes too."[1]

Delbende's unhygienic ways are responsible for a decline in the demand for his services. He talks to his dog during consultations, informing his companion of every diagnosis and asking the dog's opinion of prescriptions. The big dog cannot, of course, offer advice as it lies on the surgery floor. Nevertheless, Delbende informs his silent partner of every step taken, and at the conclusion of each interview, Delbende's pet moves towards the patient, offering comfort ("the dog came and laid its head on my knees").

God has (riskily?) entrusted the spread of the gospel to priests, parsons, popes, pious people, pew-fillers, and parishioners! The spectacularly imperfect Church is charged with the responsibility of infusing righteousness, peace, and joy. Thankfully, grace prevails, and God's people are never once abandoned in the discharge of their responsibilities. Humbly and gently, while we preach, prepare, publicise, and proclaim (and procrastinate!), the Spirit of Jesus hovers, encouraging and blessing. He is, in many ways, a silent partner, yet One who is aware of every prognosis necessary for deep discipleship and meaningful mission. In truth, he is not at all silent, for his influence upon the Church comes in the form of a still, small voice, diagnosing and prescribing as he sees fit. In reality, God's strategy is not the least risky, should we but trust the Great Physician for the healing of the nations, for with exquisite tenderness, the Spirit of Holiness draws alongside those whose spiritual health is waning, resting with us to impart a solace unavailable elsewhere.

1   G. Bernanos, *The Diary of a Country Priest* (London: Boriswood, 1937)

GRACE IRRESISTIBLE

All those the Father gives me will come to me
(JOHN 6:37 **NIV**)

Staring at a dog, eye-to-eye, is never a great idea! Prolonged eye contact between dogs is reminiscent of a scene in Quentin Tarantino's *Reservoir Dogs,* whereby a tense three-way stand-off occurs between armed men and aggression loads the air as heavily as lead as each waits for the other to make a move; the first of Tarantino's characters to avert his gaze might well end up in hospital (if he's lucky). Likewise, the dog who looks away first is the submissive one, while the dog who maintains a stare is dominant. If neither looks away, a dogfight ensues. Replicating such behaviour towards a dog is unadvisable! (On such occasions, the eyes don't have it.) However, despite my best efforts at following such wisdom on the fateful day Meg became mine, I was out-stared by a dog who wouldn't relinquish her gaze, my flag of surrender as white as Tintin's fictional terrier, Snowy. I had been wrong-footed, and our family increased by one. Emotional and tactical blackmail such as that executed by Meg should be outlawed! Jeremiah, the prophet of old, knew about her kind: "Are they ashamed of their detestable conduct? No, they have no shame at all; they do not even know how to blush" (Jeremiah 6:15 *NIV*). I hadn't exactly been sold a pup, but I certainly didn't emerge from negotiations as top dog. I had made a dog's dinner of things!

Life can do to us what Meg did to me – make us feel as though we have lost control when we would much prefer to remain in charge! Usually, the consequences are relatively unimportant, but problems arise if and when we insist on governance of our destiny, stubbornly refusing concepts of lordship and offers of help. How many of us secretly sing, Sinatra-esque, "I did it my way" while all the time realizing, deep down, that our best option is to do it God's way? We're like that, us human beings (were we not, there would be no need of a Saviour). The yoke Jesus invites us to share is easy, and the burden light; something like the harness and rein system sometimes used to keep children safe; bestowed in love for our own good by a loving Lord.

CENTRE STAGE

All of them rushed into the theatre together
(ACTS 19:29 **NIV**)

Richard Wilson, the Scots-born actor probably best known for his television role as the malcontent Victor Meldrew, is one of a number of stars who have given of their time to support a small theatre in the English town of Frinton-on-Sea, helping to secure its long-term future. The theatre has marked a special anniversary with a series of plays starring famous artistes, and Wilson had the lead in *The Dog*, a three-parter telling the story of a counsellor who likens his professional relationships with his clients to his relationship with his dog in order to give counsel. (Wilson, according to press releases, does not own a dog, but has a soft spot for Labradors.) Several dogs auditioned for the part of *The Dog*, the title role being awarded to an ex-trainee Guide Dog called Darcy (Grace in the play). Rumour has it that Darcy/Grace, a Golden Retriever, with her brown eyes and glossy coat, easily upstaged the veteran Wilson, leaving us to wonder if he used his Meldrew catchphrase, "I don't believe it!"

The Incarnation of Christ is arguably the most remarkable story imaginable; a script even the most talented playwright would struggle to create. That God should consider visiting earth in order to rekindle humankind's interest in all that is good is a storyline so wonderful it required an entire planet as backdrop. Whereas *The Dog* is a work of fiction, the drama that is "The God" is entirely true; a stunning three-parter detailing the life, death, and resurrection of the biggest name of all – the ultimate performance, with the Messiah never once coming close to being upstaged. God sent his Son to save us, then emerged from the wings, as it were, in the gracious form of the Holy Spirit, and we are invited not only to "witness" these events by reading the screenplay known as the Bible, but we are given the opportunity of adding our names to the cast list. In Christ, God has made that possible. The long-term outlook for those who embrace the biggest break of all is marvellous. Unlike Victor Meldrew, we do believe it!

SHADOWLANDS

Now we see through a glass, darkly; but then face to face: now I know in part; but then shall I know even as also I am known

(I CORINTHIANS 13:12 **KJV**)

Meg's eyesight, as she approached the conclusion of her days, was blighted by cataracts, giving her an unfortunate tendency to sometimes lurch towards traffic she hadn't seen. Despite that, Meg's eyes came in useful during those moments of awkward silence at church outreach events; Alpha meals and the like; barbecues arranged in that strange way Christians have of offering burgers and chicken legs to strangers in the hope of them (the strangers, not the chicken legs) becoming disciples – "My dog's got cataracts, has yours? Would you like to become a Christian? Scripture exposition is every third Wednesday in the month. Sausage?" Evangelical asset though she might have been, Meg was often unable to make out anything more than silhouettes, and would wander off with men who just happened to share my build (see Mark 8:24 for an insight into her world). I can but hope that if all dogs really do go to Heaven, as Disney would have us believe, then her peepers are now perfect, for the reality was that age did her few favours. The puppy had become a pensioner, then the pensioner passed away.

Unpalatable though it might be, the actuality of our existence is that we blossom as flowers, then fade. This life is but a speck on a broad canvas. The great Christian hope, though, is that those who leave this life in Christ are welcomed into an existence so wonderful he called it Paradise. I have no idea what Heaven is like, despite the Bible's best hints, but physical dimensions and tangible qualities are unimportant. It will be perfect, but that is less to do with pearly gates, streets of gold or rivers of crystal than the brilliant omnipresence of God, and those saved by grace will abide with him in uninterrupted bliss, where the tribulations of our earthly years will seem inconsequential. The sting of death is blunted. The end is seen as but the beginning. We shall be changed, in the twinkling of an eye completely free of cataracts!

LIFE PARTNERS

God said, "It is not good for the man to be alone"
(GENESIS 2:18 **NIV**)

History teaches that dogs and humans have worked in partnership for thousands of years; the dogs guarding, working as beasts of burden, and hunting or retrieving in exchange for food, warmth, and shelter. Wolves who loitered with intent around primitive areas of human habitation figured out there were leftovers available, which titbit of knowledge led them to become increasingly brave in their approach, which in turn led them to actually *want* to be close(r) to people. Those people, battling the elements in a dog-eat-dog world, realized that a livestock guardian dog was a more effective means of defence than a stick and loud voice, and a pattern of trust evolved; one which any sled driver would verify, any Royal Canadian Mounted Police Officer patrolling the inhospitable Yukon with a German Shepherd would vouch for, and any hearing impaired, visually impaired or physically handicapped person dependent upon an assistance dog would confirm. Researchers have compiled charts demonstrating which breeds are most suited to certain types of labour, and while some of their conclusions are as obvious as a St Bernard at a cat show, the research shows some wonderful partnerships have been forged.

God does not need us, but we do – astonishingly – fulfil his intrinsic need to love. He does not depend upon us, but love, by definition, cannot be fulfilled without actually loving. Hunger drove those wily wolves to approach base camps, and a fundamental hunger to love and be loved drove God to embrace the unreceptive dwelling places of his beloved; Galilee, Gethsemane, and Golgotha. Why human beings should be the object of his passion is beyond comprehension, but we are, and our understanding of matters is less important than our faith in them. To imagine that God voluntarily approached hostile domiciles as a defenceless man is – almost – beyond belief. He had everything to lose and, apparently, very little to gain. Very little, that is, until we consider the worth of our souls in his estimation.

HOME FROM HOME

Jesus said to them, "A prophet is not without honour except in his own town, among his relatives and in his own home"
(MARK 6:4 **NIV**)

Meg needed generous amounts of patience as she adjusted to bereavement, adoption, and unfamiliar routines. Her disorientation was palpable as she struggled to please, but didn't know how. Likewise, the aggression she occasionally demonstrated by way of emotional management, snapping at us as she tried to snap into a way of life that was frightening. Everything familiar had been left behind; voices, faces, games, home comforts; everyone she had known. There was a touch of the evacuee about her as she realized she would now be sleeping in a strange kitchen every night, walking new routes each day, hearing noises and smelling smells to which she was unaccustomed. A blend of love, discipline, care, and tolerance was called for as Meg settled in. Celebrity dog behaviourist, Cesar Millan, teaches that those who introduce dogs to new homes should do so gradually, prescribing guidelines for such introductions, including a walk around the block before the new pet enters one's house, so as to familiarise the stranger with the area. He also recommends giving the newcomer time to map out which odours belong to whom. I'm afraid I failed Meg in nearly all respects, and ignorance prevailed as I thrust her into a brand-new situation. Nevertheless, she coped, and slowly regained her equilibrium.

What passed through Jesus' mind as he realized he was no ordinary person? Did he glimpse his pre-incarnate existence? As the umbilical cord was severed, was there any sense in which the regal cord holding him to the splendour of his heavenly home tugged at his heartstrings? Was he homesick? Did the Christ of the human road experience flashbacks? Luke 2:41–52 is an intriguing account of an incident in the life of the boy Jesus. Aged twelve, he wanders away from Mum and Dad, who were in Jerusalem for the Jewish equivalent of Greenbelt; notwithstanding their frantic search for their missing son, it is amazing that it transpires he had been holding court in the Temple courts, debating theology! What must the theologians have made of this young pup chipping in with his two shekels' worth of insight? What might he have thought of their ponderings on the nature of God, and how many of their rules could serve as helps to holiness? Was he tempted to drop hints that he was God, sitting there, in their midst? His home was in Nazareth. His heart was in Heaven. He enjoyed dual citizenship, with a birth certificate stamped "Bethlehem" and a heart stamped "Gloryland". Wonderfully, because he entered humanity, his followers enter Paradise.

UP AND DOWN THE CITY STREETS

*"Here I am! I stand at the door and knock. If anyone hears my voice and opens
the door, I will come in and eat with that person, and they with me"*
(REVELATION 3:20 **NIV**)

As I write, HMV, the company once promoted as "the home of entertainment",
has gone bust. The demise of HMV is sad, not least because the picture of Nipper,
the HMV dog, will no longer grace our streets; Nipper, a Jack Russell, cocking
an ear to a gramophone scratching out a recording of His Master's Voice. The
Terrier that inspired the artwork (christened Nipper, incidentally, because he
nipped at the legs of people he didn't like), is buried in Kingston upon Thames,
England, where a bank stands nowadays, a brass plaque commemorating the
famous dog lying beneath the building. Someone with a fair bit in common
with Nipper is Norman Hunter, a former professional footballer with Leeds
United FC and England. Hunter played 108 games for Bristol City FC and
Nipper was born in Bristol, in 1884. Nipper defended his territory fiercely, and
Norman Hunter defended his penalty area with a Terrier-like commitment.
He also had a reputation for biting legs; not literally, of course – he didn't
ever actually sink his teeth into flesh as Nipper did, but he was ferocious in
the tackle, and was famously nicknamed "Bites Yer Legs" Hunter. Nipper and
Norman; loved by many, instantly recognized, and assured of their respective
places in entertainment history.

Nipper was made famous by promotional campaigns carried out by HMV. Norman Hunter
was known to thousands on account of his televised appearances at packed stadia and twenty-
eight games for England. Jesus, by contrast, never appeared in front of a television camera.
Neither did he preach before great crowds. No billboard publicity was given to his personal
appearances. He was largely anonymous, and even the story of his crucifixion made only minor
local news; just a matter of miles outside Calvary, it wasn't even noted. Yet, his name is the most
famous on the planet, and his gospel has filtered its way into every corner of the globe. That
remarkable fact ought to make us consider his divine power afresh. This same Jesus makes his
way into lives that will receive him; he enters hearts unseen and brings about transformation.
He doesn't nip or bite his way in, but comes full of grace and truth.

A DISAPPOINTING DEITY?

*I offered my back to those who beat me, my cheeks to those who pulled out my
beard; I did not hide my face from mocking and spitting*

(ISAIAH 50:6 **NIV**)

When I was growing up, we had two dogs. Fred, a Border Collie, my brothers
and I found wandering the streets. Whether Fred was a stray or not, we
weren't sure. He looked in good condition, but he also looked lost, so, erring on
the side of compassion, but also because it was a lark, we enticed him home
and introduced him to our parents. Mum and Dad, Salvation Army officers,
parents of five, and therefore used to most of what life had to throw at them,
received his arrival with equanimity. Fred joined our family, but was never
particularly at home with us, spending most of his time behind the settee,
eating sticky tape, before upping and leaving, no doubt in search of a less
chaotic household and more sticky tape. Scruffy, a Border Terrier, was adopted
by my parents when they rescued him from beatings on our council estate;
bedraggled, frightened, and desperately needing shelter. Scruffy attached
himself to Mum, and never really trusted anyone else, shaking whenever I
stroked him. He couldn't be trusted not to bite, and after a few happy(ish)
years, during which he never recovered from the trauma of his youth, Mum
reluctantly decided to have Scruffy put to sleep. He couldn't manage life. Mum
keeps a framed picture of Scruffy – a reminder not only of a pet who never
really stood a chance, but also of the importance of kindness.

The Gospels present a Christ who is fully God and fully man. Hebrews 4:15 tells us he was
"tempted in every way" (NIV). It is not, therefore, disrespectful to imagine he was tempted to
be terrified when he was beaten with a degree of violence so severe it would make newspaper
headlines even today, in a world inured to thuggery. Might we argue that panic ill becomes an
incarnate God? Does it disappoint us that our human God probably shook with panic as he
was punched and kicked? Do we lose faith in him because he almost certainly gave way to fear?
Not at all. On the contrary; we are drawn to love Jesus all the more because he shows us a
vulnerable God willing to undergo humiliation for our sakes, demonstrating bravery that put
his accusers to shame and courage to stay the blood-splattered course. This is our God, and
he is not even remotely disappointing.

A GRAVE CONCERN

"I was dead … I am alive for ever and ever!"
(REVELATION 1:18 **NIV**)

It could never be said that my dad was a gardener. Granted, he excelled at bringing people trays of tea as they sat in his garden, but that was the extent of his horticultural interest. He could, though, dig holes with an astute comprehension of which end of the spade should be handled and which placed in the soil, and it was as Dad was digging one day (no one knows why) that he discovered a plastic bag full of dead puppies. We have no idea how they got there, why they were buried, or who buried them, and I have no recollection of what happened next, but I do recall a sense of sadness that someone had buried six puppies. Maybe they had died naturally, and this had been a reluctant burial. Possibly, they had been killed, though it's hard to think why as, even if they were unwanted, they could have been sold for a profit. It seemed such an awful pity those puppies never had the chance to become dogs, a pity intensified in poignancy by the fact their black fur looked new, shining like their plastic coffin. Dad, not knowing what to do with his furry find, reburied the pups. The mystery continues.

A legend tells of Satan's displeasure at God's plan to brighten up the barren landscape of the newly created earth by scattering seeds. Dismayed by the fact that the seeds would produce brightly coloured flowers, Satan decided to wreck the plan by burying them deep in soil, denying them access to light. Then he covered the soil with water, hoping to rot them. This diabolical plan failed miserably as far from rotting, the seeds blossomed beautifully, turning swathes of land into God's palette. Jesus had taught on the principle of the seed being buried in order to germinate and produce new life, but how must his disciples have felt when they saw their leader's corpse being lifted into a borrowed tomb? Hope had died. Their dreams were in tatters. Praise God, though, he was crypt-confined only briefly, and up from the grave he arose, demonstrating that death is but a chapter, not the end of the story. At least that much of the mystery has been solved. It is up to us to dig deep to find out more!

TENACIOUS TRACKING

Your goodness and love will follow me
(PSALM 23:6 *NIV*)

A sketch in the television sitcom of yesteryear, *Dad's Army*, shows the hapless Private Pike at the mercy of Bloodhounds baying for his, well, blood. Pike had had to dress in the uniform of a German soldier on account of his own uniform being too wet to wear, thanks to a series of watery misadventures. Unfortunately, the uniform in question smells strongly of aniseed, highly attractive to dogs. The garb is to be used in training exercises, to assist the Bloodhounds in the capture of enemy soldiers on British soil, the theory being that the dogs would learn to ignore personnel in His Majesty's uniforms and hunt down those representing Germany. The desperate Private Pike is unable to shake off the hounds, and nothing is helped by the fact that the pack is under the control of the witless Captain Cadbury, whose ability to maintain order is severely limited. Captain Mainwaring, Officer Commanding, orders his men to cross a river in the mistaken belief that the Bloodhounds will lose the scent in water, but Pike falls headlong into the river and has to continue manoeuvres wearing only a potato sack. He does his best to march alongside his comrades, insofar as it is possible to march wearing a sack, and in the distance, it is possible to hear the howls of the Bloodhounds. They have discovered the abandoned uniform and no longer have any interest in Pike as their prey!

George Mueller, renowned for his faith, prayed for one of his friends for fifty years. Nothing happened during Mueller's lifetime, but that friend came to Christ as a result of the message preached at Mueller's funeral service. May we liken Mueller's God to a Bloodhound, insofar as he longs that not one soul should perish and is relentless in his concern? The story of the penitent thief on a cross shows us a great deal about the nature of God; he will pursue us with a deathless love even if we have just a few short breaths left in our lungs, and is truly the God of the eleventh hour. I commend to you Francis Thompson's poem 'The Hound of Heaven'. It is not a straightforward piece of literature, but worth the excavation it demands. In it, Thompson describes the chase embarked upon by God as he woos a reluctant convert; the twists and turns of the hunt as God remains on the trail throughout every hide-and-seek moment of objection, rejection, and procrastination; surely, a love that will not let us go.

IGNORANCE IS NOT BLISS

What great love the Father has lavished on us, that we should be called children of God!

(1 JOHN 3:1 **NIV**)

As I write, we are hoping to adopt Finn, whom we found on a rehoming website. We have completed the paperwork, presented ourselves as a normal family (well, they'll never know), and promised to look after Finn should he be entrusted to our care. Finn is more Shetland Pony than dog – a gentle giant; handsome, ten years old, arthritic, and placid. He doesn't enjoy great health, and on vet's orders must only walk for half an hour at a time. He is averse to anyone touching his hips, and has been known to snap at children who fail to heed warnings. Finn's owner can't be at home much, which means he (Finn) is left in the garden all day, barking quite a bit. Half Burmese Mountain Dog, his bark would come in handy up a mountain in Burma, but is a tad out of place in suburban Hertfordshire. Our hope, above all, is that Finn finds a good home, for sitting in the garden all day is a lonesome assignment – soul-destroying and entirely unsuitable, and if his heart is even half as massive as his physique, he must feel these woes keenly. If only he knew how enthusiastically we registered our interest; that would bring a wag to his impressive tail!

How it must weigh upon God's heart, that so many wander through life without realizing he longs to adopt them. What sadness God must endure, watching people meandering along, ignorant of the fact their adoption papers are already stamped with Heaven's approval. Yet, meander we do – some for an entire lifetime – fearing God, worrying about punishment, thinking ourselves beyond mercy. The mists of doubt swirl around us, shadows of unbelief obscure our vision, and we have little idea of the fact that all the love in the universe is but a whisper away. We persist in loneliness, convinced of exclusion, never daring to imagine that God might wish to embrace us, forgive us, and keep us. Finn has no knowledge of the efforts being made on his behalf, but what a tragedy it is that so many experience years in the wilderness, ignorant of the arrangements that have been made for them to step immediately into their inheritance.

LOVE AND LOYALTY

God ... will never leave you nor forsake you
(DEUTERONOMY 31:6 **NIV**)

Failing Finn, we have put our names down for Bob from Battersea Dogs' Home, an elegant, long-haired tortoiseshell boy of indeterminate breed (my guess would be Border Collie/Lady as in the film *Lady and the Tramp*, if you get the picture). No one knows much about Bob; rescued as a stray, he has chosen to keep his past private, and all the Battersea website reveals is that he is "a worried boy" demonstrating behaviour causing concern; whether he is a bank robber, pickpocket or master forger, no one seems to be aware. Neither are we told what it is he worries about; politics? The price of biscuits? The weather? Brian Clough, legendary football manager, specialized in alchemy whereby he would take on players regarded as troublemakers, rehome them in his teams, and mould gold from base materials, welcoming footballers other managers offloaded. Gamblers, drinkers, truants, smokers, overweight veterans, and those with shoddy disciplinary records were his stock-in-trade, and not only because he could pick them up without spending much. He turned miscreants into medal winners, one such player being Kenny Burns, who had a reputation as a wild-boy gambler. Clough liked him as a footballer, but was concerned about Burns' reliability, so had him followed, tracking his movements only to discover Burns drank in moderation and backed greyhounds with modest amounts. Clough bought Burns for a snip of a fee and turned him into a European Cup champion.

Perhaps the only limitations to God's grace are those we ourselves impose? Is it possible we sometimes make God in our own image and ascribe to him a meanness of spirit that finds it difficult to believe in his enthusiasm for "lost causes"? Might we even keep our Redeemer at arm's length in the belief that our sins have exhausted his capacity to restore? God is not deterred by rotten reputations, but makes it his business to spot potential, being only too willing to declare an interest in the discarded. He lovingly tracks us, aware of our failings, with the sole (soul) intention of working on our weaknesses, undeterred by what others think of us. Thank God for his wonder-working power, turning those the world regards as write-offs unworthy of a second chance into those who are more than conquerors. God's grace is such that if and when we fail or resort to old sins, he keeps faith with us; he loves, convicts, forgives, and maintains a skilled work of improvement.

CHRIST FOR THE WORLD

God so loved the world that he gave his one and only Son, that whoever believes in
him shall not perish but have eternal life
(JOHN 3:16 *NIV*)

Speaking of football (Germans and Scots may wish to look away now), England won the World Cup in 1966 with a 4–2 victory over West Germany. There was some dispute about whether one of Geoff Hurst's three goals actually crossed the line, but as every Englishman knows, it almost certainly, probably did. Unbeknown to the watching thousands that day, another drama was unfolding behind the scenes, in that the Jules Rimet trophy had been stolen from its display case at an exhibition at the Methodist Westminster Central Hall (though no Methodists were implicated). The sensational story was global news within hours, as Scotland Yard detectives launched a search, and a series of intriguing developments ensued involving mysterious telephone calls and clandestine arrangements for ransoms. The trophy remained at large until a man by the name of David Corbett was walking his dog, Pickles, a Mixed Breed Collie, when Pickles sniffed at a parcel lying beneath a hedge. There, wrapped in newspaper, was the World Cup! Pickles became a celebrity, and an embarrassing crisis was avoided. He saved the day, and the tournament! History was made.

What a marvellous rescue plan was enacted when Jesus went to Calvary! With a world in peril, God sent his Son to resolve the problem and rescue the lost. What was looking dangerously like a crashing defeat for the forces of good was spectacularly turned into a memorable victory when Jesus died to pay the price of sin, then rose from the dead to signal his triumph over the forces of evil and death. England's captain in 1966, Bobby Moore, drenched in sweat, lifted the Jules Rimet trophy high, at Wembley Stadium, as evidence of a stirring success for his team; the only Englishman ever to skipper a side to World Cup glory. Jesus Christ, drenched in blood, was lifted high, at Calvary, so that he might draw all people to himself; the only Saviour, escorting his people to Glory. His cross looms large over human history as the unmatched emblem of grace.

MISTAKEN IDENTITY

Salvation is found in no one else, for there is no other name under heaven given to mankind by which we must be saved

(ACTS 4:12 **NIV**)

This tale involves a Salvation Army lady, her husband, and their dog. The narrative is that Hubbie had "frequently" told his wife that he did not want a big dog; he had made the point in no uncertain terms, despite having a soft spot for dogs, maintaining his stance their house was too small to accommodate a giant pet. Unfortunately, his beloved fell in love with a puppy Boston Great Dane (now weighing in at fifteen stone and munching his way through £37 worth of food each week, including a cooked breakfast of four fried eggs and several sausages every morning), and told Husband her tiny 1lb 5oz surprise purchase was a Jack Russell Terrier! Now kept in a three-acre paddock for (a great deal of) exercise and protected from the British elements by wearing an outdoor horse coat, he is Britain's biggest canine. The lady in question admits she "told a little fib" in order to trick her husband but, thankfully, their unexpected guest is loved by them both, and divorce papers have not been served. (The health, or otherwise, of their bank balance remains unknown.)

We live in a pick 'n' mix society, spiritually speaking. The rule of thumb seems to be that we are at liberty to create God in our image; which, literally speaking, we are, in that we have freedom to worship a block of wood, a lump of metal, or an elephant, should we wish to, or to ascribe deity to trees, rivers or mountains. Likewise, we may choose from any number of religions on offer in our pursuit of a spiritual connection. "Two-a-penny" hardly does it justice. However, just because something or someone is referred to as a god, and revered as holy and an object of worship, it ain't necessarily so! A Boston Great Dane can be sold as a Jack Russell every day of the week, but that doesn't, and can't, make it one, as the couple in our story now know, only too well! The New Testament makes no bones about the fact that Jesus is God. There is no trickery at work, and no deception. He is who he is, eternally.

DYING TO LIVE

A man of sorrows, and acquainted with grief
(ISAIAH 53:3 **KJV**)

En route to work, I saw a Yorkshire Terrier appear as though from nowhere and run into the road. The chances of that little Yorkie avoiding the traffic were minimal, and to my horror, I watched as it went under the wheels of an oncoming van. Not wishing to paint myself as a hero, I nevertheless stopped my car and went over to see how the dog was as it lay motionless, by which time the van driver had driven off, probably not even realizing what had passed beneath his tyres. The Terrier was in a terrible state, and suffice to say, died as I stroked him. I had advised his distraught owner to fetch a box and a towel, so that we could rush him to a vet, but I'm afraid nothing could be done and, within minutes, there was no need of either box or surgery. Entirely unexpectedly, his owner then launched into quite some verbal attack on me personally (as I wiped her dog's blood from my gloves); shock and grief had hit her with considerably more force than the van ever hit her pet, and her initial outlet for same was to blame me for failing to note the van's registration number. No offence taken; it was all perfectly understandable, as healthy bereavement needs a voice, especially in the immediate, so I quietly and gently left her nursing her darling departed.

There is a line in Gone With the Wind: "Death, taxes and childbirth! There's never any convenient time for any of them." I don't earn enough to pass significant comment on paying taxes, and I certainly don't intend to make any statement on childbirth, but we all, at some time or another, encounter death, be that in the form of bereavement or the pain of standing alongside a friend as they say farewell to a loved one – or, indeed, the moment of our own Home Call. What a glory, then, that we serve a God who cares and understands. His deep acquaintance with grief qualifies him as the One to turn to in our darkest hour, and he is big enough to hear us when we cry, or shout, or berate, or vent our despairing, questioning, heartbroken fury. God knows; and that, when we sense the cold valley of death near, is enough.

BAGGAGE HANDLING

Sell your possessions and give to the poor
(MATTHEW 19:21 **NIV**)

I sometimes watch a television programme about people addicted to hoarding, and I find it fascinating, painful, and sad. Adults who hold down responsible jobs and often run families too, obsessively collect pretty much anything, from toys to yellowed newspapers to Victoriana, until their living space (and sometimes their garage or shed as well) is cluttered with dusty items. One episode featured a man unable to part with anything linked to his dog, as he was convinced throwing away anything to do with his beloved pet constituted betrayal. Empty, used dog food tins were hoarded as treasure, and as the cameras rolled, this man demonstrated emotional meltdown when asked to collect bundles of dog hair from his carpets, to be thrown away. Several football-sized amounts of the stuff were rounded up, as his dog had malted over the years without once being followed by a vacuum cleaner, and this man was distraught at the thought of relinquishing the hair to the waiting refuse bags, believing it to be part of his dog he was throwing out. He saw it as bereavement, and my heart went out to him.

None of us is too dissimilar to the televised hoarders, much as we might like to think we differ. The rich man Jesus spoke to in today's text might well have been smart and presentable, with a house/palace to match but, in essence, we all share this intrinsic problem of hanging on to worldly goods – or, at least, awarding them an exaggerated importance in our lives. Don't we? If not for its monetary value, is it possible we hold on to stuff because of its sentimental value? That new suite of furniture we simply must have; that fitted kitchen we can't live without, or those family heirlooms with which we can't bear to part; not exactly the same, granted, but similar in principle. If not items of any particular worth, what of those pairs of shoes, for example, languishing at the bottom of a wardrobe, rarely worn? What do we do if we sense that gracious little nudge from God's Holy Spirit that he has a better use for our hoarded resources? Do we sell up and give away, or do we keep? Do we hoard or help?

PULLING THE WOOL OVER OUR EYES

*Jesus said … "I am the good shepherd. The good shepherd lays down his life for the
sheep. The hired hand is not the shepherd and does not own the sheep. So when
he sees the wolf coming, he abandons the sheep and runs away. Then the wolf
attacks the flock and scatters it. The man runs away because he is a hired hand
and cares nothing for the sheep. I am the good shepherd; I know my sheep and my
sheep know me"*

(JOHN 10:7–14 *NIV*)

Japanese boffins have created machines whereby sheep might, in the future, be
rounded up by remote-controlled mini-helicopter/drones the farmer operates
from his or her living room, simply by looking out of the window. Good news
for the boffins, who stand to make a fortune. Good news too for the shepherd
who, instead of rounding up a flock of wet, muddy sheep in the rain and cold,
can stay by the fire (except, maybe, for securing the pen gate). Not such good
news for the sheepdogs! If this becomes reality, those loyal creatures are out
of a job; surplus to requirements, replaced by impersonal machines, for a
computer-operated device will never need to be fed or watered, it can be stored
in a box, and it won't need a bed. On the other hand, a robot will never care
about the shepherd's well-being, nor will it lay across the shepherd's feet of an
evening, and neither can it offer the shepherd devotion and company, trudging
across isolated fields as a friendly, ever-attentive companion.

God is not an automaton! The concept of an unfeeling, unresponsive deity is unattractive, as
sentient human beings long to engage in warm relationship with a sentient greater power; to
love, and to be loved. The prospect of God as a neutral, remote being is awful, belonging to the
realms of science fiction or cold commerce, not to the realms of emotion, spirituality, feeling,
heartache, life and love. Jesus knows the needs of his sheep, and is able to meet those needs.
The Good Shepherd longs to be intricately involved in our lives, sharing our concerns and
helping us. He loves. He helps. He is irreplaceable.

DEITY OF THE DALES

I lift up my eyes to the mountains – where does my help come from? My help comes from the Lord, the Maker of heaven and earth

(PSALM 121:1–2 **NIV**)

I'm not a fan of "bucket lists"; places to be visited, ambitions to be achieved before life ends. I've never wanted to compile one, any more than I have longed to backpack through Outer Mongolia, swim with giant turtles, hang from a bridge suspended from my ankles by elastic, or learn to speak Finnish. Nevertheless, I would quite like to meet Amanda Owen, also known as "The Yorkshire Shepherdess". Mother of eight, wife of Clive, owner of several animals, and a lady who has declined modelling contracts in order to spend her days in wellies on the farm ("at the wrong end of a sheep"), never happier than when she is feeding her flocks, her children, any number of passers-by, or rounding up herds. Amanda and Clive's Terriers, Chalky and Pippen, revel in it all, not least their responsibility to keep an eye on the local rat population. Pippen has even developed a fake limp which she puts to great effect when ramblers ramble by, soliciting food and sympathy, having perfected a successful begging routine. Chalky prefers snacks of roadkill, and has been known to wander miles away in search of flattened birds and small livestock. Both roam collar-free, given Amanda's conviction that farm dogs risk being caught up in wire fences if collars are imposed, and neither are Chalky (a dog) and Pippen (a bitch) spayed or neutered; it's just not Amanda's way. It all sounds rather idyllic, especially for two energetic, hungry farmyard Terriers!

What a life Chalky and Pippen lead! A loving home, acres of land, rats to chase, plenty of food – not even collars to worry about, all set in the beautiful Yorkshire Dales. Is it a stretch of the imagination to suggest we may catch a glimpse of Eden when we gaze at ancient mountains? When a range of unspoilt hills dominates the landscape, do we pause to regard God's handiwork in such a way that we sense a distant whisper of a world that existed before pollution, congestion, and environmental compromise? Is that why news of Chalky and Pippen's existence strikes a latent chord? In our busy lives, surrounded by concrete, fumes, and noise, do we rest in order to hear God's still, small voice? We look to the hills, either literally or metaphorically, and we relocate the presence of a God who is older than the hills; we find our Maker, and our peace.

RUNNING WELL

If anyone forces you to go one mile, go with them two miles
(MATTHEW 5:41 **NIV**)

The owner of a Springer Spaniel called Chester was puzzled by the way his dog seemed tired after every walk they took. Chester's owner was no slouch, thinking nothing of a ninety-minute walk, but Chester would fall asleep in front of the fire as soon as they returned home. Curious, Chester's master equipped the Springer Spaniel with a tracker in order to, well, track his movements in search of clues, recording details of Chester's activities as soon as he was let off the lead. An hour and a half later, the data could be studied, and whereas the humans involved in the experiment had walked a recorded distance of 4.2 miles, Chester had covered 8.8 miles, thanks to his habit of zipping about here and there, going round in circles, and searching out opportunities for fun, splashing and sniffing, exploring wayside bogs and clumps of shrubbery. Chester the lively Springer Spaniel had covered more than double the distance of his human companions! Little wonder his fireside rest was part of his routine!

Roman authorities occupied the area in which Jesus lived, and it might have been difficult to go about one's business without bumping into a Roman soldier on every street corner. Most of them were ordinary conscripts on deployment but some were rotten Romans; brutal in their occupation and suppression of the locals. One of their more unpleasant customs was to order innocent bystanders to carry heavy gear for them, irrespective of whether or not it was convenient, and those living under occupation resented this imposition. Jesus, however, instructed his followers not only to comply with the order, but to "go the second mile"; in other words, check to see if your new-found Roman friend would like you to do anything else for him, and do so willingly! The plan was, those watching on, and the Roman soldiers, would be so impressed with the grace, humility, and kindness of the "Christ-ones", and their lack of resentment, that they would show an interest in the faith. I think Chester would approve!

DAMAGED GOODS

A bruised reed he will not break, and a smouldering wick he will not snuff out
(ISAIAH 42:3 **NIV**)

We decided against adopting Bob or Finn, and made another choice – Skipper, a twelve-year-old German Shepherd Collie Cross who had languished long in the care of the Royal Society for the Prevention of Cruelty to Animals. This spell with the RSPCA was Skipper's second – he has previous! He had been placed with them when he was four, then returned to their supervision when he was ten or eleven. A combination of erratic behaviour on his part, and some unfortunate ownership, had put him once again behind bars, and our journey with him has been interesting, challenging, frustrating and, to be honest, only minimally rewarding, for Skipper is cold, emotionally, showing hardly any interest in anyone; it is as though his trust in human beings has crashed, though he is remarkably gentle. He cannot be let off the lead in public, as he is antagonistic to other dogs, cats, squirrels, and pretty much anything on four legs, and will attack without provocation. The best we can do is to keep him here and, maybe, help him to realize he is wanted. He might never be able to trust fully, or come off the lead, but we regard him as a "work in progress".

No one would recommend brokenness. From a broken leg to a broken heart to a broken mind, it has little to commend itself, speaking of fracture, unbearable weights and pressures, and inability to persevere. Whether brokenness is self-inflicted, or is experienced through external circumstances, its consequences are overwhelming. The mystery of Skipper's aloof approach speaks of a temperament that has been eroded, leading me to think of the grace of God whereby we are encouraged to come to him just as we are; shattered, demoralized, left cold. He knows why; he knows, too, what factors have played their part, but his adoption of us is instant; guaranteed, the moment we seek it. Our healing, thereafter, might be immediate, or it might be gradual, and there is the possibility that our healing might not ever be complete this side of Heaven. We are, nevertheless, most definitely worth it, in his sight.

TIDY LIVES

If ye forgive men their trespasses, your heavenly Father will also forgive you: But if ye forgive not men their trespasses, neither will your Father forgive your trespasses

(MATTHEW 6:14–15 *KJV*)

What comes next isn't my favourite subject. It's not particularly savoury, so sensitive readers may wish to leave things where they are and not pick up on anything. The officers of England's Daventry District Council have revised their Public Spaces Protection Order in relation to Dog Control Orders. In addition to orders relative to leads and children's play areas, Dog Wardens will now be deployed to make sure owners exercise their pets only once they (the owners) are suitably equipped with poop-scoops and a supply of bags so as to properly dispose of any faeces that may have been deposited: "Failing to provide at the request of an authorised officer the means to pick up after a dog ... could result in the issuing of a £100 fixed penalty notice or being taken to court and receiving a fine on conviction of up to £1000." According to Daventry District Council, fouling is the "single biggest environmental concern that people have about their local area". Citizens of Daventry, you have been warned! A telephone hotline has been established so that aggrieved parties may report their discoveries. The success of the project seems guaranteed. It's in the bag.

Tidying up – not the best part of dog ownership! But, there it is (quite literally), and it has to be dealt with. Life can be a bit like that, too, insofar as there are matters we need to resolve; mistakes, sins, hurts. We need to be forgiven and we need to forgive. And that – forgiveness – isn't always straightforward. There is no hotline as such to record our misdemeanours, but it remains the case that we need to make good, and "sorry" can be the hardest word. Jesus was unequivocal on the point; the measure of forgiveness we extend to others (for any pain they might deposit in our lives) has a direct bearing on the measure of forgiveness we should expect to receive (for any pain we ourselves have deposited). It's about making amends, admitting wrongdoing, offering contrition, and being forgiven. Let's not dodge the issue!

SPLENDOUR FOR SQUALOR

God is seated on his holy throne
(PSALM 47:8 *NIV*)

I stand second to no one in my admiration for the novelist P. G. Wodehouse. I have twenty-nine of his novels, in addition to biographies, and should I ever be stranded on a desert island, I'd ask for little more than tea and P. G. Wodehouse. Comedic taste is, though, subjective; I might find Wodehouse's works hilarious, whereas others might prefer someone else's jokes, but I warm to Pelham Grenville because he demonstrated a deep affection for dogs, particularly Pekingese. Wodehouse gave shelter to strays who wandered his way; Dachshunds, Terriers, a Boxer, and a Foxhound, and such was his devotion to his collection, he even arranged his working day around their needs; writing for a few hours before breaking off for dog-walking duties. His personal correspondence was loaded with updates on the well-being of dogs he was hosting at the time ("I wish I could convert you to Daschunds ... they really are all right"), particularly if they were ill or dying ("Poor little Wonder had to be put to sleep ... She was almost totally blind, and she developed some sort of mental trouble ... We miss her very much, of course, but ... she was so obviously suffering ... Now Squeaky is our only dog").[1] For all that, Pekingese remained his lifelong favourites.

Pekingese, or Peking Palace Hounds, were the pets of Chinese princes, and one theory suggests their bowed legs, which limit their mobility, are a result of breeding designed to prevent them wandering from Temple grounds, so prized were they. Pekingese were allowed to be kept only in the Chinese Imperial Palace, valued because of their gold colouring. Jesus Christ, at home in the palaces of Heaven, prized beyond measure, could have confined himself to the luxury of the Heavenly Temple he occupied before condescending to a Bethlehem barnyard. He could have given up in Gethsemane and relinquished Calvary; in Heaven, he was worshipped. Here, he wasn't even wanted. Yet, he came; our royal friend, and because he did, our eternal well-being is secured. Definitely something to write home about!

---

1   P. G. Wodehouse, Sophie Ratcliffe, ed., *A Life in Letters* (London: Hutchinson, 2011)

A VERY PERSONAL TRAINER

Physical training is of some value, but godliness has value for all things

(I TIMOTHY 4:8 *NIV*)

There is a fitness video produced by a pet insurance company and praised by the British Veterinary Association. It has been made in response to concerns about obesity in dogs, the idea being that a person and a dog exercise together; the human squatting while the dogs weaves between his or her legs, or doing "bicycle crunches" with the dog jumping around nearby. Such antics are designed to promote the physical and mental health of dogs, but there is no record what effect they have upon their owners, all promoted under the label "petsercise". Personally speaking, my gut feeling is that I would struggle to persuade Skipper of his need to watch a "petsercise" video, never mind actually take part! My guess is, he'd look at me, waggle his big ears a bit, then gaze out of our patio doors in the hope of a walk in God's fresh air. However, if the video sounds like something your dog would enjoy, and benefit from (it's also supposed to help with obedience), go for it. Be my guest!

I have no way of knowing whether or not "bicycle crunches" were all the rage in Jesus' time here on earth, but I expect there was something equivalent that was just as painful. The Bible recommends personal fitness, reminding the likes of me that one's body is nothing less than a temple of the Holy Spirit, to be cared for with wisdom and a sensible diet, but I can't pretend to be wildly enthusiastic about exercise videos. I do, though, have a great deal of enthusiasm for a God who takes an interest in my holistic situation. He catches my keenness because he is interested in every aspect of my welfare; my soul, my mind, my spirit, and my physical condition. God's "How are you?" means, quite literally, everything; how is your prayer life, how is your family, how are you coping, how is your job, how is church for you? Nothing escapes his loving attention. What a lovely, attentive God.

R & R

Mary took about a pint of … expensive perfume; she poured it on Jesus' feet and wiped his feet with her hair

(JOHN 12:3 **NIV**)

Should your dog not fancy exercise in front of a screen, then you might prefer to treat it to a "doggie spa", the latest idea in pooch pampering. For a fee ranging from £50 to £80 (gulp!), professional pamperers will take care of doggie and indulge his or her every whim, depending on what is required. "Treatments" such as reflexology and various therapies are on offer, and your dog will stay in a room with underfloor heating (nothing so common as a kennel or an old bed in the kitchen, then). Even a choice of menus for mutts is available! Suitably treated, your dog can then look forward to a "peticure" whereby its claws will be trimmed and polished, followed by a spell of dental care having its teeth professionally whitened before spending "relaxation time" in the heated crèche. Owners may choose which type of music is to be played while their pampered, trimmed, fed, polished, warmed, whitened (and invoiced) dog is resting!

Christians are not to judge; Jesus said so, and he had a reputation for meaning what he said. It is not therefore within my remit to form a judgment on the justifiability, or otherwise, of spas for dogs, and if owners choose to part with their money in order to indulge in a spot of luxury for their beloved pet, who am I to comment? For a dog that has been abused, beaten, starved or neglected, such a day out would probably be quite wonderful. Regular trips to the spa, on the other hand, for a dog that is already well cared for and hasn't suffered any, might be tricky to justify. So, I guess this becomes an exercise in keeping one's own counsel; in itself, a spiritual grace well worth pursuing. If to speculate is to judge, then who am I even to speculate on what motivates someone to do something that appears extravagant? Am I in full possession of the facts? Hardly ever! Whoever would have thought that a dog at a day spa might teach me something about the spiritual life?

NEVER-ENDING STORY

Why do you look for the living among the dead? He is not here; he has risen
(LUKE 24:5–6 *NIV*)

Scotland's most famous dog is probably a Skye Terrier known as Greyfriars Bobby, who came to fame keeping guard over the Edinburgh grave of his owner for fourteen years, until his own death in 1872. Bobby belonged to a man called John Gray, and when Gray died and was buried in Greyfriars Kirkyard, his devoted companion took up his post on the grave and stayed put. Some offer a cynical view of a story of romance and devotion, suggesting the real Bobby died before 1872 and was secretly replaced by some sneaky individuals in the employ of Edinburgh City Council. It is even suggested Greyfriars Bobby was one of many substitute dogs passed off as the original after his demise; tourists probably wouldn't know the difference, and their visits to Edinburgh would help swell the city coffers. Indeed, a statue of Greyfriars Bobby remains a magnet for sightseers, with many leaving behind sticks, toys and treats, or rubbing his (shiny) nose in the hope of good luck. Who knows what's actually true? Most dogs are devoted enough to do what Greyfriars Bobby is said to have done, so that part of the account is credible but, by the same token, lucrative commercial opportunities rarely remain unexploited by city councils! Quite possibly, the romantics and the cynics will never fully agree on this one!

It is not unknown for dogs to sit at the graves of their owners, or to scratch at the surface, such is their grief – not a million miles away from the bewilderment experienced by Jesus' disciples after his burial. Their hopes were dashed. Their loss was absolute. Jesus was their hero; they had invested everything in following him. They had sacrificed careers, left families, taken his teaching on board, in the hope of revolution. They were grieving for a friend, a leader, and a way of life, and we can only imagine their desolation. Death, though, was by no means the end of the story, as Jesus was to be gloriously resurrected, conquering death. We know that now, but all the disciples could see was a stone-cold tomb. Thank God for the resurrection! Thank God for eternal life!

SIGNING UP

The disciples were called Christians first at Antioch
(ACTS 11:26 *NIV*)

Harold Wilson was Prime Minister of the United Kingdom from 1964 to 1970 and 1974 to 1976. Born and bred in Huddersfield, England, Wilson supported Huddersfield Town FC, and a story exists whereby Prime Minister Wilson, keen to extol the virtues of Huddersfield, was entertaining a Russian delegation. Engaging in small talk, but aware of a language barrier, Wilson struck on the idea of football as a common denominator. Out of his pocket came a treasured picture of a Huddersfield Town cup-winning side from yesteryear, and the PM beamed as he showed the photograph to his Russian counterparts. Unfortunately, the language barrier proved to be larger than he had imagined, and the Russian thought he was being invited to autograph the snapshot, doing so with an inky flourish, scribbling his name across Harold Wilson's pride and joy! Huddersfield Town Football Club, Wilson's heroes, are nicknamed "The Terriers" in memory of "Huddersfield Ben", the first Yorkshire Terrier to be registered with the Kennel Club, and a "Yorkie" has appeared on the badge of Huddersfield Town, with the logo "The Terriers"; at one point, shirts carried a picture of a red Yorkshire Terrier above the nickname, most popular during the 1969/70 season, when promotions manager Bill Brook suggested it reflected the "Terrier-like" qualities of the team.

Wilson's cherished photograph of "The Terriers" was ruined because of a misunderstanding! There was no misunderstanding whatsoever, though, surrounding the nickname given to the early Christians, when the pagans of Antioch kept a beady eye on the conduct of the "Christ-ones". The "Christ-ones" were watched and listened to; no doubt, some of the pagans wanted to trip the believers up and expose them as frauds. No doubt, too, others studied their conduct to assess whether it might be worth signing up as followers. Their nickname, the "Christ-ones", was either thrown at them as an insult, loaded with scepticism and reproach, or offered as a compliment – a badge of honour to be carried with pride. I wonder if today's watchers will give us such an honourable nickname. What qualities do our lives reflect?

PRIZED EXHIBITS

If you, Lord, kept a record of sins, Lord, who could stand?

(PSALM 130:3 *NIV*)

Today we move from Westminster, England, Harold Wilson's domain throughout his political career, to the Westminster Kennel Club Dog Show, USA, which is held in February in Madison Square Garden and is celebrating an astonishing 140 years of dog shows, agility tests, competitions, and "Best in Show" trials. Thousands of dogs of all shapes and sizes, representing fifty American states and twelve foreign countries, compete to be judged on their looks, skills, and levels of obedience (Golden Retrievers, not surprisingly, make up the majority entry in the Obedience category). The Westminster Show is even televised live. Should I find myself with a spare $160 my pocket, plus enough for my air fare and accommodation, I might consider buying an admission ticket and heading Stateside to see what's on offer and take advantage of the "Meet the Breeds" exhibition (until then, I'll content myself taking Skipper out for his walks).

What a wonder it is there is no such selection process in place for those who wish to follow Jesus! Can we imagine how that might work? Supposing the criteria for acceptance by God was based upon the way we look, our intelligence, our level of obedience, where we come from, or the quality of our bloodline? How many of us would be selected? I'm not sure I'd stand much chance at all! Thankfully, grace prevails and our imperfections are eclipsed in mercy, for Jesus promises that no one who comes to him in repentance will be rejected, or classed as "not quite best in show". The Kingdom of Christ is not an exclusive club granting admission only to the smart and the sassy, the clever and the capable. The Westminster Dog Show celebrates almost a century and a half of exhibitions, but for 2,000 years, the cross of Christ has towered over our faults and failings as a symbol of grace and acceptance.

GUILTY AS CHARGED

With loud shouts they insistently demanded that [Jesus] be crucified, and their
shouts prevailed. So Pilate decided to grant their demand
(LUKE 23:23–24 **NIV**)

Another prominent Labour politician (Wilson was a Labour Prime Minister), Roy Hattersley, an MP for thirty-three years, was often in the newspapers, or interviewed on radio or television. Thus, he was a household name, yet in 1996, it was his dog, Buster, who hit the headlines. A Staffordshire Bull Terrier/ German Shepherd mongrel Hattersley had rescued from an animal shelter, Buster famously killed a goose in London's St James's Park – bad enough, but St James's is a royal park, making the murdered goose the property of none other than the Queen! Needless to say, given the royal connection, the story made national news, especially when Hattersley was fined £25 for allowing Buster to be off the lead and a further £50 for the demise of Her Majesty's feathered property. The blood around Buster's mouth sealed his fate, apparently; evidence enough for a verdict! Subsequently, Roy Hattersley published *Buster's Diaries*, a book purporting to be Buster's thoughts on the matter and other issues of concern to a political mongrel. (Buster himself was reunited with the goose some years later.)

Charged with crimes against geese and the royal livestock, Buster was judged guilty, and despite a plea of self-defence, fines totalling £75 were handed down and justice had been done. Thanks to the media interest, justice had been seen to be done too. Jesus, the King of kings, was sent for trial, but without any hope of a fair hearing; his fate sealed by a mob and a parade of corrupt officials baying for his blood. On his day of judgment, when he was sentenced to death by crucifixion, no one stood in his defence; no one entered a plea on his behalf. An offence against royalty was committed in public, yet no journalist wanted to know, and on that day, the innocent was slaughtered on behalf of the guilty. Thus, was our salvation procured. Hallelujah! What a Saviour!

THE GOD-MAN

Jesus knew what they were thinking and asked, "Why are you thinking these things in your hearts?"

(LUKE 5:22 **NIV**)

Was it love at first sight for you and your husband or wife? Or are you still hoping for that special encounter? If so, it might be worth asking your dog to help! Forget speed dating and/or dating websites; abandon ideas of romantic meals – dogs, apparently, put store by first sight (and smell), without much need for dinners and dates. According to animal psychologist Dr Roger Mugford and his Golden Labrador, Bounce, dogs are ultra-reliable when it comes to making an assessment of one's partner. Mumford is a renowned expert on animal behaviour, and a prolific author whose training methods receive acclaim, and is convinced dogs are blessed with an instinct enabling them to "read" faces and discern moods, and personalities, by using ultra-sensitive chemical senses. Should we, for example, be tense, then we emit a smell undetectable to each other but which would alert a dog to tension. Likewise, when our blood pressure is high, we give out an odour that would alert Bounce and his friends to a certain type of temperament. By the same token, dogs can sense a calm, friendly nature in a person. So, how about taking a dog with you on your next Valentine's Day venture?

Jesus – fully God and fully man – was uniquely able to combine and utilize his humanity and his divinity to discern the intentions of those around him, be they hostile or benign. He was no seaside-booth fortune teller, and he didn't deal in guesswork; neither was he a music hall mind reader, but the man perfectly filled with the Spirit, supremely capable of reading our hearts. The Gospels provide examples of Jesus' ability to pick up on the unspoken words of those around him; the Pharisees, for example, whom he completely disarmed when he told them what they were silently thinking and hoping to keep secret. Likewise, his encounters with Zacchaeus and the woman at the well. This same Jesus knows our hearts too. We can't kid him for a second. He knows. He loves. He forgives. He heals.

LOVED WITH AN EVERLASTING LOVE

As a dog returns to its vomit, so fools repeat their folly
(PROVERBS 26:11 **NIV**)

Skipper is a cause for concern, and we are struggling to know what to do. Walks are less and less pleasurable. He pulls on the lead (that's putting it mildly), he attacks other dogs, and his highly strung temperament means he spends an hour or so every evening pacing the floor making odd breathing noises. He is stressed, yet we don't know why, and he licks us endlessly. The paradox is, he has it made here; regular walks, company most of the time, food galore, and lots of affection, yet he remains uptight and insecure to the point of panic. From time to time, his nervousness gets the better of him, and his bowels reflect that tension. He vomits a fair bit, too, which appears to be a symptom of psychological unrest as opposed to anything dietary. We have sought advice, I have read around canine behaviour, we have tried this and that, yet we remain stumped. We shall, though, persevere, despite our frustrations and disappointments, but we are mystified; here we have a dog whose background has done him few favours, who is as gentle as can be around people, but who is patently emotionally disturbed. (If Dr Roger Mugford is reading this, he should feel free to call!)

We are, each of us, like Skipper, to greater or lesser degree. Put it down to nature or nurture, we are complex beings; some people cope better than others, some keep a lid on things, while others openly demonstrate fragile and even volatile natures. We wear masks, we pretend. Sometimes, we cope. Often, though, we privately despair and live with the lurking embarrassment of our secret failures. Weirdly, we return to sins and harmful patterns of behaviour time and time again, against our better judgment, sometimes engaging in destructive cycles of conduct. That being so, we rejoice all the more in the faithfulness of our God, whose steadfast love is utterly unchanging. He will never abandon us. He will unfailingly persevere, in love. This is our God.

HOW GREAT THOU ART

When I consider your heavens, the work of your fingers, the moon and the stars, which you have set in place, what is mankind that you are mindful of them, human beings that you care for them?

(PSALM 8:3–4 **NIV**)

We have a water colour at the foot of our stairs – *The Shedding Ring* by Andrew Hutchinson. It is an entirely pleasant work, and the £3 I paid for it was money well spent. Hutchinson is a gifted artist specializing in wildlife scenes, often setting his paintings in my beloved north of England, and I like his gentle, unpretentious style. *The Shedding Ring* is set in what looks like Yorkshire, and features a farmer, a dry-stone wall, four sheep, and a Border Collie, all against a backdrop of what I think is the Yorkshire Dales. For me, simplicity is the key as shepherd and Collie are shown working well together. The attention to detail is great, especially the hunched pose in which the painter has captured the dog, and thanks to Hutchinson's skill, it doesn't require a great leap of imagination to imagine oneself on the Dales, with the Collie focused on his work; back arched, not missing a trick as it looks to place the sheep where they need to be. I'm no art critic – I know what I like and I like what I know, that's about it – but that single black and white image of a Border Collie against the green and brown background of the rolling hills really is striking.

One person's masterpiece is another person's eyesore! What might appear beautiful to one critic may appear ghastly to another. Someone, therefore, might find my appreciation of Hutchinson's Collie puzzling, and may not be able to "place" themselves in the picture. The Bible, though, indicates that God's workmanship in creation has something to suit every taste, in order to catch their personal attention; an ink-blue sky, for example, streaked with lightning; an ocean raging; the intricacy of a petal; the burning mystery of a desert; examples of God's creative genius are endless: a parrot on the wing; an Arctic fox superbly camouflaged. I could go on! Psalm 8 touches on the splendour of God's masterpiece, gently leading us towards worship. Sometimes, simply to worship is enough; not to ask, not to petition, not to question, but to adore.

KEEPING ON KEEPING ON

Pray without ceasing

(I THESSALONIANS 5:17 *KJV*)

A funny thing happened to me as I was walking Skipper. We were wandering along, Skipper sniffing his way from curiosity to curiosity, while I concentrated on keeping my arms from being pulled out of their sockets when, suddenly, a woman appeared and asked me if my dog liked carrots. Before I had chance to reply (he doesn't, as a rule), she was, for reasons best known to someone who is patently not too concerned about thrusting her hand into a dog's mouth, trying hard to feed Skipper a carrot (or, more accurately, to stuff a carrot down his throat). No matter how many times I pointed out Skipper is a German Shepherd and not a reindeer, she was not to be deterred! Neither of us have anything against carrots; I can take them or leave them, but I'd never knowingly hurt one, whereas Skipper, not altogether illogically, prefers a juicy bone to a juicy root vegetable. Carrot Woman persisted, but Skipper wasn't interested, so we made our apologies and wandered home, hoping not to be offered any more produce on the way. To be honest, I think we were both more than a little relieved to say cheerio to our rather insistent new acquaintance.

Insistent people tend to be annoying people; salespeople who can't take "no" for an answer, for example, when we repeatedly decline their dogged offers of bank refunds, accident compensation, crazy paving or conservatories. Nevertheless, Jesus twice commended women who wouldn't give up; the story of the persistent widow referred to in Luke 18 is held up as an example of one of the ways in which prayer is practised and answered. Likewise, the account of the woman who touched the hem of Jesus' garment (see Mark 5), whose determined faith was rewarded. Such admirable persistence, though, is by no means a female preserve, as witnessed by the fearless Bartimaeus in Mark 10. When it comes to prayer (if not the distribution of free carrots), there is no reason not to persevere and keep on keeping on.

THE QUALITY OF MERCY

Thou shalt make a mercy seat
(EXODUS 25:17 **KJV**)

My parents were Salvation Army officers, used to encountering people with an enthusiastic fondness for alcoholic beverages. One such enthusiast was a chap called Basil, who roamed the streets of the town in which we lived, often hopelessly drunk, sometimes moderately drunk, but never, in my experience, sober. Basil was harmless enough, even if he didn't always understand why shopkeepers insisted on payment for the tins of lager he removed from their shelves, and was actually something of a local celebrity. As a young Salvationist, I propped up the Salvation Army band when they were desperate for players, and was therefore to be found lurking around at band practice once a week. One such evening, a heartbroken Basil wandered in with his dog draped over his shoulders, held as a shepherd holds a lamb, and made his way to the front of the hall, where the band was assembled. As Basil laid his dog on the mercy seat (prayer bench), we watching musicians realized this was in fact his dog's corpse, and he knelt and sobbed as the Bandmaster knelt with him to pray. An alcoholic, a dead dog, a mercy seat, and a praying Salvation Army Bandmaster; I have rarely felt the presence of God's Spirit closer before or since.

This may land me in hot water with those who prefer a sterner line. So be it! I know what the Bible has to say about alcoholics, and I know too of theological disputes regarding whether or not God hears our prayers depending on us being in a right state or a state of grace. My thinking, though, is that love reigns supreme, and that mercy triumphs over justice. Thus, I am convinced God heard Basil's prayer that evening. Granted, he lived many years of his life as a drunkard, and died that way too. Granted, he was a smelly, selfish nuisance. Yet, in his hour of need, when his dog died, he made his way to a Salvation Army mercy seat. In my opinion, God would have to be made of concrete to ignore his prayer, but I believe in a God whose heart is immensely vulnerable to our tears. I do not, I'm afraid, believe in a concrete deity.

AT PEACE WITH ONESELF

As far as the east is from the west, so far has he removed our transgressions from us

(PSALM 103:12 **NIV**)

Before Skipper came to live with us, we had the horrible task of saying farewell to Meg, when we agreed the kindest option we could offer her was a gentle, dignified exit from this world courtesy of a vet's needle. I was with Meg as the lethal dose was administered, and I wouldn't be in any hurry to repeat that experience. It had to be done, though, and mercy sometimes arrives disguised as steel. Meg breathed her last as I cradled her head, and even though I am convinced of the validity of our decision, I can't escape feelings of guilt; as though I had betrayed a creature who had proved herself steadfast and loyal. (Strange as it may sound, I apologized to Meg after her death.) I've no idea whether or not dogs have souls and are able to hear people speaking to them once they are deceased but, nevertheless, I offered her an apology. On her last day, I treated her to a meal of all the things she wasn't supposed to eat any more, but which she still loved, feeling like some kind of lowlife cheat. I still have Meg's old collar but, sometimes, looking at it (which I don't, very often), I feel terribly guilty.

The Bible is saturated with verses talking about forgiveness. John 3:16 is the jewel in the crown, but is by no means the only text offering the reassurance of being forgiven, as the crimson thread running through Scripture declares forgiveness at every turn. We are happy to share this message with others; evangelists relentlessly preach the gospel of forgiveness; that same gospel is shared from pulpits week after week; we are usually – by and large – willing to forgive others. Yet, we find it difficult to forgive ourselves! The spiritual and humane logic we apply to the sins of others, we find hard to apply to our own, and self-forgiveness can be the hardest thing to embrace. As we reflect on the mistakes we have made, the sins we have committed, and the regrets we have, may God grant us grace to receive for ourselves the same inner healing we wish to see bestowed on others.

TELL ME THE STORIES OF JESUS

"Very truly I tell you," Jesus answered, "before Abraham was born, I am!"
(JOHN 8:58 **NIV**)

For my dad's sixty-fifth birthday, I treated him to a guided tour of the Houses of Parliament. It was great, as Dad graduated in politics, and we spent a lovely time being shown around such a beautiful building. One of the myths surrounding the Houses of Parliament, we discovered, is that the Cavalier King Charles Spaniel is the only dog allowed access to those hallowed halls. The myth persists that King Charles II was so fond of his Spaniels, he published a decree stating the King Charles Spaniel should be accepted in any public place, even in the Houses of Parliament, where animals were not usually allowed. I'm afraid there is no such decree! As a rule, dogs are not allowed to run freely in the Palace of Westminster, but this is simply a health and safety concern, and has nothing to do with King Charles II! On the contrary, former Labour Home Secretary, David Blunkett, who is blind and dependent upon a guide dog, has brought six different dogs into the Commons over the years; Ruby, Teddy, Offa, Lucy, Sadie, and Cosby, usually sleeping at his feet as debates went back and forth. On one occasion, Lucy (a black Labrador Curly Coat Retriever Cross) vomited during a speech by a Conservative member! A party political animal, maybe!

Someone once said that if people didn't stand for something, they would fall for anything. Quite often, myths and half-truths are given a better reception than truth itself; such is human nature! Fiction and fable do the rounds and gain greater acceptance than reason and fact, and stories about Jesus are no exception. Serious schools of thought claim he never existed, or that if he did, he taught nonsense, while other stories make him out to be merely some kind of angelic being on a par with an alien from another planet. Some refuse to accept his divinity, insisting that Jesus is only one of many great spiritual teachers. Let us, though, in the midst of that milieu, hold fast to the truth that Christ is Lord.

REQUIESCAT IN PACE

Give me property among you for a burying place
(GENESIS 23:4 **ESV**)

My paternal grandparents owned a Border Collie called Willie. I can't pretend to have known Willie all that well, as my grandparents lived in London throughout my childhood, whereas I lived in the north of England for much of that time. However I always sensed Willie the Border Collie was loved and appreciated, never more so than when he was attacked one day by a rat he had cornered in the garden, and had to be put to sleep urgently, so great were the injuries to his throat. To this day, I believe, Willie lies in a grave in that same garden, where Grandad marked his resting place with a beautiful display of Sweet William flowers. He and my grandmother have since passed on, but that little patch of London still belongs to their much-loved pet. The current occupants of Nan and Grandad's house almost certainly have no idea of the existence of Willie's grave, and I quite like the idea of him resting in peace in a secret location. (The rat escaped without charge!)

I am intrigued by obscure references throughout the Bible regarding the final resting places of different people, or stories of memorials set in place to mark the life of the deceased. One such memorial, a mound of stones, stands on the Isle of Gigha, in the Hebridean Islands. Visitors add their own stones or pieces of slate to the mound and, gradually, the pile grows. These stones and slates are usually painted with messages or pictures commemorating their visit or memorializing a loved one, and each crude marker represents a life, even if that life is unknown to many who inspect the stack. Our need to commemorate the lives and loves of those we hold dear is perfectly natural, be that with a headstone, a stone, a bed of flowers, or some other token of loving remembrance. Those Bible references reassure me that God understands.

GOD OF THE SECOND CHANCE

The disciples picked up twelve basketfuls of broken pieces that were left over
(MATTHEW 14:20 **NIV**)

Charity shops are a feature of most British high streets. I love them, and not many weeks go by without me popping in to snoop for bargains. In fact, most of my clothes and shoes come from charity shops, enabling me to parade around in designer labels for a fraction of what such items would cost new, with the added satisfaction of knowing what is spent aids a good cause. Two of my best deals came in the form of second-hand books (another love of mine); dog-eared, maybe, but none the worse for that. One was Phil Drabble's *One Man And His Dog* and the other, Jan Fennell's *The Practical Dog Listener*. I nabbed both for the price of a decent cup of coffee, and was delighted, when I got home, to discover they were signed by their respective authors. That which someone else had donated to the charity shop – the unwanted and no longer needed – is of some value to me.

In the story of the feeding of the 5,000 there is mention of the fact that twelve baskets of leftovers were collected. Crusts? Fish heads? Who knows! All I know is that I am as delighted to read of those surplus morsels being collected as I am to find a steal in a charity shop. It pleases my heart that the Gospel writer saw fit to include the remnants of the meal in his story. Why? Because it reassures me that in God's Kingdom, no one need be on the scrapheap. I believe in a God who recycles lives others abandon; a Kingdom where those no longer regarded as fit for purpose are made useful again. God gathers those whom society discards, specializing in grand redesigns, and his unrivalled ability to make good that which is regarded as junk is a hallmark of his love. If we look carefully, we might even spot his signature somewhere – written in red. Even the vilest offender is of inestimable value to him. This is God.

HELP!

Very truly I tell you, when you were younger you dressed yourself and went where you wanted; but when you are old you will stretch out your hands, and someone else will dress you and lead you

(JOHN 21:18 **NIV**)

Skipper continues to prove challenging. He is lovely, but emotionally damaged and not sure how to give or receive love. He will, for example, ignore people he knows well. Conversely, he will often crave attention, licking us unmercifully in some kind of desperate attempt either to make amends or seek reassurance. Walkies can be difficult, such is his tendency to pull hard and disobediently on the lead. To that end, we are seeking (more!) help, this time via a website whereby people who are dog-friendly but can't own a dog themselves make themselves available as dog-sitters and dog walkers. Subscribers either offer their dog for "borrowing" or offer themselves as "borrowers", so, in order to give ourselves some respite from Skipper's trying ways, we have offered to lend him to people who agree to take him out for walks; we need a breather, and they need a dog! We have been perfectly honest about his funny mannerisms and a full declaration of his disorderly conduct has been published! Even so, we have received offers, and Skipper is all set to be farmed out from time to time. Plenty of love and exercise for him, and a break for us equals a win-win situation. Some, we realize, may disagree with our stance, but we see it as a useful step forward – one that might possibly help preserve our sanity!

Asking for help doesn't always come easily, does it? Quite rightly (up to a point), we like to do things for ourselves, preferring to rely on our own abilities. We have to admit, though, there are (or will be) those times when we need help. When we are ill, maybe, and a neighbour offers to do a bit of shopping for us. When we are struck down, possibly, and need to be spoon-fed. Pride kicks in! We wish we could do everything independently (especially in more personal matters), and we resist offers of assistance. Maybe we resent the fact that support is necessary, and we find our dilemma frustrating or embarrassing. It is right and proper that we do all we can for ourselves while we are able to, but should that day arrive when our mobility is limited, or our physical, mental and emotional capacities lessened somewhat, then may God grant us the grace to reach out, to confess our need, and to give thanks that there is some kind of relief available.

FIGHT THE GOOD FIGHT

What causes fights and quarrels among you? Don't they come from your desires that battle within you?

(JAMES 4:1 **NIV**)

Our letter box somehow attracts all sorts of unsolicited leaflets, junk mail, and promotional offers of one kind or another. I do, apparently, qualify for large pizzas at a number of venues all across town, at bargain prices. Likewise, I appear to have people queuing up to buy my house. I have even been invited to join a Guitar & Bass School, which promises to help me "conquer my dreams" (not entirely sure what that means), with "books included"! Such is the deluge, I am beginning to wonder if I need ever leave my in-demand house again; perhaps I can live my life simply by sitting beneath my letter box? One such leaflet offers "Doggy Day Care!" and/or a "Drop and Shop!" service (with no shortage of exclamation marks) which wants to "make my life easier" by looking after Skipper while I shop and, if I pay a bit more, will treat him to "lots of cuddles" and the opportunity to "socialise with other dogs!". It's a useful option, and I admire the entrepreneurial spirit behind it all, but the fly in the ointment is the "other dogs" bit. As pleasant as it sounds, Skipper wouldn't enjoy that as socializing would stress him massively, and any number of dog fights would almost inevitably ensue. (I think I'll engage in another spot of leaflet recycling.)

There has not, apparently, been one single day in the last 250 years when the world has been entirely at peace, without one conflict taking place. Much as I believe in the fundamental desire of most human beings to live at peace with their neighbours, history slams down the irrefutable fact that the absence of battle is the exception, not the norm. Skipper will bite and fight, other dogs will retaliate, and a vicious circle begins. Not dissimilarly, any number of dictators, bullies, tyrants, and warmongers (including those who make their millions from arms sales) will agitate for power through violent means, careless of the bloodshed and misery created. Reluctantly, we sometimes have no choice but to recycle, or even to scrap altogether, plans for peace. Shall we cease the snapping and snarling? Let there be peace on earth, and let it begin with us.

ONLY THE LONELY

God's love has been poured out into our hearts
(ROMANS 5:5 **NIV**)

In the UK, 14 February is Valentine's Day, in honour of St Valentine, who courted unpopularity with the Roman authorities of his day by performing Christian marriage ceremonies at a time when such religious duties were frowned upon. He also annoyed the powers-that-were by offering practical assistance to persecuted Roman Christians. Nowadays, couples wishing to celebrate their devotion to one another will often do so with a romantic meal or the exchange of gifts, but the Romans took a dim view of St Valentine's rebellious efforts at promoting love and marriage, and he was beheaded for his troubles. Rather bizarrely, given the serious nature of Valentine's execution, there are now Valentine's Day courses for those who wish to learn how to love their dogs in ways that dogs really appreciate! Such as, for example, with the absence of hugs; these, apparently, are alright for human couples, but dogs care not to be hugged; they would much prefer to be left hug-less, however much we might regard a hug as a sign of affection, for a hugged dog tends to be a frightened dog; it feels trapped, and anyone enrolling for a Valentine's Day Dog Training Course will be advised on such matters. (I think I'd prefer a restaurant booking with my wife, to be honest.)

Learning to love can be difficult. Maybe it's easy to love those we like, but the trick is to love (and even hug) the unlovable; the aggressive, the demanding, and those whose awareness of social norms is lacking. The writer Adrian Plass coined the phrase "hugs without history", explaining his reluctance to embrace people with whom he had no significant history of friendship.[1] Many of us share that aversion. Nevertheless, maybe there are those out there who are aggressive and demanding, etc., precisely because they have never been loved, or even wanted. There is truth in the saying that "hurting people hurt" and possibly, for them, Valentine's Day is the day in the year they feel most painfully aware of their unpopularity. God's tender touch can heal the broken-hearted. Ours can help, too.

---

1   From a private conversation.

MY, MY, MY DELILAH

Speak, Lord, for your servant is listening
(1 SAMUEL 3:9 **NIV**)

A story floated across my radio airwaves, of a deaf dog who has been resident in a shelter for seven years, being rehomed. Seven years! Prospective owners were discouraged from adopting Delilah, a white English Bull Terrier Staffordshire Cross, because she suffers from congenital deafness, hence her prolonged stay in care, and a staff member from the rehoming centre said: "Unfortunately the condition isn't uncommon in white dogs, and often results in many ending up in rescue centres or abandoned when breeders are unable to sell or find homes for them." Quite wonderfully, the highly intelligent Delilah has learnt a lot of sign language, and responds to a variety of commands and instructions, taking particular delight in earning a thumbs-up sign from her trainers, when she knows she is doing well. Now that she has been adopted by a retired gentleman who can spend a lot of time with her, Delilah's future is assured. Her silent world will be happy, and the signs are looking good!

I wonder how God must feel when he tries (repeatedly) to get through to us! Given that he appears not to speak verbally often, he is confined to grabbing our attention by way of signs and "hints"; a word from the Bible, perhaps, that leaps out of the page and speaks to us, or a point in a sermon that strikes us as relevant and helpful. Maybe God engages in repetition because we choose not to hear him the first time, or because, if we do hear him, we lack the conviction to respond to the messages we pick up? Quite legitimately, we hesitate as we try to decipher what might be God speaking to us and what might be wishful thinking, and such caution has merit. By the grace of God, though, he communicates time and again, bearing with us in our hesitancy, until we are attuned to his "sign language". Thankfully, all throughout, despite our faltering ways, we receive his thumbs-up.

RSVP

A wedding took place at Cana in Galilee. Jesus' mother was there, and Jesus and his disciples had also been invited to the wedding

(JOHN 2:1–2 **NIV**)

Just for the record, most dogs (I'm generalizing) respond much better to being invited to approach someone (an encouraging pat on one's thighs, for example) than they do to being approached. Instinctively territorial creatures, canines don't always feel comfortable when the likes of you and I encroach upon "their" little patch, however kind and benign our intentions may be. Personal space matters, and it is better by far to stand at a respectable distance and wait to see if doggie chooses to approach you; to issue an invitation instead of considering yourself invited! Standard practice, really, in the business of making friends and influencing not only dogs, but people too.

Jesus was the invited guest at a wedding in Cana. Invited! Can we catch the irony there? God in the flesh, entitled to go anywhere he liked, without any need of an invitation. The fact he humbled himself to take on the role of invitee is glowing testament to his grace, and tells us much about Christ. Meekness and majesty indeed! Our incarnate God entered humanity to such a stunning degree, he never thought of throwing his weight around, arrogantly making himself at home but, instead, waited for an invitation. It brings to mind Holman Hunt's painting *The Light of the World* in which Jesus is depicted knocking at a door, that door representing a human heart. He waits until admission is granted, such is his humility, such is his patience. Revelation 3:20 is the backdrop to that picture of a gracious Saviour who treats us with underserved courtesy and respect, yet longs to come into our lives. Likewise, James 4:8 – "Come near to God and he will come near to you" (NIV) – which is not merely a suggestion, but a lovely reminder of God's innate charm.

VISITING ORDER

I was ill and you looked after me, I was in prison and you came to visit me
(MATTHEW 25:36 *NIV*)

Friends of ours have owned King Charles Spaniels over the years. They have brought their owners a great deal of satisfaction, but they have also been employed (voluntarily) as PAT dogs – Pets As Therapy. Strictly known as Animal Assisted Therapy, this is a charitable endeavour whereby people who are, say, housebound or in hospital are visited by people like my friends and their dogs. The therapeutic power of being able to stroke a dog, or cuddle a lapdog, is immense, and can play a part in physical and emotional healing, so much so that thousands benefit from such visits; in residential homes, hospitals, hospices, schools, day-care centres, and prisons. It is quite astonishing how much joy, comfort, and companionship can be brought to individuals, just by making it possible for them to stroke (pat) a friendly animal whose love is given unconditionally. Subject to certain conditions, all kinds of dogs can become "PAT" dogs, with the latest innovation being the introduction of dogs as reading companions to children who struggle to learn to read. The presence of a non-judgmental companion eases stress levels considerably, aiding the learning process by some degree.

Jesus was outspoken on the subject of visitation. His words on the importance of visiting the sick, the lonely, and the imprisoned leave little room for misunderstanding, and it appears we serve him best by serving those whose need for companionship, company, and care is urgent. Would it be right to say that pastoral visitation is perhaps the poor relation when it comes to Christian ministry? Possibly, in our drive for, say, fundraising and even our promotion of outreach (nothing wrong with either), we sometimes, inadvertently, overlook those who hardly ever see another living soul from week to week, for whom loneliness is crippling, or for whom pain is a daily enemy. How can we deny the worth of a visit from a caller to a prisoner whose years ahead behind bars will not include huge amounts of warmth and concern?

RULES AND ROLES

Submit to God and be at peace with him
(JOB 22:21 **NIV**)

Eddie the Jack Russell is one of the stars of the US TV sitcom *Frasier*. Trained to a high degree, Eddie, owned (in the programme) by Martin Crane, plays an integral part in the storylines. Martin Crane lives with his son, Dr Frasier Crane, an eminent Seattle psychiatrist and radio broadcaster, who takes fastidiousness to a new level; ultra-fussy about his appearance, his Armani suits, the décor in his apartment, his imported coffee, and his inflexible routines. Eddie, responsive and obedient only to Martin, exasperates Frasier by leaving hairs all over furniture he isn't supposed to sit on, licking up morsels of food from the immaculately cleaned and polished-to-within-an-inch-of-its-life expensive wooden flooring, and ignoring the good doctor even at his most frustrated and angry. Eddie's speciality is fixing Frasier with a long, hard stare, driving him to distraction, often leaving the learned psychiatrist with little option but to slam the door as he storms out of his apartment. Quite remarkably, even though a starry host of internationally renowned thespians make up the cast of the series, Eddie received more fan mail than any of them!

Rule-breaking, Eddie's favourite pastime, is our common lot! We like to do our own thing, go our own way. We provoke God with our stubborn ways and our very DNA seems reluctant to embrace any proposals of proprietorship. Thankfully, God is not in the habit of slamming doors and storming out of our lives, despite our tendency to exasperate him and our strange, almost inexplicable ability to submit to his Lordship. Eddie, though, adores Martin Crane, and a fundamental component of his expressed adoration is obedience. What Martin says, Eddie does; not because he has to, not because he is frightened of Martin (who loves Eddie, regardless), but because he wants to. Similarly, in willing compliance lies freedom, peace, and security. If we did but know it, God is our greatest fan; he's even written to us!

OUCH!

Grow in the grace and knowledge of our Lord and Saviour Jesus Christ
(2 PETER 3:18 **NIV**)

A growing craze in Hong Kong is "*doga*", an initiative in holistic well-being for dogs whereby canine participants are massaged, twisted, and stretched in yoga-like poses intended to aid relaxation and better equip dogs to cope with the high-pressure-fast-pace life Hong Kong offers; *doga* can make all the difference, reducing stress levels and introducing health benefits. An added bonus is that owners are given time, during the classes, to bond with their pets, as the norm in Hong Kong, especially in commuter areas, is for professional dog walkers to be responsible for walkies because their owners are busy working. *Doga* therefore helps relationships too, but much as I wish for a better relationship with Skipper, I can't see us signing up for *doga* classes any time soon! I do not condone yoga as a practice compatible with Christianity, but I am in favour of anything making life better for dogs. However, something tells me a German Shepherd with an attitude problem might not take kindly to being twisted and stretched. I wish every dog in Hong Kong every happiness, but they will need to enjoy their classes without Skipper's company!

Comfort zones – we love them, and being taken out of our comfort zones is not something we crave. Yet, how often do we find God "stretching" us; nudging us towards an experience that will make us uncomfortable but which will do us good? An experience in prayer, perhaps, where we are challenged to step out in faith? An opportunity to trust God for something, even though we hesitate? I wonder if the great Biblical characters were really all that different from us in such ways. Would those spiritual giants have enjoyed the stretching of their belief? Or was it more the case their convictions – and their reputations – grew as a result of their increasing confidence in the promises of God? Had they opted for their comfort zones, their reliance upon God might never have been reinforced, and we might be deprived of their example. Time to stretch?

LOST PROPERTY

He was lost

(LUKE 15:32 **NIV**)

Portuguese football manager, José Mourinho, is, to put it mildly, no stranger to controversy. An outspoken individual, Mourinho has clashed with referees on numerous occasions, publicly disagreeing with their decisions. Phenomenally successful, he speaks his mind and appears not to care about the consequences (usually a fine or a touchline ban). On one occasion, though, José Mourinho was in hot water not with a referee, but the police, who had visited his London home, when he was managing Chelsea FC, to remove his Yorkshire Terrier, Gullit (named, presumably, after former Chelsea and Netherlands star Ruud Gullit). They were keen to quarantine Gullit (the dog, not the Dutchman) because they had reason to believe it had been taken abroad and brought back into England without vaccinations, thanks to a mix-up over the requisite documents for veterinary regulations. Unfortunately, as the police struggled to forcibly remove Gullit from Mourinho's home, the Yorkshire Terrier ran away into the busy London streets, prompting an appeal in national newspapers for the safe return of Jose's missing Yorkie. To be continued …

Paul and Timothy wrote to Philemon, a leader in the Early Church, on behalf of another runaway, Onesimus. He (Onesimus) was a slave/servant belonging to Philemon, and he ran away under suspicion of theft. On the run, or in prison, Onesimus encountered Paul, and his meeting with the evangelist led to his conversion and a new friendship. Appealing for clemency, Paul advised Onesimus to return to Philemon, sending him away with a letter of commendation aimed at effecting forgiveness and reconciliation. The runaway had been found, and Paul gladly acted as advocate on his behalf, commending him as a "useful" person (Onesimus means "useful"). In like manner, Jesus acts as our Advocate and Mediator, pleading our case in the heavenly realms and effecting our forgiveness. We are declared "not guilty" in Christ! Our letter of pardon has been signed in blood.

A GOOD RESULT

Now he is found

(LUKE 15:32 **NLT**)

All is well! Despite rumours that Arsenal FC had kidnapped José Mourinho's Yorkie in an attempt to derail Chelsea's season, and claims that the police had no leads, I can report that this special dog was found, returned, and declared to be safe and well. The paperwork issues were resolved and national football was at liberty to continue unabated. José, on good form, fired a few blistering volleys at members of the press because of what he considered to be their intrusion of his and his family's privacy because photographers had more or less camped on his doorstep, zoom lenses snapping away at every move his family made, and the great manager resented this. However, this was a happy ending. An unsuspecting Yorkshire Terrier that had unwittingly become the subject of frenzied media attention could once again take up its daily routine, unaware of the furore surrounding its famous owner. A story of two halves!

Isn't it intriguing, the way in which human beings know when they are lost, literally, physically, but have little or no idea of being lost, spiritually? Supposing we find ourselves in a strange town, looking for a particular venue. Should we lose our way, we will (eventually!) ask for directions, consult a taxi driver, or buy a map. Chances are, with a bit of help, we will find our way again, by acknowledging our need and approaching someone we trust to redirect us. Do we, though, quite so readily seek spiritual help, so that we can find our way to (or back to) God? I would hazard a guess that for some inexplicable reason, we are more relaxed in that respect, and tread more slowly. Mercifully, though, grace prevails, and our loving Father watches our wandering footsteps with compassion. What a struggle it must sometimes be for him not to interfere when we go astray, like the proverbial backseat driver! Thankfully, he remains faithful, and is only too willing to steer us through life's furore and bring us safely home.

GUARDIAN GUIDE

The Lord himself watches over you! The Lord stands beside you
(PSALM 121:5 **NLT**)

A friend of mine depends upon a Guide Dog in order to get out and about and retain a level of independence. My friend is visually impaired, and her eyesight is deteriorating. Thus, her need of a Guide Dog is increasingly essential, and Vicki, the Labrador in question, does her job well, including guard dog responsibilities. As gentle as Labradors are, Vicki is trained to protect and will bark a warning to anyone who oversteps the boundaries. Her care of my friend, a single woman, combines gentleness, intelligence, and appropriate strength, but I possess a secret weapon that comes into play whenever I want to, say, have a cup of tea with my friend without being regarded as a dangerous suspect (by Vicki). On account of owning a dog-walking coat with pockets that are usually stuffed with dog treats, there is a residue of biscuit crumbs and meaty-flavoured bits lining the pockets, and even Vicki, as obedient and well-trained as she is, will treat me with a little less suspicion when she smells my dog-coat. She is a delightful creature, but not entirely above being bribed! God bless Vicki and Guide Dogs everywhere – they do a first-class job.

Except for her susceptibility to tasty titbits and biscuit bribes, so much of Vicki reminds me of God. She is rarely far from my friend's side, and God has promised never to leave us or forsake us. She is entirely at my friend's disposal, and Jesus said he came not to be served, but to serve. She is utterly devoted to my friend, and Calvary's stained and spattered cross convinces me of God's devotion to us. She is strong and protective, even to the extent of making herself vulnerable if it means offering protection; God is our shield and defender, and, in Christ, made himself vulnerable to the point of death. How marvellous! How wonderful! What a friend!

SWEET AND SOUR

When the woman saw that the fruit of the tree was good for food and pleasing to the eye, and also desirable for gaining wisdom, she took some and ate it. She also gave some to her husband

(GENESIS 3:6 **NIV**)

We have a stomach-sinking feeling Skipper may have blotted his copybook with a previously untraumatized person who looked after him when we were on holiday. He's a handsome boy, and he knows very well it is not at all difficult for him to inveigle his way into the affections of the unsuspecting and altruistic. One such beguiled person of goodwill, whose friendship we can only hope to retain, helped us by giving Skipper B & B while we went away to dog-free zones. All did not go well, not least in regard to Skipper's interest in some nectarines our friend had in a fruit bowl in her living room. Skipper, so we were told, developed a habit of helping himself, despite there being an array of snacks available – more appropriate/normal dog snacks, I mean – and with his new-found taste for nectarines, he made quite a mess (in more ways than one); this in addition to the aggression he showed to a neighbouring dog. We collected him with the distinct impression that we shouldn't expect any such hospitality again, and even now, I have an inkling we don't know the full story, our friend having opted for Christian diplomacy in her account of matters.

Whatever made Skipper raid the fruit bowl is beyond us, given that he is a German Shepherd/ Collie Cross, not a baboon. Most people, with a dog in the house, wouldn't worry about hiding the nectarines; the sausages, maybe, or a lamb chop, but fresh fruit? The attraction of forbidden fruit, is that it? That which we don't necessarily need or even want, to begin with, but which grows ever-more alluring, until it's all we can think about … Adam and Eve knew a bit about that, and so, if we're honest, do most (all?) of us. In Skipper's case, the consequences were bemusing but not ruinous, whereas in Adam and Eve's case the fallout can still be felt and has echoed catastrophically down the centuries. Lord, lead us not into temptation, but deliver us from evil!

PAVING THE WAY

I will surely bless you and make your descendants as numerous as the stars in the sky and as the sand on the seashore

(GENESIS 22:17 **NIV**)

Visiting someone in hospital, I stepped off the train at the station nearby, and stopped to watch a pavement artist sculpting a dog from damp sand. It was a work of art, and he deserved every penny of the money dropped into his hat (which was on the pavement, not his head). By the time I arrived, most of the sculpture was in place – a Greyhound, I think, unless he had underestimated how much sand he would need and it was in fact a malnourished Labrador. The artist's skill was evident, and I couldn't help wondering why such a gifted individual was obliged to earn a meagre living courtesy of a cold, hard pavement. His attention to detail fascinated me as he carved the Greyhound's/Labrador's nostrils with a spatula, making the dog's face appear realistic. Granted, keeping sand damp in England in winter is not incredibly difficult, but his creation was quite something, nonetheless. (I resisted the temptation to ask if his dog was called Sandy.)

Abraham must have received God's promise of descendants as numerous as the grains of sand on the seashore with astonishment – incredulity, even. Firstly, he had something of a chequered past, which must have made him question his worthiness to receive such a promise; then, secondly, wandering in the desert, or taking a dip in the sea, he might have wondered if he had heard correctly, for the promise would have seemed unbelievable. Have a look at a beach next time you are near one, and contemplate that sandy shore. Think of those occasions when your sea-wet feet have collected a lining of sand, and imagine trying to count even that relatively small number of grains! Impossible! In Abraham's story, we see the limitless grace of God at work; a grace that trumps unworthiness, and we realize it is similarly impossible to count the ways in which he clings to our lives in order to bless us. That is to his glory and our benefit.

FIGHTING FIRE WITH FIRE

Samson went and caught three hundred foxes, and took torches, and turned the foxes tail to tail and put one torch in the middle between two tails. When he had set fire to the torches, he released the foxes into the standing grain of the Philistines, thus burning up both the shocks and the standing grain, along with the vineyards and groves

(JUDGES 15:3–5 **NASB**)

On a trip into London, I heard a noise as I stepped off the train. It sounded like an animal in distress; a high-pitched screeching noise, so I stopped to have a look around, and eventually spotted two foxes in the tangled mass of unkempt brambles growing by the tracks. Are foxes dogs? Some, apparently, belong to the *Canidae* family (wolves, foxes, jackals, coyotes), and others to the family *Canini* (dog-like mammals and some kinds of fox), whereas true foxes take pride in the title *Vulpini*. These two in the bushes (urban red foxes) were – how shall I put it? – "courting" – well, to be more specific, the male fox was, in the time-honoured fashion of male/female courtship rituals, being rebuffed by the female object of his desire. To say she was playing hard to get would be doing her an injustice, but he was not to be deterred, though he did eventually give up his pursuit and wander away, disappointed and embarrassed. The screeching noises were mostly hers, as she rejected his advances and bared her teeth. I wandered away, as did he; having seen her teeth and witnessed her temper, I didn't fancy my chances as relationship counsellor.

Samson, like the vixen in our story, was upset. He was yet again at war with the Philistines. He and they were always baring their teeth and growling murderous threats towards each other, and in the course of one such period of aggravation, Samson hatched a plan for revenge involving catching 300 foxes and setting fire to valuable Philistine crops by letting the foxes loose with flaming torches attached to their tails. We can only imagine what expensive damage ensued – not to mention the pain and terror inflicted on the foxes. In my opinion, Samson should have been arrested for cruelty to animals, and if he had a quarrel with the Philistines, perhaps he should have approached them with an offer of reconciliation instead of allowing himself to become so fired up. His actions solved precisely nothing. What might we learn from this?

HAPPY DAY!

The Spirit said to Philip, "Go over and join this chariot." So Philip ran to him and heard him reading Isaiah the prophet and asked, "Do you understand what you are reading?" And he said, "How can I, unless someone guides me?" And he invited Philip to come up and sit with him

(ACTS 8:29–31 **ESV**)

Meg, queen of my heart, was too old for boyfriends. I can't vouch for her younger days, but what happened in the past, stays in the past, and we are all entitled to the grace of discretion. In her later years, though, she had little patience with suitors, whom she regarded as beneath her dignity, and should any guys persist in their attentions, she would snap at them as a warning of her displeasure. She was too old, too blind, and too arthritic to be enthusiastic about their passion, so imagine my surprise when, on a day out, Meg was approached by a playful Irish Wolfhound. I had a word with him, advising him of the futility of making his feelings known, but his cheeky Irish nature refused to give way, and I marvelled as he charmed Meg and persuaded her to play along. For the first and only time, Meg revelled in the company of a beau, and it has to be said, she demonstrated excellent taste; the Wolfhound was impressive, with a delightful temperament and a silver-grey coat lending him an air of distinction. I could see why she might have fallen for him. Sadly, though, we had to leave for home before the burgeoning relationship could develop ...

Might Meg and the Wolfhound have become pals? Would their destinies have changed course, had we lingered? Acts tells of a meeting between Philip the Evangelist and an Ethiopian court official, a bureaucrat in the court of Queen Candace, who was trundling along in his chariot one day when Philip was prompted by the Spirit to catch up with him and explain the writings of Isaiah the official was reading. In one unexpected conversation, the spiritual destiny of the aide was changed as Philip told him about Jesus. A chance encounter? Someone once said coincidences occur when God chooses to remain anonymous! Thank God for Philip. Thank God for a life-changing gospel.

IF RELIGION WERE A THING THAT MONEY
COULD BUY …

*When Simon saw that the Spirit was given at the laying on of the apostles' hands,
he offered them money and said, "Give me also this ability so that everyone on
whom I lay my hands may receive the Holy Spirit." Peter answered: "May your money
perish with you, because you thought you could buy the gift of God with money!"*
(ACTS 8:18–20 **NIV**)

Mention of sculpted sand dogs the other day led me to research the subject, and it turns out the sculptures are almost certainly a scam, whereby the dogs aren't sculpted at all, but made from moulds filled with damp sand, then laid on a pavement, with the "sculptor" merely adding a few "finishing touches" such as nostrils, for example. I might be wrong, but the evidence is pretty overwhelming, and I have seen pictures of identical dogs appearing in different places of the country, hundreds of miles apart, at the same time, the odds of which happening must be nigh on impossible. Sadly, the "artists" give every impression this is their handiwork, whereas they are conning people. I feel annoyed, but saddened, too, that people stoop (literally) to such levels in order to take home a few pennies. It's a pity, too, the artistry I admired is little more than the product of a factory-produced plastic mould. No doubt I shan't be the only one taken in before the deception is publicized and stopped, but what grieves me is that the "sculptor" I saw was begging outside a hospital, where visitors and patients are likely to be vulnerable, emotionally, and more likely to feel sympathy than they might otherwise.

The opportunity to make a "fast buck" is tempting. It's wrong if that buck is made fraudulently, but it is not for me to judge anyone who finds it necessary to sit on a rock-hard, cold pavement, begging. So what if it is part of a bigger scam? It's still not a great option. Simon the sorcerer earned a living performing tricks, and was regarded as a great man (see Acts 8), but coming into contact with Christians demonstrating the authentic power of Christ, he offered them money for the secret of their authority, thinking the grace of God could be purchased, offering money in exchange for their miraculous abilities. Peter was having none of it, and wasn't even tempted to con Simon out of his cash, but rejected the opportunity to turn a quick profit; instead, pointing the sorcerer to the source of truth. The free grace of God is all too often regarded as too good to be true. Yet, it is true! Acts 8:24 leads us to believe that Simon was warming to this glorious fact. Let's hope so!

CELL GROUPS

Taste and see that the Lord is good
(PSALM 34:8 *NIV*)

Convicted drug barons in South American prisons are permitted to use dogs as food tasters, as a precaution against poisoned goodies being smuggled in. Prison authorities are anxious that rival drug barons still at liberty should be prevented from poisoning their imprisoned "business" rivals, then inheriting their clients (victims). Therefore, when food is eaten, the first mouthful is tasted (tested) by a dog, and only when everyone is satisfied the dog has not suffered any ill-effects will the rest of the meal be eaten by the convict. Not much of a job for any dog but, on the plus side, those prison canines probably get to eat much more than their friends on the outside! We have a similar problem in our family, in that Skipper has appointed himself as Food Taster In Chief, despite having his nose tapped whenever he commences his official duties. Not, I hasten to add, that we are drug barons; it's simply the case that Skipper will sniff around anything on offer in the hope of a free sample. Occasionally, he will steal a roast potato and run away with it, fully aware of his guilt, and at such times, I am tempted to book him a flight to South America and offer his services to the prison authorities.

It would be good to offer a prayer for drug barons everywhere; for their customers whose lives are at the mercy of lethal substances and spiralling debts, and for prison warders. May they all experience abundant compassion to assist them. Imprisonment is always bleak; literal incarceration, of course, but also captivity that might not involve prison bars and guards, but which can be demoralizing; the misery of mental health issues, for example, whereby fear and paranoia enchain and oppress. Those who are isolated because of physical ailments limiting mobility and social opportunities can feel imprisoned, and our prayers this day could include the request that all such imprisoned will taste and see the Lord's great love. Freedom might not arrive overnight, but grace cannot be restrained by high walls and barred windows.

WHAT A LOAD OF RUBBISH!

Everything else is worthless when compared with the infinite value of knowing Christ Jesus my Lord. For his sake I have discarded everything else, counting it all as garbage, so that I could gain Christ

(PHILIPPIANS 3:8 **NLT**)

Yorkshire folk, in the north of England, have a saying: "Where there's muck, there's brass" – meaning, don't be afraid of getting your hands dirty if you want to make money, "brass" being the old name for copper and bronze coins. As John Ray expressed it in his 1678 *Collection of English Proverbs*, "Muck and money go together"; where there are grimy jobs to be done, there are lucrative opportunities to be had. Two hundred miles south of Yorkshire, in Bedfordshire, there is a plan to phase out dog poo bins and replace them with "dual use receptacles", but locals have registered concerns at this proposal, fearing it might make messy Bedfordshire streets worse. Bedfordshire Borough Council, though, is standing firm, claiming budget cuts can be made by doubling up and that this scheme will save £30,000 annually. Despite this claim, many locals are poo-pooing the project and would prefer litter bins to remain for litter only. A council spokeswoman said: "We are consulting on increasing the number of standardised bins for dual use with litter and dog waste in suitable areas. This will provide greater access for users and for collection crews, increasing efficiency and saving money."[1] The citizens of Yorkshire might be right, after all!

When Paul assessed his spiritual journey from persecutor of Christians to evangelist, he considered his qualifications to be just so much rubbish, compared to the saving grace of knowing Christ. Scholars tell us we should not baulk at the idea of Paul listing his credentials under "D for Dung", such was the contrast he was at pains to illustrate, between his old way of life and his behaviour as a convert. Theologian, teacher, Jew of Jews, intellectually gifted; yet, he regarded all things as fit only for the bins for the sake of knowing Jesus. Paul wasn't dismissing intelligent study, but pointing out that a saving encounter with Jesus Christ was of paramount importance. All we hold dear is of no eternal worth in that light. Exactly what decision Bedfordshire Borough Council arrives at remains to be seen, but Paul made the most important decision of his life when he decided to follow the Nazarene.

1   BBC Three Counties Radio. Date unknown

SO MUCH MORE TO SEE

Now we see through a glass, darkly; but then face to face: now I know in part; but then shall I know even as also I am known

(I CORINTHIANS 13:12 *KJV*)

Skipper's latest attempt to win universal unpopularity comes in the form of abusing the hospitality of a friend who looked after him for a weekend. Our friend is no stranger to dogs, but Skipper did his best to see himself expelled from his temporary guest house by launching himself at the large window facing the front garden; whenever a dog, cat or squirrel wandered past, he would throw his not inconsiderable frame at the glass in the hope of starting a fight or killing something. Thankfully, the glass held firm and withstood his best efforts at pretending to be a flying dog, but we are left with the impression that the longer we keep Skipper, the fewer friends we shall have; there is a ratio now in existence whereby his behaviour corresponds directly to the number of acquaintances we retain. What to do? Well, we can't very well ask our friends to draw their curtains whenever we visit with Skipper in tow, nor can we impose a curfew on local wildlife. If only he would just sit and look out of the window, without succumbing to the urge to hurl himself through it.

I visited a museum which featured the type of hand "mirror" women carried in St Paul's day. It was a cute little thing – the size of a pocket mirror, made of polished metal; like a reflective dessert spoon, and I could see my reflection in it; a mirror without glass, but still very effective. The card in the display case informed me this type of looking "glass" was commonplace in Roman times, and I couldn't help but think of Paul's words, which might have referred to something similar. Looking out of life's window, so to speak, we see but a partial picture of what our existence is all about – a glimpse. What we perceive here is not the full picture, and Paul frames his conviction that we enjoy only a limited view in our three score years and ten. There is more to come, in the life hereafter, and by the grace of God, all will be revealed one day. When we all get to Heaven, what a day of rejoicing that will be! We shall see!

DOING WHAT COMES NATURALLY?

Jesus was led by the Spirit into the wilderness to be tempted by the devil. After fasting forty days and forty nights, he was hungry
(MATTHEW 4:1 *NIV*)

I saw a van advertising a dog food product claiming to have a "natural dog food taste" and was struck by the irony of a commercially manufactured product claiming to taste "natural". It begged the question: if one is interested in one's dog food purchases having a natural taste, then why not buy natural ingredients? Why go to the trouble of manufacturing something that is, by definition, manufactured, then marketing it as "natural"? Dogs are, by nature, carnivorous; they prefer raw meat and bones, but will also eat some plants. Skipper, for example, eats grass if his tummy is out of sorts; it's a natural instinct. Wild pups feast on their mother's regurgitated meals, and wild dogs eat chickens, birds, and rodents; all perfectly natural! Left to their own devices, dogs then fast for a couple of days, to allow their digestive systems to rebalance, and a fasting (domesticated) dog should not necessarily be rushed to a vet. Wild dogs know when their stomachs need a break, and benefit from going for a while without feeding; their colonic equilibrium is naturally regained. As nutritious as the dog food advertised on the van no doubt is, it is probably some way from being natural!

I wonder how Jesus survived his time fasting in the wilderness. What did he eat when angels looked after him after the period of his temptation? Did they bring food? He must have been starving, and I personally wouldn't care much for an angel who forgot to bring rations! Would that have been all-natural food? Pomegranates, perhaps, and figs? That month in the wilds would have been almost intolerable, especially when Satan tempted him with bread. Half-starved and possibly delirious, we couldn't have blamed him for throwing in the towel, but Jesus overcame the strongest, craftiest wiles of the tempter, showing us that victory is possible; that defeat is not inevitable. As we continue on a diet of prayer and Bible reading, may we draw strength from our undefeated Saviour.

THE RIGHT MOVE

Let the peace of Christ rule in your hearts
(COLOSSIANS 3:15 **NIV**)

In 1975, a Dutch footballer, Willem van Hanegam, was approached by Marseilles to sign for them and leave his beloved Feyenoord, for whom he had first signed in 1968. He anguished over this proposition because Marseilles had made him a great offer and he would have the opportunity to pit his wits against the biggest names in French football, but set against that was his strong emotional attachment to Feyenoord. The midfield maestro was faced with such a conundrum he invited friends to a picnic so they could chat over the options. All to no avail! As pleasant as the picnic was, van Hanegam was no closer to choosing between Marseilles and Feyenoord, but then he hit upon the idea of asking his dog's opinion! Turning to his pooch, he said, "It's up to you now. If you want to go to Marseilles, bark at me." For the next few minutes, the dog didn't move, neither did it bark, leading WvG to stay put. He went on to make a career total of 298 appearances for Feyenoord, becoming their manager in 1992, winning the League in 1993, and the Dutch Cup in 1994 and 1995. Well done, that silent dog!

How do we make decisions? A picnic with friends? I think most of us would draw the line at consulting a dog regarding a career move! The Bible encourages us with the thought that there is wisdom in many counsellors, but we also believe in the Holy Spirit as our infallible Counsellor. Is a combination of good advice and prayerful guidance therefore acceptable? The disciples of the Early Church cast lots on the matter of choosing a replacement for Judas on their team, and we have no reason to believe the Lord disapproved of their actions or failed to honour their request (significantly, though, this took place before the dispensation of the Holy Spirit, which might have ruled out the need for any such practices thereafter). I feel God is only too willing to guide us even when our most sincere guesses are incorrect, so long as we are intent on his will being done. Our perplexity is his chance to reassure us. Prayer gently lifts us from earth's confusion.

ANOTHER FINE MESS

I will instruct thee and teach thee in the way which thou shalt go: I will guide thee with mine eye

(PSALM 32:8 *KJV*)

Back to Vicki the Guide Dog. My friend told me about her working relationship with Vicki's predecessor, Laurel the Labrador. She hadn't long been using a Guide Dog, and was still becoming accustomed to the rules of successful Guide Dog management – trusting the dog implicitly and becoming used to the fact your Guide Dog won't let you down, even if you can't understand why, for example, it might suddenly stop walking and expect you to halt too. The secret is to trust and obey, to relax in your dog's care; it is a well-trained employee, and it knows its job. Problems occur when a novice Guide Dog owner insists on overriding the dog's instincts. Problems, such as, in my friend's case, walking into a brick wall Laurel had tried to steer her away from. He had stopped when he saw the wall, but my friend, thinking he was inexperienced and making a mistake, tugged him along and collided painfully with some rather solid bricks held together by some equally resistant cement. Problems such as allowing Laurel to wander too far from her side one day, which led my friend to walk into an immovable concrete bollard placed at the end of a road to stop traffic. Ouch! Fortunately, lessons were learnt, and Laurel proved himself to be reliable and trustworthy – as is Vicki.

Walking into a wall or a bollard is painful and embarrassing, but not the end of the world. It is, though, symbolic of those times we think we know better than God; when our distance from him is greater than it should be. God wishes to guide us in good ways, and never has any intention of harming or misleading. He wants to steer us along paths of blessing. He wants us to stay close by, precisely because he is aware of the unseen pitfalls ahead; the further we are from him, the weaker our devotional life becomes, the more likely we are to fail to heed his warnings and wind up bruised. What shall we do with God? Relax with him and respond to his guidance? Stop when he tells us to? Keep him close? We need no assistance to work out the answers to those questions!

AWAY WITH THE MANGER!

Rejoice with those who rejoice
(ROMANS 12:15 *NIV*)

A Greek legend provides the phrase, "A dog in the manger." On first reading, this saying doesn't make sense, insofar as dogs are rarely found in mangers. It is attributed to the Greek novelist, satirist, and playwright, Lucien (c. AD 125 – c. AD 180), who used it as a metaphor to describe those who prevent others from having something for which they themselves have no use; that is, a dog lying in a manger would have no use for the grain upon which it was lying, but a horse would find that grain inaccessible. Quite why a dog in particular would wish to do this is not clear (dogs not being vindictive creatures), but the metaphor makes the point of spitefulness. The writer of the apocryphal Gospel of Thomas ascribes the saying to Jesus, who is alleged to have said (to Thomas), "Woe to the Pharisees, for they are like a dog sleeping in the manger of oxen, for neither does he eat nor does he let the oxen eat." It's about envy, jealousy, malice, and pride; not wanting others to do well, or to be happy. The late Commissioner Vic Poke, an Australian Salvation Army officer, once spoke about gum trees which, he said, refuse to tolerate the growth of other plants within a certain radius by emitting a chemical discouraging the appearance of anything much else. Honesty compels me to say I have sometimes fallen prey to the nasty traits of "gum tree-ism"; may God forgive me.

Begrudging another's success is childish and pointless; the colleague who is promoted, for example – can we honestly say it never crossed our mind to wonder why it was him or her, and not us? The neighbour whose house/car is bigger/grander than ours, and so on. We're like that, I'm afraid (well, I am). It's one thing to feel jealous, but another to put obstacles in the way of another's well-being; to play dog in the manger when we don't gain anything by doing so. In fact, we suffer because of our self-inflicted distress! We have a gracious God who knows quite a bit about mangers, which means we can bring all our pettiness to him and instead of acting like dumb gum trees, celebrate each other's achievements altruistically.

TAKING OUR BOW

It is better to go to a house of mourning than to go to a house of feasting, for death is the destiny of everyone
(ECCLESIASTES 7:2 *NIV*)

Should you be in Scotland, you may wish to find the grave of The Great Lafayette, a music hall entertainer, one of the highest paid of his era, friend of Houdini; his illusions were the talk of the town when he was booked to appear in Edinburgh in 1911. The Great Lafayette lived with Beauty, his Cross-bred Terrier, and he doted on her; Beauty slept on velvet cushions, dined at the same table as Lafayette, wore a solid gold, diamond-studded collar, and even the radiator ornament on Lafayette's limousine was a statuette of Beauty, who had her own rooms furnished with dog-sized furniture and baths. A plaque over Lafayette's home was inscribed, "The more I see of men the more I love my dog." Just days before The Great Lafayette was due to open in Scotland, Beauty died, and Lafayette was so heartbroken he persuaded Edinburgh City Council to grant permission for the embalmed Terrier to be buried in Piershill Cemetery. Astonishingly, the showman himself died that same week, in a fire, when a prop dislodged a hot light and the theatre burned down. The first car in the funeral cortège was Lafayette's Mercedes, the sole passenger a Dalmatian; Beauty's coffin was opened and Lafayette's ashes placed inside. Houdini sent a floral representation of Beauty to the service.

Poor Beauty! Not a great ending for Lafayette, either, but none of us knows when God will call us; when our souls will be required. The writer of Ecclesiastes visited graveyards, and Skipper and I do the same thing – we stroll around graveyards (him on a lead), and I inspect the tombstones. I find it interesting, but also a reminder of one's mortality, as our three score years and ten will pass very quickly! Is that a gloomy thought or a useful spiritual exercise? The Great Lafayette had no idea that his appearance in Edinburgh would represent the final act of his life; that the curtain would fall just moments later. May God grant us the grace to be ready for his summons.

FACING GIANTS

David triumphed over the Philistine with a sling and a stone; without a sword in his hand he struck down the Philistine and killed him. David ran and stood over him. He took hold of the Philistine's sword and drew it from the sheath. After he killed him, he cut off his head with the sword

(I SAMUEL 17:50–51 ***NIV***)

A big story on my local radio station in 2015 was that of a lady called Lynette, fined by her council for letting her Miniature Schnauzer off its lead in a graveyard. A council employee informed her she was breaking the law, but Lynette's defence was that there were no signs at the cemetery telling her she wasn't allowed to do this. Despite pleading this case, she received a £50 penalty, and was warned that this would increase to £75 should she fail to pay within two weeks, and that if she further refused to pay, she would be given a criminal record. After months of escalating threats, the case was dropped, but not before Lynette had suffered a huge amount of stress. Sasha the Schnauzer was brought into the offices of the radio station for a guest appearance as the story became massive news, the miniature dog making big headlines. A lawyer took on Lynette's and Sasha's case, eventually making the council abandon its pursuit, and he was so appalled by the unfairness of the charge he acted for Lynette without claiming any fee (pro-bono, if you'll excuse the pun), and I am delighted to report Sasha the Schnauzer is now at liberty to visit the graveyard whenever Lynette takes her there – on a lead!

Listeners following this case were captivated by a sense of injustice; the notion of an ordinary woman taking on the council, with huge financial resources at its disposal. Callers to the radio station offered to pay Lynette's fines, so strongly did they feel about what they regarded as her persecution; she was viewed as David taking on Goliath. In the original narrative featuring those two, David (on paper) never stood a chance – a stripling lad up against an enormous man, a shepherd boy taking on the pride of the Philistines. I expect David gulped as he faced his opponent, before flinging his stone and hoping/praying for a direct hit. As we know, Goliath was well and truly stoned and eventually lost his head, the implication being that David had God on his side and couldn't fail. Lynette and Sasha succeeded against the odds because of Lynette's courage, but also because a lawyer intervened. Need we ever doubt that God himself will step in on our behalf as we too stand for truth and righteousness?

NO PAIN, NO GAIN

Carrying his own cross, he went out to the place of the Skull (which in Aramaic is called Golgotha)

(JOHN 19:17 **NIV**)

Meg was all set to come on holiday with us. We were used to taking her everywhere in the car, without a moment's trouble; she would sit or lie in the back, and be no problem at all – an excellent traveller; never car-sick, and willing to put in the miles as long as she could be with us. We packed the car then went to fetch Meg, expecting her to agree, as usual, to be lifted into the hatchback space and sleep for the journey. This time, though, she wasn't interested, despite our efforts to coax her into the vehicle. For the first and what proved to be the last time, Meg walked away, asking to be let back inside the house. She knew the routine, but was trying to tell us this was one journey she wouldn't be making, and when I picked her up, she yelped in pain as I cradled her legs into my embrace. Her travelling days were done, arthritis had the better of her and, as we subsequently discovered, would eventually immobilize her. She conveyed the information that her end was nigh; no more trips, no more holidays; not even managing to stand successfully very often.

Can we imagine how Jesus might have felt as he made his (reluctant?) way along the Via Dolorosa? We can try, and in doing so, appreciate his sacrifice all the more. Limping along what is known as "The Way of Sorrows" in Latin, or "Painful Way" in Arabic, on his final journey, what might have gone through his mind? He headed to "The place of the Skull" where no holiday awaited him, but only the macabre hell of Calvary. Did his legs give way? Definitely, as he stumbled beneath the weight of his cross; a burden not only of physical proportions, but of spiritual magnitude too. (It is estimated Jesus' cross weighed something like 300lbs.) Did he long to turn back? I think so. Largely immobilized by a beating that took him to within an inch of his life, Jesus knew his departure was just a few more painful footsteps away. Yet, for the joy set before him (the joy, that is, of redeeming us), he endured it all. A great Saviour!

WALKING WELL

Can two people walk together without agreeing on the direction?
(AMOS 3:3 **NLT**)

Walking Meg was, well, a walk in the park. She would amble along, checking back every so often to make sure one of us was still within reach, she could be let off her lead with no threat whatsoever, and in her younger days, could chase a ball or a stick with the best of them. We even bought her one of those flingers whereby a ball is loaded into one end, which can then be flung at speed courtesy of a long handle – a poor man's clay pigeon thrower. Then, her energy was boundless, and I have fondest memories of taking her for late-night walks if I had something on my mind, which helped clear my head and which gave her a bonus outing. Skipper, on the other hand, presents some challenges! His walking style is zigzag haphazard, and we daren't let him off the lead. He resents any hint of restraint, and I can see the day coming when my left arm (my lead-holding arm) is significantly longer than my right one! I long for the carefree days of walks with the docile Meg when, if I happened to meet a friend out walking, I could stop and chat, instead of being yanked hither and thither. What to do? Answers on a postcard, please ...

At my grandmother's funeral service, we used Commissioner Theodore Hopkins Kitching's hymn, "How Wonderful it is to Walk with God" (best known to Salvationists, I imagine). Commissioner Kitching wrote about walking with God, and painted a picture with his lyrics born, no doubt, of his personal experience of pilgrimage. A friend once gave me a bookmark, and written on it were these words:

Don't walk behind me; I may not lead. Don't walk in front of me; I may not follow. Just walk beside me and be my friend.[1]

It's slightly different with God, because he expects us to follow, but I love the idea of also walking alongside God as his friend. How sad it is when I zigzag my own way along my own routes, distracted by the sights that dazzle and the tempting sounds I hear. May God help us each to walk with him this day.

---

1   Source unknown

THE WHOLE STORY

Jesus did many other things as well. If every one of them were written down, I
suppose that even the whole world would not have room for the books that would
be written

(JOHN 21:25 ***NIV***)

Flicking through a magazine (pretending to be researching this book), I found an article about a "dog blog" with a picture of a Springer Spaniel plodding along an isolated beach. It's a website devoted to bloggers wishing to write about their experiences of a particular English coastal county in respect of their dogs, and short features are invited recommending dog-friendly places, beaches, hotels, pubs, and eateries – the key word being friendly. (For example, are dogs allowed in the grounds of, say, a stately home and, if they are, will they also be welcome inside?) One blogger listed "five dog-friendly pubs with roaring fires" and there is advertising space for items made in that county that have dog appeal; locally produced goods supporting a local economy. The "dog blog" is keen to hear from visitors who have discovered places where dogs were welcomed, and although the website is apolitical, it will feature issues such as beaches with dog bans in order to save people wasted journeys. I hope the idea catches on as a handy repository for useful snippets and memos.

Blog contributors are encouraged to keep their contributions brief, and low word counts are preferred. It seems as though John, the Gospel writer, was working under similar restraints, albeit self-imposed. Half the skill of being a successful writer, I guess (I wouldn't know!), is understanding what to leave out, as much as what to include, for long-windedness tends to bore, and it would be a crime for any of Jesus' followers to portray him – of all people – as boring. Could that happen? Can the God-man be made to look dull? Well, maybe we have all experienced sermons during which the preacher seems to be on a mission to present Christ as the dullest man ever! I think it's a pity John excluded stories of which he was obviously aware, and I wonder what he knew, but didn't record. Perhaps he had an editor breathing down his neck, carefully watching his use of parchment and ink. We'll probably never know for sure. However, if what we do know about Jesus – his miracles, his love, his revolutionary teaching – isn't the full story, then we can but praise him all the more, because what we know is marvellous enough, and we therefore marvel that there is extra news of him, as yet untold!

SAUSAGES AND SUCCESS

The chief jailer did not supervise anything under Joseph's charge because the Lord
was with him; and whatever he did, the Lord made to prosper
(GENESIS 39:23 **NASB**)

It wasn't often Marilyn Monroe and Fred Astaire were upstaged, but Uggie the Jack Russell managed to do just that by becoming the first canine to print its paws on Hollywood Boulevard, where the handprints of Monroe and Astaire also appear. The first Terrier of Tinseltown, Uggie was quite an actor, starring in hits such as *The Artist* (in which he played "The Dog"!) and *Water for Elephants*. Uggie's acting skills included playing dead, hiding his head in his paws, and walking on his hind legs – some repertoire for a rescue dog saved from incarceration by Omar Von Muller, who trained the two-year-old in the thespian art. So popular did Uggie become, he even published an "autobiography": *Uggie: My Story*, ghostwritten by Wendy Holden, detailing the tale of a reject who became a star. Uggie was rejected by his first two owners as being wild, but Von Muller said of his little friend, "He was a crazy, very energetic puppy, and who knows what would have happened to him if he had gone to the dog pound. But he was very smart and very willing to work. One of the most important things is that he was not afraid of things. That is what makes or breaks a dog in the movies, whether they are afraid of lights, and noises and being on sets. He gets rewards, like sausages, to encourage him to perform, but that is only a part of it. He works hard."

At the heart of the gospel is the story of humankind messing up, then being rescued by a God who is so desperate for reconciliation he dies for his beloved. It's not so much about how we start, as how we finish. We might get into all sorts of scrapes – some self-inflicted, others no fault of our own, but what matters is that we allow a loving Father to lift us out of the incarceration of sin and into his care. Paul wrote about reaching the finishing line; leaving the past behind, pressing on in the grace of God. That's not to say we will have trouble-free lives when we come to God, but we will be helped and redirected, if necessary. Does your past haunt you? Memory is a wonderful faculty, but we will often remember that which we would rather forget about ourselves. May I encourage you today to receive the forgiveness of God? We all need to do that, then move forward.

WITH NO-ONE THERE HIS SORROW TO SHARE

He was despised and rejected – a man of sorrows, acquainted with deepest grief
(ISAIAH 53:3 **NLT**)

What qualities come to mind when we think of military leaders? Courage? Strength? The ability to lead without fear or favour? Perseverance? Conviction? A refusal to admit defeat? Logistical awareness? Leaders need to possess such attributes, especially in the heat of battle, where their decisions can be crucial, and one such figure was Napoleon; famously ruthless, cunning, calculating, and intelligent in terms of strategy; able to identify weaknesses and exploit them. Even Bonaparte had a softer side, though, and he is recorded as describing the saddest moment of his life: "On the battlefield, this dead soldier I realised must have family and friends at home and friends in his regiment. Yet he lay there deserted by all except his dog. I looked on unmoved by battles which decide the future of nations. Tearless, I had given orders which brought death to thousands. Yet here I was profoundly stirred, stirred to tears. And by what? By the grief of one dog."[1] The image of a dog beside his dead master, licking his face, haunted Napoleon for the rest of his days.

Jesus died alone, albeit surrounded by friends and family, but not one of them was able to touch him, soothe his forehead, or embrace him as his life slipped away. How he must have longed for his mother's tactile love as his heartbeat slowed and his breathing became agonal, yet even the physical comfort of human contact was denied our dying God. Napoleon – tough, brutal, hardened by war – cried at the sight of a grieving dog, but can we imagine the waves of grief that would have overwhelmed Mary and Jesus' disciples, and his loved ones, as they stood helplessly at the foot of his cross? How they must have longed to reach out to the Saviour, even just to hold his hand as the Incarnation reached its conclusion, set in blood. Here we see the Man of Sorrows bowing his head in dreadful isolation as he died for the sins of the world. His was the last word in rejection.

1 www.goodreads.com

STORM AND A TEA CUP

My sheep listen to my voice; I know them, and they follow me
(JOHN 10:27 **NIV**)

From time to time, people invite me into their homes to lead house groups and/ or Bible studies. I arrive early, not only because it means I am offered an extra cup of tea, but also because I can get to know my hosts and settle my mind on what is expected of me. On one such occasion, I met Storm, a lively and lovely black Labrador who gave every impression of being a fierce guard dog, barking at me as I arrived, but who was in reality a big softie. Despite his pretend protestations, he was soon licking my hand and lying on the floor asking to be stroked, and even allowed his owner to place a woollen monkey on his head and leave it there, without a flicker of protest. Storm, I learned, had been selected for training as a Hearing Dog for the deaf, when he was a puppy, and all was going well until his trainers realized he was demonstrating unsuitable behaviour towards his fellow students; conduct that eventually ruled him out. In every other respect, he was an ideal candidate, but he has found a new life now as a much-loved pet. My only gripe with Storm was that he kept up his phoney guard dog act every time someone came near the house! His bark was convincing – though not entirely conducive to the success of a reflective house group! – but his bite was nonexistent. (My guess is, he just didn't really fancy working for a living!)

Storm left his studies because he demonstrated traits unacceptable in a dog hoping for a career with the hard of hearing. It worked out well for him in the end, so no great harm done! What about us, though? Our text today states that we will recognize the voice of Jesus when he speaks to us; regarding guidance, perhaps, or sin, maybe – whatever he needs us to listen out for. How is it, then, we sometimes make out we can't quite hear what he is saying? When, for example, a verse from the Bible "speaks" to our heart, and the Holy Spirit works overtime to impress it upon us – yet we "fake" a kind of deafness. Or, say, a hymn strikes us right between the eyes; is that Jesus trying to grab our attention? Do we still wander around with our spiritual ears stuffed, even going so far as to blame God for not speaking up? Maybe, if we act upon what he has said to us in the first place, we would hear a bit more, subsequently? Oh, for a responsiveness to divine breathings.

DON'T RULE OUT LOVE

These are the commands, decrees and laws the Lord your God directed me to teach you to observe

(DEUTERONOMY 6:1 *NIV*)

My parents-in-law, formerly Salvation Army missionaries in Kenya, kept a dog by the name of Mbogo, which, in Swahili, means "African buffalo". By and large, Kenyan tradition is to keep dogs as guard dogs, rather than pets, and Mbogo served such a purpose; a cross between an Elkhound and an Alsatian who was friendly, intelligent, and responsible, but not a beast to provoke. His chosen method of guarding his loved ones was not to display overt aggression, but to circle visitors as they arrived, conveying the subtle greeting that they may approach so far, but no further without his permission. Round and round their legs he would go, sending a warning that this was his territory and he was protecting his pack – the rest was up to the visitor! A deep sea diver once issued a similar note of caution, advising trainee snorkellers that they should feel free to dip their flippered feet into the ocean, but what happened after that would rest entirely with the great creatures of the sea at perfect liberty to nip, sting, or even swallow whole! The divers were, after all, like Mbogo's callers, splashing around as guests in someone else's domain!

God is a gentle rule-giver, but a rule-giver, for all that; Governor of the universe, First Sea Lord, King of Kenya. The Bible speaks of his care, his patience, his grace, and his tremendous ability to keep his temper despite our best efforts at making him lose it. The same book, though, also tells of his fury, his anger, and his devastating vengeance. It's a balance, and we find ourselves faced with a similar situation to callers to Mbogo's yard; whether to test the guidelines, or to abide by the rules. If we choose to ignore God's instructions, there is of course the deep ocean of his mercy still to plunge into, but it makes sense not to risk his displeasure in the first place. More to the point, why would we want to deliberately upset and grieve a loving Father, who has our best interests at heart? Ours is a tender and compassionate God. The rest is up to us!

HELD TIGHT

I am the Lord your God who takes hold of your right hand and says to you,
Do not fear; I will help you
(ISAIAH 41:13 **NIV**)

My father-in-law, until he required surgery on a knee, was a keen walker. Given a choice between walking and taking a car ride, he would opt to walk, encouraging others to follow suit and wondering why God gave some people legs, such was the scarcity of their usage. Until I wised up, I sometimes accompanied him, and on one occasion fell for his line that we (me, him, and a few more innocents) should go for "a short walk" in the Scottish countryside. It started well; the scenery was edifying and the weather was agreeable, but what appeared to have become lost in translation was a reasonable definition of the word "short". Hours later, we were still exploring what little part of Scotland we hadn't already seen, so we stopped by a loch in order to recover the will to live. Alistair, our son, followed his energetic grandfather into the water for a refreshing dip; at which point, the attentive Meg waded into the loch to "rescue" Alistair, whom she thought was drowning. Meg was distressed, seeing it as her duty to pull him ashore by gently clamping her jaws around his arm. Then it was Alistair's turn to be distressed, as he couldn't understand why such a placid dog had decided to bite him. All was well in the end; we convinced Meg there was no need of her heroics, Alistair realized what had happened, and we continued with our world tour.

Poor Alistair! He suffered no scarring, physical or emotional, as a result of Meg's intervention. She was doing her best to keep him from meeting a watery end, but hadn't realized he was merely cooling off. Had Alistair actually been in trouble, then Meg would have earned her place in our family history as his brave rescuer. God already holds that title, thanks to the day he intervened in our lives and rescued us from the deep. Our eternal souls were in danger until he dragged us to safety, spiritually speaking. Grace marvellously prevailed, and we are hauled by love to that heavenly shore, safe in his grip. He won't let go.

SAINTS ALIVE!

Make disciples of all nations
(MATTHEW 28:19 *ESV*)

The seventeenth of March was my grandad's birthday, also celebrated as St Patrick's Day, particularly in Ireland. Patrick's story is fascinating, not least the part where he is said to have banished snakes from the Emerald Isle. Whether they were actual snakes or not remains a matter of conjecture as diehard devotees of Patrick dismiss arguments suggesting there were no snakes in Ireland in the first place, whereas others believe "snakes" was a euphemism for the druid priests whom St Patrick deposed. Whatever the facts, Patrick made his mark as a Christian giant, to such an extent there are now even pub quizzes named in his honour! One such is "Irish Dog Breeds for St Patrick's Day", featuring questions about The Glen of Imaal (a working Terrier), The Irish (Red) Setter, The Irish Terrier, The Irish Water Spaniel, The Irish Wolfhound, The Soft-Coated Wheaten Terrier, and The Kerry Blue Terrier. Accompanying pictures of these breeds show them to be amongst the most handsome in the canine kingdom – all in honour of Patrick! Snakes or no snakes, the quizzes affirm St Patrick certainly did not drive dogs from Ireland, and for that, we are grateful! (Seventeenth of March is said to be the date of his death.)

St Patrick sailed to Ireland on missionary service, taking up Christian arms against druid forces that held the people in thrall (some of whose members, incidentally, made up nasty and insulting limericks about the man who was to become the first Bishop of Amargh, Primate of Ireland). We thank God for those who leave homes, loved ones, and families to take the gospel to lands that are not their own, as missionary endeavours can sometimes be a costly and thankless task as new cultures, diets, and customs have to be assimilated. As someone once said, "An evangelist must have a face for any weather, a back for any bed, and a stomach for any food." So too, missionaries. Their labours are long, but their joys unique. God be praised for those who cross continents and boundaries for the Kingdom's sake.

MESSAGE IN A BOTTLE

For we are to God the pleasing aroma of Christ among those who are being saved and those who are perishing

(2 CORINTHIANS 2:15 **NIV**)

A friend of mine is a keen walker, hiking up hills and down dales, conquering impressive heights, and walking miles as he exercises. On one hike, he found himself being slowly pursued by what appeared to be an excitable pack of Foxhounds. Unable to understand their interest in him, he began to worry, fearing they were after him and wondering if things might turn nasty, so he hurriedly posed a question on a social media website, asking if anyone could shed light on the mystery. The general consensus of opinion seemed to be that the Foxhounds were probably "scenting" the route – the layout – of a hunt set to take place in a day or two; the tactic being that Foxhounds in pursuit of a fox are less likely to be distracted by smells on that way if they are already familiar with them. Working on a process of elimination, the Foxhounds are then better able to sniff out the fox, given that its scent wasn't there previously; the new foxy odour grabs their attention. My friend's fragrance could therefore be eliminated on hunt day as one with which they were already acquainted. Phew!

An intriguing incident took place when I was clearing my grandad's bathroom cabinet after his death. Unbeknown to me, he and I had been wearing the exact same brand of aftershave for years. Human beings have an "emotional scent memory" whereby we associate certain smells with people or events. It's part of our survival mechanism, enabling us to remember whiffs that might indicate danger (the smell of something burning, say) or aromas reminding us of something pleasant (rice pudding). It seems my emotional scent memory had, when I was a boy, noted Grandad's aftershave, leading me to prefer that style years later. What, then, of the fragrance of Christ in my life? Will anyone note that? What thoughts of Jesus will linger in the responses of my friends, because of me? I hope people like my aftershave, but, more importantly, I hope something about me reminds them of the Saviour.

ROCH OF AGES

When Jesus landed and saw a large crowd, he had compassion on them and healed those who were ill

(MATTHEW 14:14 **NIV**)

Have you heard of St Roch, the patron saint of dogs? He was, if pictures are anything to go by, a swashbuckling sort of saint; more Hollywood than holy man, and looked like one of the cavalier soldiers associated with kings Charles I and II, complete with dark beard and dashing demeanour. Stories abound regarding the astonishing ministry of Roch (or Rocco), but one in particular is relevant here. St Roch was ministering in Italy, in Piacenza, when he became ill with a contagious virus and the townsfolk threw him out. Expelled and sick, he withdrew to the trees, making himself a shelter and surviving on water from a nearby spring. According to legend, he would have starved had not a passing dog supplied him with a loaf of bread; furthermore, that same dog licked his infectious wounds clean and healed him, and paintings and statues displayed thereafter in honour of Rocco nearly always portray him with a dog nearby – sometimes carrying a loaf of bread for good measure!

I once cut my knee playing football with a friend. My friend's black Labrador (which was, tragically, shot dead by a farmer some time later) saw my knee was bleeding and came over to lick it clean (I hesitate to mention this, but I was wearing shorts). He liked the taste of my blood, and licked my knee until the bleeding stopped, so that, remarkably, the wound healed up rapidly, and the scab shrunk quicker than it might otherwise have done. That is my only (tenuous!) link with St Roch, but it does lead me to wonder about healing miracles in the Bible. They are everywhere. I love them and I believe them because they speak volumes about a God who heals; not every time – we all know that – but when he chooses to. (Don't ask me why he doesn't heal on other occasions, because I haven't a clue.) I suggest a perusal of healing miracles in Scripture. Maybe, too, we could spare a few moments to pray specifically for someone who is ill?

WAITING FOR GOD

Thou wilt keep him in perfect peace, whose mind is stayed on thee: because he
trusteth in thee
(ISAIAH 26:3 *KJV*)

At this time of writing, I have just taken Skipper to the vet because his stomach (Skipper's, not the vet's) is bloated, and refuses to un-bloat. Early indications point to liver problems, resulting in a build-up of fluid, and for all that he drives me to distraction with his neurotic behaviour, I wouldn't wish this upon him. As I write, I am awaiting the results of tests, and this situation will go one way or the other; either Skipper's liver will be coaxed back to health, or the condition will signal his demise. Skipper himself seems unconcerned, except that he is, uncharacteristically, off his food and unable to lie down properly, due to the size of his gut, so my dilemma is whether or not to engage with a series of expensive treatments, given that Skipper is already in the autumn of his days. To put it bluntly, would that be cost-effective? Would I spend on costly remedies today, only to find I need to do so again tomorrow? Skipper has gone for a lie-down. I think I would too, had I been inspected with a rectal thermometer and deprived of a syringe-full of blood. Now, we wait and see ...

The anxiety of waiting for news can sometimes be worse than actually receiving that news. We seem better able to cope with bad tidings than the apprehension of wondering what those bad tidings might be. If things are grim, our nerves can become shredded as we wait for the telephone to ring or a letter to arrive; the result of a job interview, perhaps, or a hospital report. We worry, fingernails are bitten, we lose sleep, and anxiety can dominate. Much as we hate to admit it, prayer doesn't always help, immediately. In most cases, we imagine worst-case scenarios, and what a relief it can be when the news isn't as dreadful as we first feared! Isaiah wrote about perfect peace, the original language of his words literally translating as "A steadfast disposition thou guardest in constant peace for it is trustful towards thee". This day, our thoughts are with those who are worried; may the God of peace minister to their needs.

CRIME PREVENTION

The thief comes only to steal and kill and destroy
(JOHN 10:10 **ESV**)

My wife and I used to work for The Salvation Army in Scotland, living in Glasgow, which is where today's story is set. I can't vouch for its veracity, as I believe the tale also exists set in other major cities, but I tell it as it was told to me. A lady had collected her dearly departed dog from the vet's, where it had been euthanized. Distressed, she wanted to bring her dog home before organizing cremation, and had opted to do so by using her shopping trolley as its means of transport. As she trundled the trolley along, a man asked if he might help carry what he assumed to be her shopping up a flight of steps. Grateful for this offer (the dog was no lightweight), she accepted, only to see the man running away with her trolley and its contents. He thought he had grabbed himself a free week's supply of shopping, whereas all he had managed to steal was a canine corpse! Imagine his shock when he looked inside, expecting to find a few tins of soup, or a loaf of bread and some milk, and found, instead, only a deceased dog! What happened next is not recorded, but I can only hope our chancer had the decency to return the stolen property, or at least to grant the dog a Christian burial.

The devil comes to steal, kill, and destroy – our faith, our charity, our hope, our peace of mind, and our joy. He wants to rob us of all that God wants us to enjoy, then he will then pile in with despair, hopelessness, and feelings of abandonment, running away with blessings that are legitimately ours, by grace, then kicking us while we are down. Look at Abram in Genesis 15:8–12, for example, who set out his stall of obedience and sacrifice and was immediately set upon by birds of prey. The symbols of his devotion were targeted and it was only Abram's vigilance that saved the day as he waved the predators away and went on to receive great blessing. What a battle the Christian life can be! An ongoing war against the predatory forces of evil, no less. When the sneak-thief appears, may God grant us the presence of mind Abram displayed, and the courage to preserve and protect that which God has ordained. God help us!

TUMOURS AND TRUTH

In the midst of life we are in death
(THE BOOK OF COMMON PRAYER, 1662)

It is with sadness that I report the sudden demise of Skipper, the strange German Shepherd we adopted just a year ago. His tummy had expanded to a remarkable degree, and the vet confirmed his liver had been savagely and irreparably hijacked by a large, aggressive tumour. Not only that, he was carrying almost forty mini-tumours, and was diagnosed as having only two months to live, making surgery unethical. Shocking news, as apart from a large stomach and a loss of appetite, he had displayed no other symptoms, but I was also informed our unusual dog was "very senile" – which news arrived as significantly less surprising. The vet advised Skipper's cancer would become quickly worse, and that he would collapse in pain and possibly die – or, if not die, be left in agony, so the kindest thing was to have the old boy put to sleep. I couldn't face the dread moment, so my wife, whom Skipper had never liked anyway, took him for his last walk. It's a lot quieter without him sniffing around and barking, and I miss him more than I thought I would. Goodbye, Skipper. I hadn't realized to what degree you had made your way under my skin.

Some brave souls delight in circulation-shocking Boxing Day dips into the chilly English Channel, in the name of fun and fundraising, but on the whole, shock is no fun at all. Shocking news is unsettling, and leaves us sad and unnerved. Scripture, though, repeatedly warms us with words of comfort, encouraging us to trust God even in our darkest, coldest moments. I believe such verses but, to be candid, they don't always help much, immediately. Rather, my experience of God the Comforter is that he takes a back seat in the immediate, allowing us to come to terms with our feelings so we can then make our way intelligently towards him. God treats our suffering with integrity, allowing us to navigate our problems in order to then discover him in all his patience. I like his style, and I wouldn't be all that keen on a God who rushed me into counselling, even his. He won't interfere, but will allow us time to grieve, weep, and think; all the time gently and unobtrusively making himself available. This is my God.

WELL, WELL, WELL

The Samaritan woman said to him, "You are a Jew and I am a Samaritan woman.
How can you ask me for a drink?" (For Jews do not associate with Samaritans.)

(JOHN 4:9 *NIV*)

I saw a photograph of a Staffordshire Bull Terrier sitting in a tiny pink plastic swimming pool, cooling down in the water, its tongue hanging out, and the contrast amused me, the bright pink serving as an unlikely background to a muscular, no-nonsense Staffie. This wet, warm, and weary dog was taking a break from a "Pooch Parade", a charity event whereby dog owners meet to walk their dogs at least 2.5 km in return for a guaranteed amount of sponsorship. I assumed the Bull Terrier was being walked on a particularly hot day! One such parade took place on this day in 2015, in London's Battersea Park, with instructions being issued that dogs who didn't get on well with other dogs should be muzzled or, preferably, left at home. Thousands of pounds and dollars are raised by these parades, and they are an excellent way of exercising one's pooch while making friends and enjoying the sunshine, but English dog walkers shouldn't expect too much of the latter! Perhaps you will want to investigate the possibility of supporting a charity by looking up "Pooch Parades" to see if there is one taking place where you are. (Do, though, take a bottle of water with you! Better still, one for you and one for your pooch!)

Grace follows in Jesus' wake. Take, for example, his encounter with the woman at the well in John 4, and highlight the glimpses of grace sparkling throughout. Jesus, a Jew, was talking to a despised Samaritan whom other women would have preferred stayed indoors, out of sight and out of their lives; socially muzzled. Note his charm as he speaks to a lonely outcast quenching her thirst in the midday heat. He knows her sins – they have been committed in the full glare of village life and gossip, which shone as relentlessly as the burning sun. He is aware of her reputation. Yet, he offers compassion and forgiveness. He does not reject or condemn, or abandon her to swelter under her weight of guilt, but imparts news of life-giving spiritual refreshment. This is our God.

BRAND NAMES

"Nazareth! Can anything good come from there?" Nathanael asked
(JOHN 1:46 **NIV**)

Staffordshire Bull Terriers have been given a bad press in the UK. Granted, they were, originally, bred for fighting or bull-baiting, but their reputation has been tarnished by legislation tarring all Bull Terriers with the same unfair brush. Dog fighting and bull-baiting are activities (I shan't refer to them as sports) the majority of dog owners consider barbaric, but tabloid headlines highlighting Bull breeds as "Devil Dogs" have done nothing to help. Likewise, the urban myth that Staffies and Pit Bulls have jaws that lock into place when they bite, when the truth is, they have an exceptionally strong grip; nothing more sinister than that. Any dog will attack if it is sufficiently provoked and/or trained to be aggressive, or treated in such a way it adopts a default position of defensiveness, and the fable that Bull breeds are permanently hostile to all and sundry is an exaggeration. Staffordshire Bull Terriers, if they are loved, respected and trained, make excellent, fun-loving pets, protective of children and doggedly loyal. They are by no means the domain of thugs who see them as an extension of their (supposed) toughness and street cred. Government legislation remains in place regarding the ownership of Staffies and Pit Bulls, but it is possible the Dangerous Dogs Act will be sensibly and carefully reviewed at some point. I hope so!

A bad reputation can be difficult to shake off! If we Christians sing, "The vilest offender who truly believes, That moment from Jesus a pardon receives" then it behoves us to put our hymnology into practice, does it not? Saul had quite a task persuading the early Christians of his change of heart, when he was converted and became Paul. Mud stuck, and he was kept at arm's length as people were afraid of him. Which of us, though, is sufficiently holy to be entitled to pay more attention to reputation than truth? Would it not be worth our while getting to know someone whose standing has been damaged, and who is labouring under the burden of suspicion and polite rejection? The moral character of Nazareth was proverbially bad, and to be a Nazarene was to be treated with contempt by people from other districts. We can, therefore, understand Nathanael's question; his astonishment (disgust?) at the thought of the Messiah coming from a place regarded as wicked, but this mode of judging relies not upon evidence, but prejudice and ignorance. May God preserve us from lazy and incorrect assumptions about anyone we meet; especially, perhaps, those who are looking to our churches for the possibility of turning over a new leaf.

ARE YOU SITTING COMFORTABLY?

Who hath despised the day of small things?
(ZECHARIAH 4:10 *KJV*)

It was not uncommon, in the nineteenth century, for shepherds in the Scottish Highlands to arrive at church accompanied by their sheepdogs, who sat quietly at the feet of their masters as the service proceeded. Come the benediction, though, there was a great deal of stretching and yawning, and some barking, as the dogs got ready to run out – so much, in fact, that one congregation expressed their concern that the dignified services their minister prepared should close in a more fitting manner. The minister agreed, and met with the shepherds in search of a solution. The next Sunday, he was astonished to find the sheepdogs sitting still throughout the entire benediction, demonstrating no impatience. The secret was that the wily shepherds had agreed to remain seated when the benediction was pronounced, as opposed to standing as they usually did, thus depriving the dogs of their cue to scamper noisily down the aisle. One shepherd looked up at the pulpit, and in his broad Highland dialect, said, "Say awa' sir. We're a' sitting to cheat the dogs." Problem solved, dignity recovered, minister and congregation happy!

Basic common sense, such as that demonstrated by the shepherds, is an underrated spiritual gift! The more spectacular gifts attract our attention easier than those to do with everyday life – the mundane and ordinary. There's nothing wrong with an evangelist, say, appealing to hundreds with the message of salvation, and there is a great deal to say for a preacher blessed with the gift of healing. Likewise, someone gifted with a beautiful voice can share the gospel through performances that fill large venues. Marvellous! We might want to reconsider, though, the usefulness of talents that rarely attract the attention of the public, and are usually practised in quiet, unseen ways, and not to underestimate their value. God bless evangelists, preachers, healers, and singers who serve Christ well, but God bless, too, those who clean, care, cook, and counsel well beyond the glare of the spotlight, applying humble wisdom to their unsung ministries.

LOVE IN THE FAST LANE

Jesus said, "Father, forgive them"
(LUKE 23:34 **NIV**)

As I write, police officers in Wales are under fire in the media, as complaints are being published about a runaway Foxhound being deliberately run down by a police car. The officers responsible have, somewhat ironically, been referred to the police watchdog, but they maintain the Foxhound was loose on a major road, thereby representing a significant hazard to safety. Terrified, it had bitten one of the officers, who say they had little option but to kill as this, apparently, was their only safe option. Firearms personnel also attended, but were concerned they would not be able to get a safe shot. The owner of the Foxhound, which had broken away from a hunt, has responded to criticisms of the police with magnanimity, stating he feels they made the correct decision in an impossible situation, and he too has expressed his concern that the dog might have caused an accident otherwise. Doubtless, the police did not take their decision lightly, and it seems they tried to control the hound and had no alternative but to execute. Perhaps the only saving grace is that the Foxhound was run over at such a speed that it did not suffer, and as both officers have their own dogs, we can assume they would have agonized over their actions. An investigation will follow, taking into account complaints from members of the public and animal welfare charities, but whatever the outcome, this is a sad report with an unhappy ending.

I shall swerve out of the way of pontificating on the actions of the police as the last thing this debate needs is my contribution. I wasn't there, I didn't see what happened, and I cannot imagine the pressure of having to make such a decision, so my ignorance of the facts disqualifies me from passing judgment. What, though, impresses me is the generosity of the owner of the Foxhound. Given the fact he would have been in shock, we would understand if he angrily vented his fury at the officers, but he seems astonishingly willing to understand and defend the people who had just killed his pet. I can't help thinking of Jesus' words, "Father, forgive them" as he hung on the cross. Granted, the context was massively different and the circumstances not the same by a long chalk, but the underlying principle of forgiveness and grace under pressure is worthy of comparison, and quite challenging.

PETS AND POETRY

*The righteous care for the needs of their animals, but the kindest acts of the
wicked are cruel*
(PROVERBS 12:10 **NIV**)

I am delighted to see the League Against Cruel Sports mobilizing itself in
opposition to dog fighting. LACS is concerned that public awareness of this
clandestine activity is lacking and has commissioned a report to highlight
the problem. I shall spare you the ghastly details, but criminologists spoke
to people involved in dog fighting, examining the practices, motivations, and
extent of the practice, discovering that organized dog fighting is common in
urban parks, empty buildings, and on housing estates, with people betting
thousands of pounds on fights which occur somewhere in the United Kingdom
every day. These are professional fights organized by carefully managed
dog rings, and the entire enterprise is sickening, with no legitimate place in
civilized society. Owners train their dogs to be ferocious scrappers, entering
them in deadly competitions, and such people should never be allowed
anywhere near such sensitive creatures as dogs. They are not worthy of canine
devotion. Thankfully, these barbaric activities are coming to light, and I hope
the police will prosecute. I hope too, that LACS is successful in its efforts.

Hear our humble prayer, O God, for our friends the animals,
Especially for animals who are suffering; for any that are hunted
Or lost or deserted or frightened or hungry;
For all that must be put to death.
We entreat for them all thy mercy and pity
And for those who deal with them we ask
For a heart of compassion, gentle hand and kindly words.
Make us ourselves to be true friends to animals
And so to share the blessing of the merciful.

(Although not written by Albert Schweitzer, 1875–1965, it follows his ethic of
"Reverence for Life")

GOD'S GUIDANCE

The Lord is my shepherd … He makes me lie down in green pastures
(PSALM 23:1 ***NIV***)

A lady responsible for keeping Guide Dog puppies called a radio gardening programme for advice. The lady serves the Guide Dog cause by giving a home to several puppies at a time as they go through their training, before they are allocated to visually impaired owners, but the puppies were slowly ruining her garden. Much as she loved them, she was frustrated by their boisterous behaviour as they ran, scratched, dug, and trampled all over her lawn and her flowerbeds. She told the gardening experts she wanted to keep providing the hosting service, but that she would also like her garden back, so expert counsel was dispensed, including tips from dog-owning panellists. Trees! The enquirer was advised to plant strategically placed trees to distract the puppies from the lawn, trees being much more interesting and useful – and considerably hardier! Further advice came in the form of borders of flowers protected by small fences acting as "no-go barriers". The puppies were to be told off if they ventured into flowered areas in the hope they would learn to respect boundaries. I hope the advice worked, and that the lawn and the flowers are once again looking healthy.

At my father's funeral service, I spoke from Psalm 23, likening the psalmist's description of green pastures to the prospect of Heaven. I have no idea what this lady's lawn looked like, but I imagine it to be lush and spacious; not unlike the thoughts I entertain about Paradise. Personally, I like the idea of verdant spaces in which to stroll and worship in God's presence. Amy Carmichael wrote, in her lovely poem "Moss", that followers of Christ should be content to be as moss beneath his feet if it meant serving him well; "Cool for thy feet sore wounded on the cross." It's a beautiful thought, though I believe gardeners are not usually fans of moss in their pristine lawns! Am I content to serve my Lord Jesus as lowly, quiet moss? If it means the feet of the divine are cooled, then I would like to be satisfied in that role; it would be a privilege. God help me become as moss in his service.

DAD, DOGS AND DIABETES

The lame walk

(MATTHEW 11:5 *NIV*)

My dad was a disobedient diabetic who couldn't relinquish his love of wine gums. We used to find half-eaten bags of them in his pockets but, sadly, diabetes contributed to the demise of his legs, which died some time before he himself did. Thus, he was unable to walk properly for the last year of his life, and we experienced a few adventures as Dad attempted to venture out in his motorized wheelchair! He couldn't get out much, but I am pleased to report a growing marketing trend to supply disabled dogs with carriages, carts, and wheelchairs so they need not suffer a similarly frustrating fate. It is one thing for an elderly man not to be able to walk, but Dad could at least still read, watch TV, write letters, ponder crossword puzzles, and chat on the phone. It is more trying for a dog to be confined to barracks, so selling wheels for dogs whose legs no longer work, or who have suffered spinal injuries, is big business. Dachshunds and German Shepherds thrive if supplied with "wheelchairs" to alleviate the symptoms of arthritis common to those breeds; a harness with a supporting structure and wheels taking the place of arthritic spines and paralyzed legs. It is wonderful that all this can be done for dogs who might otherwise be kept indoors, bored and listless.

Three days after Dad's departure, my wife and I attended a performance of Handel's *Messiah*. Heather had purchased tickets some time before Dad died, but I didn't really want to go as grief had the better of me, and an evening out was the last thing on my mind. I am, though, grateful I went along, because the Holy Spirit took hold of Handel's setting of Isaiah's words, "Then the eyes of the blind shall be opened, and the ears of the deaf be unstopped. Then shall the lame man leap as an hart, and the tongue of the dumb shall sing." Tears flowed, not only because I felt the Lord comforting me by describing my dad's new legs in Heaven, but also because of the promise that, one day, all will be well. We might hobble our way through this life at times, but that hope remains, and in the words of the author Brennan Manning, we "limp victoriously"![1] Hallelujah! In the life to come, we shan't limp at all.

---

1 B. Manning, *The Ragamuffin Gospel* (New York: Multnomah Books, 2005)

A HEALTHY DIET

You who are thirsty, come to the waters; and you who have no money, come, buy
and eat! Come, buy wine and milk without money and without cost
(ISAIAH 55:1 **NIV**)

Skipper could find food in the most unlikely places! It didn't seem to matter how well concealed titbits were, Skipper could sniff them out, and he once tracked down half a meat pie in, of all places, the doorway of a house, gobbling it up with the glee. Skipper's liver failed, but his nose didn't, and his final journey, en route to the vet where he was to be put to sleep, included the find of half a roast chicken beneath a bush. Why someone should have hidden this in the shrubbery is beyond me, but this constituted the equivalent of a final meal for a condemned man, and Skipper was allowed to die on a full stomach. Doubtless, purists will complain about the lurking dangers of abandoned meat pies and unwanted poultry, but I am not a dog pedant and I remain unrepentant, especially in view of Skipper's happy farewell outing. I retain a great deal of satisfaction from knowing that Skipper met his end with a bulging belly, thanks to another good haul.

Skipper was at a healthy weight, but his appetite was insatiable. I couldn't eat so much as a slice of toast without him appearing by my side, asking for his share. What, though, has his tummy to do with my spiritual life? Good question! Heather and I bought a painting recently: *Feeding the Hungry After the Lord Mayor's Banquet* by Adrien Emmanuel Marie, and it fascinates me not only as a reminder of the privilege of helping the poor, but as a work of art representing the gospel, insofar as it depicts beggars queuing to be fed, receiving food left over from London's annual Lord Mayor's feast. You see, I too am a beggar, hungry to be fed, and the good news is that when I queue at the wondrous cross, with my hands open, I am fed with spiritual blessings. Never mind the Lord Mayor – we are invited to feast at the banquet of the Lord himself!

NO OTHER ARGUMENT; NO OTHER PLEA

Salvation is found in no one else, for there is no other name under heaven given to mankind by which we must be saved

(ACTS 4:12 **NIV**)

Skipper was no saint! I do, though, know about a dog who was/is venerated as saintly; St Guinefort, a Greyhound, who belonged to a French knight. One day, said knight left his baby son in Guinefort's care, while he went hunting, and a dreadful sight greeted his return – the baby's cot was overturned, the boy was nowhere to be seen, and Guinefort had blood around his jaws. The knight immediately slew the dog with his sword, decapitating it in the belief it had attacked his son, only to then hear the child crying. He was hidden beneath the cot, safe and sound, along with the corpse of a giant viper, which was covered with bite marks. Oh dear! Overcome with remorse at having slaughtered his brave and innocent dog, the knight dropped the Greyhound's body and decapitated head down a well, covered it with stones, and planted flowers nearby, instituting the shrine of St Guinefort the Martyr, regarded as a site of prayer for people whose babies and children were sick or in peril. In 1879, the folklorist Vayssière is said to have passed through "St Guinefort's wood" and discovered it still to be intact.

Who am I to say what happened with the knight, the snake, the baby, and his dog? It is not for me to pass judgment on the preferred religious practices of others, as my responsibility is to point people to Christ, then leave the rest to the Holy Spirit. How people outwork their faith thereafter is their prayerful business. I have no objection to, say, the rituals of Anglo-Catholicism. Likewise, I respect the way nonconformists go about things. What I do regard as nonsense, though, is pseudo-religious superstition such as horoscopes and tarot cards. More sinister still are Ouija boards and séances, and I state unapologetically my belief that any noises emanating whenever boards are consulted and séances held are generated by malevolent counterfeit spirits misleading the gullible and the desperate into false beliefs regarding the afterlife. Christ is all. The cross is magnificently sufficient. I may not know what the future holds, but I know who holds the future. The gospel is no ancient legend, but solid truth for this life and the next.

A WING AND A PRAYER

The fool says in his heart, "There is no God"
(PSALM 14:1 *NIV*)

In many countries, today is April Fool's Day, when jokes are played on unsuspecting victims, and it is the easiest thing of all to fall for well-planned jests, however determined we are not to be caught out. These range from harmless tricks to elaborate hoaxes attracting publicity, and one such prank was staged by an international airline. Looking at the promotional angle, this airline announced the opening of its new airport lounge dedicated to dogs, offering world-class amenities exclusively for pampered pooches. The announcement was accompanied by videos showing glamorous air stewardesses resplendent in their uniforms, serving up high-class meals and offering dogs a hairdrying service following a shampoo and rinse. In one clip, a Labrador and a puppy are being served dinner, and the Labrador is shown looking very happy as a smiling stewardess treats him to a blast of the hairdryer. The luxury lounge was said to have been strictly for these privileged passengers and their attendants, and of course the story grew wings and a number of excited people spread the news before that horrible crushing feeling entered their souls as they realized none of it was real! The airline came clean on 2 April – there was no such lounge, the publicity was bogus, and the Labrador and the puppy were hired actors!

I'm glad I didn't fall for that one! It all looked so credible and convincing. The Bible pulls no punches in describing those who reject ideas of God's existence as being fools. Harsh language, maybe, but we cannot dispute the fact those words are there. Perhaps, though, the description of unbelievers as fools is only the opinion of the psalmist, insofar as the Bible is inclusive of all types of opinions and generously reflective of the breadth of human experience. God wants us to be ourselves. Granted, he works on us to make us better versions of ourselves, but the Bible demonstrates his gracious willingness to take on board all our feelings, sentiments, and attitudes. He might not agree with us, but he loves us – even fools!

THE MARKS OF JESUS IN ME

Whoever says he abides in him ought to walk in the same way in which he walked
(1 JOHN 2:6 **ESV**)

I was invited to participate in a "Dogs & Daffs" walk whereby I could join with other dog walkers (and their dogs!) to stroll around the gardens of a stately home. I'd like to go, but I would feel conspicuous arriving *sans* Skipper, so I shan't. It should be quite an occasion, though, as proud owners can enter their faithful friends in competitions to find the "Most Handsome Dog", the "Prettiest Bitch", and even the "Dog Most Like Its Owner"! Souvenir photographs will be available. I regret not having a reason to go along, but I can't pretend I regret not being compared to Skipper in a lookalike contest, given his long nose and hairy ears. (We did have grey hair in common, but that was about it.) I hope the "Dogs & Daffs" event is an enormous success, and I only wish I had access to the snapshots of the competition winners! They would make interesting viewing!

A Salvation Army prayer chorus includes the words: "To be like Jesus, This hope possesses me." Scholars reckon Jesus was somewhere between 5 ft 8 in and 6 ft 1 in tall, Middle-Eastern in appearance, athletic in build (given his fondness for walking and climbing mountains), and suntanned, but that's roughly all we know about him. Thankfully, then, our resemblance to Jesus has nothing to do with physical appearance, but everything to do with his image being stamped upon our natures. Becoming like Jesus is no stroll in the park. That said, it is worthwhile if it means we adopt some of his beauty, so maybe we could pray for each other today, with that in mind? "To be like Jesus" is a chorus, not a competition, but the prize on offer is worth everything. Jesus invites us to walk with him, taking on his characteristics as we do so.

FIRST SEA LORD

The ship ... ran aground
(ACTS 27:41 **NIV**)

Supposing you had to travel from the UK to the USA, and wanted to take Fido with you. Airlines carry canine cargo, but that would mean your dog being kept in a crate for the flight, although some airlines will allow your dog to sit next to you, provided it is strapped in and you don't mind paying for an extra seat. Allow me to recommend the option of a luxury cruise ship! The Queen Mary II, for example, makes the crossing several times a year between New York and Southampton, and may be the answer to the problem. Dogs are not allowed in cabins, but there are kennels on board, and owners may visit their dogs there, and may walk them, on a leash, to their heart's content, so there is no reason why owners cannot be with their dogs whenever they want to. The voyage lasts six days, so it would make for a lovely week's sailing. If ever I am adopted by another dog, and if ever my life takes me to America, then I might ask my publisher if there is space in the budget for such a convenient (and luxurious!) option ... Well, it's worth a try!

American lawyer and hymn-writer Horatio Spafford and his wife, Anna, decided on a family holiday in England, so he sent his wife and four children across the Atlantic on a steamship, planning to join them when his business was concluded. Tragically, the steamship was struck by another vessel and all four daughters drowned, though Anna survived. Subsequently, grief-stricken, Spafford sailed to England, going over the location of his daughters' deaths, which must have been a traumatic experience. According to Bertha Spafford Vester, a daughter born after the tragedy, her father penned what is probably his most famous hymn "It Is Well with My Soul" on this actual voyage. What a testimony! I am humbled and challenged by the strength of belief expressed by Horatio Spafford in the throes of bereavement, as he clung to gospel truth despite enormous heartache. You may wish to read the hymn as an encouragement to faith in the face of adversity. God bless those who struggle today and whose faith is severely tested.

ONE LIFE TO LIVE

Jesus went to a town called Nain ... As he approached the town gate, a dead person was being carried out – the only son of his mother ... When the Lord saw her, his heart went out to her

(LUKE 7:11–13 **NIV**)

On the subject of transport, Laika comes to mind. Laika was a mongrel, part Husky, part Terrier, who became famous in 1957 when she was sent into space by the Russians, and died in orbit. Her death was distressing because she overheated and ran short of oxygen, and I can't shake off the feeling that Laika wasn't really as heroic as mythology surrounding her story would have us believe. She was a stray, found on the streets of Moscow and regarded as suitable for rocket travel because of her size, but her three years on this planet, and off it, came to an end on board Sputnik 2, in geocentric orbit, but only after a cruel training regime. It is of little consolation to me that a monument in Laika's honour stands near the research facility that prepared her for flight, though I am heartened to discover that one of the scientists took Laika home to play with his children, shortly before the launch of her capsule. In a book chronicling the story, Dr Vladimir Yazdovsky wrote, "I wanted to do something nice for her: She had so little time left to live."[1] Good man.

I realize it is a leap of thought to move from a three-year-old mongrel dog to a human being, but the brevity of Llaika's life moves me to consider the despair faced by parents whose children's lives are equally brief, or even briefer, when there was once the expectation those children would become adults. Likewise, the horror of stillbirth. Doubtless, many gifted and sensitive writers have tried to encapsulate at least something of the swirling emotions surrounding such tragedies. Some will have penned their words from awful personal experience, and may even have come close to placing their deepest heart-thoughts on paper. The strong likelihood, though, is that even the most tender lines and paragraphs, though they be well-meant, will fall short of successfully capturing the depths of pain experienced. Words and thoughts may fail us; God the Father will not. He will – always – hear our prayers, whether those prayers be spoken, sighed, or sobbed. The Lord is near.

1   USAtoday.com

ALL THINGS WEIRD AND WONDERFUL

In all thy ways acknowledge him
(PROVERBS 3:6 *KJV*)

I know of a man who carries his dog for a while, then drops it, almost throws it, to the ground, so that both of them can walk together. His West Highland White Terrier doesn't seem to mind, not even yelping when it lands from a height of roughly three feet, but why this man doesn't allow his dog to walk the length of the way puzzles me, as does the fact he never places the dog down carefully. I can only assume the Terrier has strong ankles, as he trots off happily every time. By much the same token of what appears to be eccentric, inexplicable or odd behaviour, I read about a letter Michael Ramsey once received, when he was Archbishop of Canterbury. Someone wrote to him at Lambeth Palace with a complaint about "a lady the other side of the river [Thames] from Lambeth who pushed a pram with three cats in it and two dogs on leads", imagining that Ramsey was the best person to cope with the lady. I am not privy to whatever reply the Archbishop was able to offer, but what this had to do with the Primate of All England is anybody's guess. (It probably had little to do with the letter-writer, either!)

Aren't human eccentricities baffling and bizarre? (Other people's, of course!) Each of us has traits that make others smile; a habit, perhaps, a turn of phrase, a mannerism; something that speaks of our humanity and individuality, however sophisticated or normal we like to think we are. I wonder what the society of his day made of Jesus, for his teaching was countercultural, his demands intense and dramatic, and his claims quite extraordinary! He would have been regarded as an oddball by many; at best, ignored, and at worst, tolerated – more's the pity, for his difficult and unique ministry represented salvation for the world; for the sane and the insane, conformists and nonconformists, for the stiflingly dull and the splendidly creative, for Archbishops and pram-pushers. What a Saviour!

THE CURE OF SOULS

He is the Rock, his works are perfect, and all his ways are just. A faithful God who
does no wrong, upright and just is he
(DEUTERONOMY 32:4 *NIV*)

Along the road from me, there is a shop selling unusual things, and one such piece is a silver hip flask engraved with "Hair of the dog" and a picture of a Terrier. Where, I wonder, does that expression "Hair of the dog" come from? That it should be inscribed on a hip flask is appropriate, as the colloquialism refers to alcohol consumed in the (optimistic) hope of lessening the effects of a hangover, its origins emerging from the method of treatment of a rabid dog bite whereby hair from the dog in question is placed in the wound. The Scots apparently introduced the phrase to Britain, according to Ebenezer Brewer, who wrote in the *Dictionary of Phrase and Fable* (1898): "In Scotland it is a popular belief that a few hairs of the dog that bit you applied to the wound will prevent evil consequences. Applied to drinks, it means, if overnight you have indulged too freely, take a glass of the same wine within 24 hours to soothe the nerves. If this dog do you bite, soon as out of your bed, take a hair of the tail the next day." The earliest reference to the cure, though, is from ancient Ugarit (Arabic) dating from the second millennium BC, in which the god 'Ilu becomes hungover after a drinking session! A salve was recommended, to be applied to the god's forehead, consisting of "hairs of a dog" and parts of a plant mixed with olive oil.

Silly old 'Ilu was a deity fond of a tipple! He or she was a binge-drinker – not much of a god at all, then, but I hope the remedy was successful, as I wouldn't wish a thumping headache on anybody. Whatever our personal thoughts on alcohol, I take pride in the fact that my God is entirely upright, reliable, and perfect. Were he not, he wouldn't merit my devotion. Some people make ill-informed comment on Psalm 78:65, claiming it shows God up as an 'Illu-like drunken layabout, whereas it does nothing of the sort, and is merely a descriptive turn of phrase. God is without fault and worthy of worship. Interestingly, the Chinese translation of "Hair of the dog" is something akin to "Soul restorer". Our God is indeed the restorer of souls, but he is certainly not the God of magic potions and well-meant fables!

LED BY LOVE THAT LOVE TO KNOW

He said, Go forth, and stand upon the mount before the Lord. And, behold, the Lord passed by, and a great and strong wind rent the mountains, and brake in pieces the rocks before the Lord; but the Lord was not in the wind: and after the wind an earthquake; but the Lord was not in the earthquake: And after the earthquake a fire; but the Lord was not in the fire: and after the fire a still small voice. And it was so, when Elijah heard it, that he wrapped his face in his mantle, and went out, and stood in the entering in of the cave. And, behold, there came a voice unto him, and said, What doest thou here, Elijah?

(1 KINGS 19:11–13 **KJV**)

I met a man wearing a medallion portraying an image of Emperor Haile Selassie, and when I commented on this he was (overly) impressed by the fact I had recognized his spiritual mentor (he needn't have been – it was a lucky guess). We chatted, then went our separate ways, but the encounter reminded me of Haile Selassie's fondness for his Chihuahua, Lulu, regarded as part of his royal entourage. The Emperor was a fan of dogs, but Lulu, a tiny, frog-eyed creature, was trusted by the superstitious monarch to scrutinize visiting dignitaries. Haile Selassie would encourage her to wander around the legs of officials at state receptions, because Lulu was said to know if, say, an official was harbouring ill-will towards their host, and if the Chihuahua touched the foot of the unfortunate individual with her paw, that dignitary was never trusted again and diplomatic relations were abruptly brought to an end!

With respect to the memory of the Emperor, my guess is that Lulu was not so much performing a mind-reading act at formal functions, as searching for snacks on the carpet, so it was unfortunate for the dignitary whose foot Lulu trod on in pursuit of a stray sausage roll that he or she would thereafter be ostracized from the Emperor's enclaves, all for the want of not having pulled a foot out of the way in time. Having said that, decision-making can be tricky, but I recommend simple, trusting faith when guidance is sought. In some mysterious, nagging, whispered way, God speaks direction to those who seek his will with a pure motivation, and does not deny his counsel to those who need it. Maybe we should pray today for those looking to be led. Centuries ago, Elijah sensed the still, small voice of God, and the wonderful thing is that Elijah's God, then, is our God, now. He didn't fail Elijah, and neither will he fail us.

SUNDAY SCHOOL SANITY

Dear friends, never take revenge. Leave that to the righteous anger of God. For the
Scriptures say, "I will take revenge; I will pay them back," says the Lord
(ROMANS 12:19 **NLT**)

Lulu's fortune-telling antics came to an even more abrupt end than the diplomatic careers of the dignitaries whose doom she sealed. Her demise was violent and, we can only assume, brought about by jealousy. Paul, you see, a Great Dane "palace dog" identified in Ethiopian folklore as her murderer, had had enough of the favouritism shown to his house-mate, Lulu, and decided to break her neck with a sudden bite of his giant jaws, then swing her to and fro until her lifeless body hung limp from his mouth. The Emperor was heartbroken as he stared down at the corpse of his Chihuahua, and "Lulu *finite*" was his comment. There has been no official comment, though, on what became of Paul after he had committed his deadly deed, but rumour has it he was ejected from the palace and condemned to wandering the streets, a Great Dane in not so great circumstances.

If jealousy was the reason for Paul's downfall and eviction, then he is not alone. If envy turned him into a strangler, then he is not the first to have been overcome by that dreadful emotion, and he won't be the last, for history is littered with tales of plotted revenge. The Bible reveals no end of stories about decent people who gave way to distrust, hatred, and a bitter desire to get even. Resentment, unchecked, can wreak horrible results, and we should tread with caution, lest we feel ourselves above such base emotions. Maybe we envy someone their good fortune or status? Isn't there something in the Scriptures about a couple of individuals wanting to sit either side of Jesus in the Kingdom of Heaven? Incredible! Yet, we deceive ourselves if we think we are exempt from similar feelings. Can the words of the old Sunday school chorus become our prayer today? "Envy, jealousy, malice and pride, they must never in my heart abide."

FASHION AND FLOODING

He restoreth my soul
(PSALM 23:3 *KJV*)

In West Yorkshire, England, the 2016 Canine Fashion Show has just taken place, featuring a Cocker Spaniel looking dapper in black suit and bow tie, a pair of Dachshunds looking pretty (well, ridiculous) in frilly pink tutus, and a Lurcher looking depressed and not very gangsterish, dressed as a gangster. The Lurcher's owner wore a rubber Lurcher mask and, granted, it was an excellent mask, but the effect was spoiled somewhat by the fact it was worn by a man who stood upright and was otherwise wearing a tracksuit top and jeans. Not to worry, as the parade was organized as a fundraising event in support of locals who suffered devastating losses as a result of the nearby Hebden Bridge Boxing Day floods, and whose homes were in need of restoration. I hope they raised lots of money, and I hope the man enjoyed his day.

I do it, and I daresay you do too. Dress up, that is, if not literally, then metaphorically. We wear masks that help us along in society, and even at church. The classic "mask" is the one we adopt when someone asks us how we are and we answer, "Fine." We might well be fine, but we tend to give that reply even if we're not, so why the pretence? Well, sometimes we don't like to trouble others with our burdens, and at other times, our worries are too personal to share. Rarely, therefore, do we show ourselves as we really are, and even spiritually, too, we play the dressing-up game. Maybe we haven't prayed for weeks on end. Possibly, we have neglected our Bible reading. Yet, when our friends at church watch us singing hymns, they would have no idea that, spiritually speaking, we are as dust inside. The good news is God sees far beyond the disguise. God knows. Is this you, this day? In a mess? Pretending? Dried up? No matter – you still belong to God, so tell him all about it, and ditch the mask, for he loves you as you are.

SLEDS AND SALVATION

Father, if you are willing, take this cup from me; yet not my will, but yours be done
(LUKE 22:42 **NIV**)

At this time of writing, I am fifty and am, apparently, supposed to be experiencing a mid-life crisis (by which reckoning, I'm set to live to 100). This will, I am told, entitle me to buy a flashy car or start a new life somewhere, but my nineteen-year-old car will do, and I don't wish to be anywhere else. One woman who shares my age, though, has treated herself to a "mid-life crisis birthday present" of competing in a 1,000-mile Arctic dog sled race, and is heading for the tundra, where sixteen trained dogs will pull her along a route north of Anchorage, Alaska, in the hope of completing the course in fewer than nine days and establishing a record. Sleeplessness, hard work, and temperatures as low as -50°C await as she navigates frozen rivers, forests, and mountain passes. She is utterly dependent upon her team of Alaskan Malamutes and Siberian Huskies, and those magnificent beasts, equipped to run for long periods of time in extreme temperatures, hold her destiny as they race. If, for example, one of them chews through the leash and runs away, then the sled is disqualified. Likewise, if one is injured, valuable time is lost. I can but hope this feat helps her come to terms with having reached such a monumental age!

Jesus knew nothing about being pulled along the ice by Malamutes and Huskies, but he knew all about what we might call his mid-life crisis, albeit it took place before his thirty-fourth birthday when, in Gethsemane, with the weight of the world's sin on his shoulders, he knelt and prayed that the burden of his vicarious death be relieved. An agonizing death awaited him, with no one arriving to set him free and allow him to run away. The record of history – his story – shows that he emerged from his dark night of the soul to endure the cross, for my forgiveness, and yours. This, surely, was the feat of all feats.

TRULY AWESOME

Learn from me, for I am gentle
(MATTHEW 11:29 *NIV*)

There is a man who keeps two Alaskan Malamutes in a nearby town to mine. They sit together in a doorway, and he places an upturned cap on the pavement, so I suppose he is begging, except that hardly anyone seems to give him anything and it doesn't appear to be the object of the exercise as most people just chat and admire the dogs; they really are magnificent. One man often buys each dog a pie, and the gentleness of these giant creatures as they eat from his hands is something to behold – they could easily tear his arm off, but they might as well be suckling lambs, and what especially impresses me is the sheer depth of their fur, which grows up to eight inches (experts say it is a mistake to cut or shave this fur). These two bark a lot, but I am told this is par for the course with Malamutes and not necessarily a sign of distress or aggression – they are not a quiet breed, and some believe they have the most extensive "vocabulary" of any dog. Apparently, they dislike being left out of conversations, so it stands to reason that if people stop to talk to their owner, they will want to join in! These Alaskan Malamutes are gentle giants, but I'm not about to risk upsetting them!

Few match Bishop Timothy Dudley-Smith when it comes to writing inspiring hymns. One of his compositions includes the words "loveless in strength" and I have been fascinated by that turn of phrase for years as I think of political/military dictators who fit that description and consign thousands to miserable lives, or totalitarian regimes where brute strength is employed to suppress the masses, with love playing no part in society.[1] How different is the rule of Christ, whose strength is only ever exercised on the side of right, and justice. In theory, there is nothing preventing him unleashing his awesome might in merciless anger; nothing could stop him. Christ, though, rules strongly, but gently, with love as his guiding force, and his meekness is not weakness but, rather, the exercising of controlled power. This is our God; lion and lamb, mighty yet tender.

---

1   Timothy Dudley-Smith (b. 1926), "Lord, for the Years"

FICTION AND FACT

He was in the form of God

(PHILIPPIANS 2:6 **ESV**)

We therefore decided that we would sleep out on fine nights; and hotel it, and inn it, and pub it, like respectable folks, when it was wet, or when we felt inclined for a change. Montmorency hailed this compromise with much approval. He does not revel in romantic solitude. Give him something noisy; and if a trifle low so much the jollier. To look at Montmorency you would imagine that he was an angel sent upon the earth, for some reason withheld from mankind, in the shape of a small Fox Terrier. There is a sort of Oh-what-a-wicked-world-this-is-and-how-I-wish-I-could-do-something-to-make-it-better-and-nobler expression that has been known to bring the tears into the eyes of pious old ladies and gentlemen. When first he came to live at my expense, I never thought I should be able to get him to stop long. I used to sit down and look at him, as he sat on the rug and looked up at me, and think: "Oh, that dog will never live. He will be snatched up to the bright skies in a chariot, that is what will happen to him." But, when I had paid for about a dozen chickens that he had killed; and had dragged him, growling and kicking, by the scruff of his neck, out of a hundred and fourteen street fights; and had had a dead cat brought round for my inspection by an irate female, who called me a murderer; and had been summoned by the man next door but one for having a ferocious dog at large, that had kept him pinned up in his own tool-shed, afraid to venture his nose outside the door for over two hours on a cold night; and I had learned that the gardener, unknown to me myself; had won thirty shillings by backing him to kill rats against time, then I began to think that maybe they'd let him remain on earth for a bit longer, after all.[1]

In the preface to the tale, the publisher wrote: "The chief beauty of this book lies not so much in its literary style, or in the extent and usefulness of the information it conveys, as in its simple truthfulness. Its pages form the record of events that really happened ... George and Harris [the other sailors] and Montmorency are not poetic ideals, but things of flesh and blood." The "simple truthfulness" of the matter is that he lived, he died, and he rose again, and he was indeed "flesh and blood". What a glorious reality! The Incarnation is no mere poetic ideal, but much more than that – love so amazing, so divine.

1   J. K. Jerome, *Three Men in a Boat* (Ware: Wordsworth Editions Limited, 1993)

WHAT SHALL WE WEAR?

These are they who have come out of the great tribulation; they have washed their
robes and made them white in the blood of the Lamb

(REVELATION 7:14 **NIV**)

Montmorency & Co. were planning to stay in hotels en route sailing from Kingston upon Thames to Oxford, and back again, but had they sailed north instead, they might have discovered the delights of Whitby, a port-town on England's north-east coast. Montmorency, a Fox Terrier, would have loved it there, because Whitby boasts a luxurious dog spa, where, for a fee, besuited men will relieve you of your doggie duties by taking your pet for a stroll in the grounds while you relax. Once strolled, nothing is too much trouble for canine guests, and ladies in tailored uniforms, complete with satin neckwear, will rush to be with your dog, making sure it lacks nothing. I can only wonder what Montmorency would have made of it all, given his reputation for chicken-and-cat murdering and a fondness for rat-hunting. Maybe, though, dressing up in a suit or the costume like that of an air stewardess would not have been the ideal attire for walking him across the Whitby moors or along the beach, and I would suggest boots instead of brogues and scarves instead of suits. (That, though, may risk lowering the image of the establishment!)

"Sunday best" conjures up images of Christians in suits and dresses, does it not? I dress smartly when I attend church because it's something I prefer but, should you wish to sit alongside me in your ripped jeans and hoodie, then please do so as we worship together. Some priests like the whole robed effect. Fine. Others prefer casual clothing. No problem. Isn't it sad, though, when we Christians sometimes get all hooked up on secondary issues, and in doing so, replicate the behaviour of the Pharisees over things that don't matter in eternity? Priestly garb is important to some people, and I respect that. What is more important, though, is that we unite at the foot of the cross to adore the Saviour, where all that is of concern, ultimately, is that our clothes are clean; spiritually speaking, that is. Thanks to Jesus, they are.

DAISY, DAISY

The angel of the Lord encamps around those who fear him
(PSALM 34:7 **NIV**)

I am impressed with the work of a photographer who keeps *The Photographic Diary of a Dog-Walker on the Northumberland Coast.*[1] Frankly, I do well to tell one end of a camera from the other, and it would be fair to say there are not hordes of people queuing up asking me to capture their image. This guy's work, though, is something else – a visual delight – and Daisy, his Lurcher/ Irish Wolfhound cross, plays her part to perfection, featuring in various poses, including a shot of her captioned "Racing on the Howick shore but Daisy loves the wind in her fur" and another snapshot accompanied by the words, "Today I completed my first 5K run after 6.5 weeks of training. My time was 31 mins 31 secs. Daisy ran way more than me of course but here she stands looking not very tired!" Daisy looks lovely, and the backdrop of a windswept Northumberland suits her perfectly. Does she, I wonder, realize she is a model?

Almost certainly, all Daisy really cares about is another walk along the coast! The breeze through her coat is of more importance to her than photographic fame, and the lenses mean little to this Lurcher. Isn't it something, though, to remember that God has us in his sights 24/7/365? Sadly, that fact is often taken to mean he is obsessed with spying on us, waiting for us to make a mistake so that he can punish us, when quite the opposite is true. God has his zoom lens, so to speak, focused in our direction because he loves, and he can't bear for us to be out of his sight, not because he is "Big Brother-Eye-In-The-Sky" waiting for us to mess up. He watches as an attentive parent brooding over his children. Daisy is entirely unaware of the commercial reasons behind her owner's interest in capturing her on film. Wouldn't it be tragic if we spent our lives similarly unaware of God's goodwill?

1   Northumberland360.blogspot.co.uk

I'LL WALK WITH GOD

These things happened so that the scripture would be fulfilled: "Not one of his bones will be broken"

(JOHN 19:36 ***NIV***)

A consequence of Skipper's death is that I am putting on weight. Granted, the Good Book does say that "Godliness with contentment is great gain" (1 Timothy 6:6, KJV) but I am not convinced that text refers to ounces and calories! Skipper used to take me for two walks every day – one for half an hour, and then another, later on, for an hour, and as we have established, walking Skipper was never a stroll – more workout than walk! – but now that he walks no more, neither do I. For all that I am a believer in church growth, I'm not sure this counts, so I shall have to think about an alternative form of exercise. God has given me two legs that at the moment work well, and the day may come when I am in need of hip or knee replacements, so it does appear somewhat ungrateful to use the legs I have only to walk to and from my car. I shall give the matter some thought!

God gave Moses and Aaron the Passover rules, including the prohibition against breaking any bones of the lamb that was sacrificed. The command that the Passover lamb should not have its legs broken is rich in symbolism because when Jesus, the Lamb of God, was crucified, not one of his bones was broken. When the Roman soldiers came to break his legs to hasten his death, they found he was already dead, so they pierced his side with a spear instead, hence John's testimony, our text for today. The Passover rule of Exodus 12:46 is echoed in Psalm 34:20: "He protects all his bones, not one of them will be broken" (NIV). Jesus fulfilled the prophecies concerning the Messiah, thereby verifying evidence for his deity. There, on Calvary's hill, hung a God no longer able to walk, who couldn't have exercised even if he had wanted to. This is my God; crippled, disabled; dying to save me.

WOULD I LIE TO YOU?

They began to accuse him, saying, "We have found this man subverting our nation. He opposes payment of taxes to Caesar and claims to be Messiah, a king"
(LUKE 23:2 ***NIV***)

I find it fascinating, listening to *Gardeners' Question Time* on BBC Radio Four as the panel of experts (including the superbly named Bob Flowerdew) deal with queries covering lawns, lilies, grass, and gladioli. One listener asked for help with his parents' lawn which had, he said, stunk of dog urine for years, even though the dogs they had owned died some time ago. The general feeling was that the lingering odour was nothing to do with the departed dogs, given that rain would have washed their urine away, but everything to do with foxes marking their territory or, possibly, certain shrubs or hedges which have been known to cause this problem. After much discussion, it was decided the dogs had been unfairly accused in being held responsible for the posthumous pong. Having exonerated the dogs, the panel then offered solutions. (Lavender was suggested as a good option.)

False accusations are nothing new. Liars have given dodgy evidence in courtrooms ever since courtrooms were invented. "Kangaroo courts" have existed for centuries, and corrupt governments stage mock trials to convict innocent people, where trumped-up evidence is the norm. Jesus was arguably the most famous victim of a bent jury the world has ever known; the fall guy for half-truths and scurrilous accusations. People who could see only the guilty verdict they were determined to produce were fanatical in their desire to have him convicted, and truth became irrelevant. Hardly anyone spoke up for him, yet he faced every charge without protest; like a sheep before its shearer, he remained dumb. Why, though, didn't Jesus simply speak up for himself? American pastor Rick Warren comments on this stunning dimension of grace: "He allowed himself to be put on trial so there would be no doubt about who he was. He could have stopped the trial at any moment; he knew he would be proven guilty and put on the cross. But he allowed it to happen. It was all part of the plan" – the plan, that is, of our redemption; the innocent sacrificed for the guilty. Ours the transgressions, his the deadly pains.[1]

---

1   www1.cbn.com *What's so important about Easter?*

THAT HE WOULD COUNT ME FAITHFUL

Twenty-two thousand men left, while ten thousand remained
(JUDGES 7:3 **NIV**)

An enterprising head teacher of a junior school has entered her pupils in an attempt to break a world record. As it stands, the record for the largest gathering of people dressed as dogs (yes, I know) is 264, and the teacher is calling on pupils, siblings, and parents to meet in the school hall on a certain date, at a certain time, dressed in their canine clobber. It's all part of World Book Day (the book being the *Guinness World Records*), and prizes will be on offer for the best costumes. Participants are encouraged to "release their inner dog" and "join the pack" to see if the feat can be achieved, so we can but guess as to the range of outfits that will appear! Cartoon dogs will no doubt feature prominently, alongside pupils dressed, maybe, as their pets or their favourite canines. Great fun!

I hope lots of people take part in the attempt – at least 265, but crowd events can be unpredictable; a football match, for example, watched by thousands of people all packed together, can go off without a hitch, or the curse of hooliganism can strike. Billy Graham had a tremendous ministry of reaching out to millions of people around the world, yet a parish priest, say, with an equally faithful ministry and with exactly the same gospel to proclaim, might count himself fortunate to see a dozen people in his congregation. Thankfully, Kingdom "success" is not always measured in numbers, and we rejoice in the way in which God has used Billy Graham, but we know God regards the ministry of the dedicated priest as equally precious. Kingdom economics are often as difficult to predict as the dynamics of crowd interaction, and were we to judge the work of God using only statistics, we might be disappointed. The likelihood is, the Church will break few world records. No matter. God will not necessarily call us to account for souls won or pews filled, but will examine our hearts for the hallmarks of Christ. Grace counts us worthy.

CARS AND CAMELS

*I tell you, it is easier for a camel to go through the eye of a needle than for
someone who is rich to enter the kingdom of God*
(MATTHEW 19:24 **NIV**)

Skipper's absence has created a problem in regard to the type of car I drive, in that we Poxons make our way north a fair bit, visiting family and venturing out on camping expeditions. To that end, I invested in an old estate car that could manage a) long journeys b) four people c) camping equipment and d) a German Shepherd/Border Collie cross. I found just the car. Then, as we know, the vet intervened and Skipper's space was no longer required. Without his presence, we can manage with a run-of-the-mill saloon car. For the time being, therefore, I am trundling around in a car big enough for points a), b), c), and d), but overlarge for everyday needs. The problem is, though, I've come to like it because I'm almost 6ft 3ins and I love the legroom my estate car offers. Are the seductive tentacles of materialism reaching out to ensnare me, or do I have a reasonable case for not offloading my super-sized car?

Jesus spoke frankly to a rich young man who approached the Master for advice. He was a decent chap, but seemed unable to relinquish his worldly goods in order to follow Christ. Jesus counselled using the "eye of the needle" illustration, pointing out that material possessions can block our entrance into the Kingdom if we hold them too tightly. Did Jesus use the word "kamelos" (camel) or "kamilos" (rope) when he spoke? We don't know, but the latter explanation would make sense, although one theory suggests Jesus might have been referring to a gate in Jerusalem which opened after the large main gate closed, the moral of the story being that a camel could only pass through this smaller gate and enter the city if it had its baggage removed. Semantic speculation will rumble on, but the point remains that our "baggage" – our disproportionate attachment to the things of this world – can sometimes have a detrimental effect on our spiritual health. I shall need to think carefully!

BY PRISON BARS RESTRAINED

For Christ's sake, I delight in weaknesses, in insults, in hardships, in persecutions, in difficulties. For when I am weak, then I am strong

(2 CORINTHIANS 12:10 **NIV**)

Skipper loved going for a walk, and would happily have spent whole days outdoors. Stella, on the other hand, has spent the last years in a cage – a Pit Bull-type dog caged under the Dangerous Dogs Act who hasn't been properly exercised since 2014. Her story turns my stomach because her incarceration is unnecessary, and she must be depressed to the point of despair. If she really is such a menace that she can't even be trusted out of her prison on a leash, then she should be humanely destroyed, but if that is not the case, then she should be released to responsible owners. I intend writing to the police force responsible for keeping Stella in a concrete cell measuring 3ft x 9ft, to find out the facts of the matter, but also to protest. There might be much more to the story than has met my eye, but something has to be done. Poor Stella.

People, as well as dogs, are locked up for all sorts of reasons. The prison population is rising, and will continue to do so. God bless, therefore, prison chaplains and prison visitors. The Apostle Paul was chained up on account of his faith, as the gospel he preached was regarded as dangerous. However, he continued to witness. I can't say what his conditions were like, but the denial of one's liberty is never going to be a bed of roses. All the more remarkable, then, that Paul's writings from confinement indicate his confidence in God remained intact, and that witnessing for Jesus was still his priority. Doubtless, he wanted to be free again, but even at the mercy of jailers, Paul was, first of all, a Christian, and then a prisoner. We might want to pray for prisoners in general, and perhaps especially for those who languish in cells on account of their Christian stance. God bless them.

GOD IS KEEPING HIS SOLDIERS FIGHTING

Abram said to Lot, "Let there be no strife between you and me, and between your herdsmen and my herdsmen, for we are kinsmen"

(GENESIS 13:8 ***ESV***)

A court case has reached the airwaves of local radio, as two dog owners are in dispute over who was at fault for an incident which left one of them needing surgery. A man received puncture wounds to his arm after his Husky, Apache, scrapped with a Staffordshire Bull Terrier called Dot Com. In the fracas, Dot Com (allegedly) grabbed Apache by the neck and Apache's owner was bitten by his own dog as it panicked (he alleges Dot Com bit him too). The case rests on whether or not Dot Com was on a lead and controlled in a proper manner. Police have told Dot Com's owner to keep him leashed and muzzled when in public places, otherwise he could be destroyed, and Apache's owner was asked by police whether he thought she should have the dog taken away, but he signed a document to say she should be given another chance, saying, "I didn't want that on my conscience. It's not the dog's fault."[1] The squabble continues!

There are some people we probably won't ever get along with! Dot Com's owner and Apache's owner won't be spending an enormous amount on Christmas cards for each other, and even in church life, we encounter people who rub us up the wrong way. By the same token, we rub people up the wrong way from time to time! Not even the Reverend John Wesley and the Reverend Augustus Toplady, Anglican contemporaries, saw eye to eye, but disagreed over doctrine, exchanging bitter correspondence, until Wesley refused to write any more, so we are at least in good company when we disagree with someone! The words "Take it to the Lord in prayer" come to mind, whether our upset is over people, politics, pews, pooches, or prayer books.[2] Irritations won't magically disappear when we pray, but we may find ourselves better able to cope, and grace might just be unleashed.

---

1   BBC Three Counties Radio. Date unknown
2   J. M. Scriven (1819–86), "What a Friend We Have in Jesus"

COME, BEAUTIFUL CHRIST, RADIATE THY BEAUTY IN ME

The Lord does not look at the things people look at. People look at the outward appearance, but the Lord looks at the heart

(1 SAMUEL 16:7 **NIV**)

I love Stan Laurel and regard him as a comedy genius, especially as much of his work was original and because he was, by all accounts, a lovely, charming fellow and a great clown. One of his and Oliver Hardy's films is *Laughing Gravy*, featuring a little dog of the same name whom Stan and Ollie are trying desperately hard to conceal from their vindictive landlord, who refuses to allow pets into his seedy boarding house. Clowning calamities ensue, involving a broken bed, a dog in a cupboard, a dog (and Ollie) in a tin bath full of soapy water, Ollie locked outside in the snow, and so on – all good, clean fun! Laughing Gravy was, incidentally, the dog's real name (as opposed to a stage name); a cross between a Cairn Terrier or a Norfolk Terrier with a little Pekingese thrown in, who had been rescued from the dog pound because he was exactly the scruffy, docile, and compliant pooch the studio was looking for. He certainly had the last laugh! (I just wish I knew what was behind such an unusual name.)

Try to find a picture of Laughing Gravy; there is something winsome about him that would melt all but the hardest hearts. There is a saying: "Fortune favours the pretty" (a corruption of "fortune favours the bold") and there is a measure of truth in that – the most photogenic candidates will invariably be selected as, say, Members of Parliament, and psychologists tell us first impressions count (at interviews, for example). Thank God, he looks for beauty in our hearts, and his criteria seems to be how attractive we are on the inside; how much of Christ we carry with us. Laughing Gravy looked into camera and stole the show, with a face that became his fortune. For those of us who aren't invited to appear on catwalks, though, or in magazines – and for those who are – the beautiful truth is that God wants to cultivate his image within us. Laughing Gravy stared into camera and built up a fan club. We gaze at the Saviour and build on his likeness in our conduct.

MY CHAINS FELL OFF, MY HEART WAS FREE

When Jesus got out of the boat, a man with an impure spirit came from the tombs to meet him. This man lived in the tombs, and no one could bind him anymore, not even with a chain ... he tore the chains apart and broke the irons on his feet. No one was strong enough to subdue him. Night and day among the tombs and in the hills he would cry out

(MARK 5:2–5 *NIV*)

There was a lady who went by the name of St Quiteria, also known as the Virgin Martyr, and amongst the miracles attributed to Quiteria is one concerning two rabid dogs who attacked her one day, but were put off from doing so by nothing else than the sound of her sweet and gentle voice urging them to cease and desist. On account of such a miraculous happening, St Quiteria is depicted nowadays, in icons and paintings, with a dog lead in her hand, or with a dog on a lead, as a symbol of her placid and saintly influence. I'm not entirely sure what St Quiteria might think of this, but she is now the patron saint of rabies, whose powers, apparently, can be invoked by anyone bitten by an infected dog. Let's hope none of us ever has to test that theological theory!

Rabies is a dreadful disease that sends even the most loving dogs wild and insane. Jesus encountered a man who fitted that description, whose life was in a terrible state; possessed by demons, making his life a misery. Like a rabid dog, this man had a reputation for being fierce and out of control, to such an extent he was chained up and expelled to a cave. What a desperate existence; a life ruined by evil forces; little more than a plaything in the hands of Satan – until, that is, Jesus intervened, taking control and bringing the poor wretch to his senses, offering victory, pardon, deliverance, and release. The Miracle Man with a heart for the marginalized, the trapped, the demonized, the unwanted, the unwashed, and the chained – Christus Victor!

BEGGING FOR LOVE

Even the dogs came and licked his sores
(LUKE 16:21 **NIV**)

I do not suggest that street people mistreat their dogs – quite the contrary, actually, in my experience, as people who keep a dog for company while they make their beds on the pavements are often extraordinarily caring towards their companions, even making sure they are fed before they themselves are, from what scant supplies might be available. Nevertheless, it's still not much of a life for a dog, any more than it is for a human being, to spend days and nights with only a cardboard box and a blanket for shelter, having makeshift meals only every so often. Such dogs are undoubtedly loved, but the fact is, homelessness is a plight no person or animal should have to face. We can but marvel, though, at the steadfast manner in which a dog whose only home is a shop doorway will stick by the side of the owner it loves. Such love! Even better that the feeling is mutual!

A pitiful story exists in the New Testament, in which a beggar called Lazarus sits outside a rich man's house, hoping (without success) to find compassion. Not unlike a homeless person hoping to receive a few coins or something to eat or drink, Lazarus begged for what might have fallen from the rich man's table, metaphorically speaking, and with a great sense of pathos, the gospel writer tells us that "even the dogs came and licked his sores". Why did those dogs come to lick the sores of the beggar? Perhaps they cared for him when human concern had run its course, or maybe they sensed his loneliness as he lay there, unwell, unwanted, and undernourished, with that sensitivity dogs possess. Either way, this account shows dogs in a much better light than humans, who appeared to be content to allow Lazarus to sit there begging. May God bless the charities and individuals who are affected by homelessness and minister to those existing without walls to protect them and roofs to keep them dry – and their dogs!

TAKING CENTRE STAGE

Jesus said to him, "Away from me, Satan! For it is written"
(MATTHEW 4:10 **NIV**)

We have a celebrity in town! We are delighted to welcome a famous dog called Pudsey to these parts! Winner of a television talent show and now a professional entertainer, Pudsey has gone from strength to strength, and is now even accepting pantomime roles! His act, performed with his trainer, is a song and dance/comedy routine (but Pudsey can't sing or tell jokes), with backing tracks setting the scene as the Border Collie/Bichon Frise/Chinese Crested Powderpuff Cross takes to the stage, sometimes in costume. He demonstrates not only an aptitude for learning but a fabulous bond with his owner/trainer, who has invested the best part of a decade in teaching Pudsey the ways of show business, although he has only been performing for four years. Pudsey is, apparently, now worth a cool £1 million, and in 2012, even published his autobiography! (Though I'm not quite sure what happens at book signings.)

Pudsey is a bright creature, and it's paying dividends, quite literally. As long as he's happy, I wish him and his owner well as he learns his lines, his fan base grows, and the coffers swell. Jewish children were encouraged to learn their lines too, memorizing Scripture by heart; and Jesus' childhood would have been no exception. He would have been trained in Jewish laws and customs from when he was a boy. Therefore, when Jesus the man was tempted in the wilderness, he was able to refute Satan's attacks by quoting Scripture; his second language, so to speak. In every battle with the Pharisees, the Scribes, and the Teachers of the Law, Jesus was able to add all the weight and wisdom of his divinity to that which he had learnt as a boy, teaching with authority and lifting the Law from formal legalism to something touching on the very motives of human behaviour. What of us? What of me? Is Scripture ingrained in our thinking?

IT IS NO SECRET

To him who is able to do immeasurably more than all we ask or imagine, according to his power that is at work within us, to him be glory
(EPHESIANS 3:20–21 **NIV**)

As a boy, I devoured Enid Blyton's adventure books *The Famous Five* and *The Secret Seven*. I couldn't get enough of them, and would panic when the characters were faced with, say, a villain on a beach, wondering what they would do if he drew a pistol, or how they would survive locked in an airtight basement. Gripping stuff, but quite how two groups of people became involved in so much trouble every summer while the rest of us failed to encounter any criminals at all never crossed my mind, and neither did I query the numbers of mad professors, burglars, poisoners, and smugglers they met with alarming regularity. Decades later, I can still recite the names of The Famous Five: Julian, Dick, Anne, George, and Timmy the Dog! Did you spot the identity of the fifth gang member? A dog! To be honest, Timmy – a mongrel of indeterminate breed – was the most intelligent member of the quintet; as while George (his owner) and the others blundered around all over the place, clueless, Timmy could sniff out a rogue at fifty paces. Indeed, the presence of Timmy was probably the only reason a bunch of kids were at liberty to roam around such dangerous places as deserted castles and caves without parental supervision or even awareness!

Enid Blyton was the queen of my childhood reading, allowing me to enter a world of thrilling danger that kept me glued to her books, following every plot, and my imagination developed largely thanks to Blyton's works. I still like to use imagination – though not, any longer, in relation to dastardly deeds! I imagine this, and I imagine that, and then I find myself stunned by today's text, where the Scriptures clearly tell us – so clearly that even Julian, Dick, Anne, and George could figure it out – that God can do more than we ask or imagine. My imagination is strong, yet God promises blessings over and above whatever scenarios my mind's eye might create. What might God have in store for us on the next page of life, as it were? Whatever it is, it will be written with love. Imagine that!

BEING BRAVE

Do not fear, for I am with you; do not be dismayed, for I am your God. I will
strengthen you and help you; I will uphold you
(ISAIAH 41:10 **NIV**)

Skipper, unlike the gang members of *The Secret Seven* and *The Famous Five*, who spent entire summers together and loved each other's company, was never taught to socialize, and when we collected him from the rescue centre, we were advised he showed little sign of ever having mixed with other dogs, and that his was a default position of defensive aggression. He knew none of the enjoyment of play and social interaction. I longed to let him off the lead, but I daren't, because he would fly at any dog within 500 yards – whole fields to walk in, to run in, to enjoy, as a dog should, yet, he could never be more than the length of his lead away from me, unable to run for a ball, fetch anything, or exercise at more than my walking pace. I so wish I could have explained things to him, as he must have thought me a spoilsport, when quite the reverse was true; I would have loved nothing more than to set him free.

Fear blights lives, keeping its captives in a state of anxiety. A psychiatrist once told me that decisions should only be made out of wisdom and humility, never out of fear, because it is not, apparently, a valid emotion in terms of decision-making with regard to careers and the like (though it's probably wise to decide not to stick one's hand in a fire if fear is telling you not to do so!). What are we afraid of? Other people's opinions? Criticism? Ridicule? Not fitting in? What fears act as straitjackets? A lack of confidence? Concerns about the unknown? Rejection? The Bible tells us "perfect love casts out fear" (1 John 4:18, ESV) – banishes it, excluding it from our mental processes. A love, that is, which comes from God and emboldens us so we can run and not be fearful – a love which reassures us of God's presence; that fills our hearts with the conviction that Christ will not fail us; a love that helps us to overcome. We need not fear.

APRIL 27

KEEPING UP WITH THE TIMES

David … served God's purpose in his own generation
(ACTS 13:36 **NIV**)

I wonder what prompted Noël Coward to write his song, *Mad Dogs and Englishmen*. He composed the entire song in his head while driving from Hanoi to Saigon, without the aid of pencil and paper, drawing on his experiences of that part of the world and committing it all to memory! I have put together a few published songs, and I can tell you that to remember all the lyrics in one go is no mean feat, never mind doing so while driving in a foreign country! The implication within those lyrics is that only those unaccustomed to tropical climates would be foolish enough to venture out in the heat of the midday sun, while locals remain indoors. Quite how I feel, as an Englishman, about being put on the same par as an insane canine is a moot point, but I assume Coward's inspiration came from seeing hapless individuals struggling to cope with uncomfortable temperatures. Following its publication, the song was sung whenever it featured in sketches written by Coward; performed by "English missionaries" in pith helmets, clerical collars, shorts, and, sometimes, wellington boots – complete with an umbrella to finish off the look!

Robert Morley played such a character in *The African Queen*, starring alongside Katharine Hepburn and Humphrey Bogart in a wartime epic set in the African jungle. Morley and his sister (Hepburn) are devout missionaries out to convert Africa by playing a portable organ in the middle of nowhere and sweating their way through British hymns, Morley refusing to remove his jacket. Their piety cannot be doubted, yet their cultural irrelevance is staggering. Robert Morley played the Reverend Samuel Sayer excellently, but everything about his outreach pointed to a white, middle-to-upper class English congregation – not to the bemused Africans gathered around him, handling their hymn books with bewilderment. It's only a film, but it begs the question of our relevance in the community, whether we are in Hanoi or Hartlepool, Africa or Aberdeen. Are we perhaps enthusiastic but slightly irrelevant? Maybe it's worth thinking about, as we too set about the business of soul-winning.

IF YOUR HEART'S ALRIGHT, YOU'LL DO

Since I myself have carefully investigated everything from the beginning, I too decided to write an orderly account

(LUKE 1:3 *NIV*)

Away from stage and screen, the actor Robert Morley was an entertaining character, with a giant heart to match his massive frame, and a genial wit based upon goodwill and friendliness. He was remarkably and unusually well-read, able to quote Homer, Cicero, and Shakespeare at will, but his intellect never prevented him enjoying simple comic limericks and poems. Whereas some scholars might have despised the silliness of "lowly" works, Morley, almost certainly, would have enjoyed and appreciated many of the quirky works of the poet, Ogden Nash, who sometimes wrote about dogs, and even once used his own, personally invented, words in order to describe the difference between canines and human beings: "People may be reprehensibler, but that's probably because they are sensibler"![1] Great stuff!

It is hard to think of anyone who strangled the English language as much as Ogden Nash! His invented words and passion for assonance was all part of his charm, and no one can deny this poem captures the spirit of dogs! Luke, on the other hand, doctor turned Gospel writer, was a stickler for detail; read his Gospel and the book of Acts, which he also penned, and you'll notice his insistence on keeping facts straight, employing a high form of Greek in elegant eloquence. When it comes to the gospel, I'm all for both styles, Nash's and Luke's; the converted chimney sweep who is barely literate but knows the love of God written upon his heart, and the saved professor who can add "Ransomed, healed, restored, forgiven" to his list of credentials.[2] Christ is for everyone, not just the clever or the rich, but the penniless and uneducated too, and for all sorts in-between; a Saviour for the slapdash and a Messiah for the meticulous, those in silk, those in rags; stately homes and tents. This is a gospel of grace, and in that, we all rejoice.

---

1   *The Golden Treasury of Poetry* (London and Glasgow: Collins, 1968)
2   C. Wesley (1707–1788), "Love Divine, All Loves Excelling"

POETRY AND PEOPLE

When King Hezekiah was well again, he wrote this poem

(ISAIAH 38:9 **NLT**)

For years we've had a little dog, last year we acquired a big dog;
He wasn't big when we got him, he was littler than the dog we had.
We thought our little dog would love him, would help him to become a trig dog,
But the new little dog got bigger, and the old little dog got mad.
Now the big dog loves the little dog, but the little dog hates the big dog,
The little dog is eleven years old, and the big dog only one;
The little dog calls him Schweinhund, the little dog calls him Pig-dog,
She grumbles broken curses as she dreams in the August sun.
The big dog's teeth are terrible, but he wouldn't bite the little dog;
The little dog wants to grind his bones, but the little dog has no teeth;
The big dog is acrobatic, the little dog is a brittle dog;
She leaps to grip his jugular, and passes underneath.
The big dog clings to the little dog like glue and cement and mortar;
The little dog is his own true love; but the big dog is to her
Like a scarlet rag to a Longhorn, or a suitcase to a porter;
The day he sat on the hornet I distinctly heard her purr.
Well, how can you blame the little dog, who was once the household darling?
He romps like a young Adonis, she droops like an old moustache;
No wonder she steals his corner, no wonder she comes out snarling,
No wonder she calls him Cochon and even Espèce de vache.
Yet once I wanted a sandwich, either caviar or cucumber,
When the sun had not yet risen and the moon had not yet sank;
As I tiptoed through the hallway the big dog lay in slumber,
And the little dog slept by the big dog, and her head was on his flank.[1]

It's a funny poem, isn't it? Yet, it makes serious points not only about dogs, but human nature too, as resentment is touched upon – hatred, even. Violence is mentioned, as is, we can infer, jealousy; having one's nose put out, name-calling, cursing, the issue of strength versus weakness, the disruption of harmony, and resistance to change. However, in the final couple of lines, we read something warmer and less hostile. None of Nash's themes here are absent from Biblical accounts of God's dealings with humans. Not one of these messages is omitted from Scripture, even if they do sometimes portray Homo sapiens in a negative light, because the Bible tells our story "warts and all". Here we have it – the narrative of God's ways with us, and ours with him, because at the heart of the Bible is the embrace of love offered to imperfect people. Can we see ourselves in the picture and in the prose?

1   www.poemhunter.com/ogden-nash

LIVES SAVED

"He saved others," they said, "but he can't save himself! He's the king of Israel!
Let him come down now from the cross, and we will believe in him"
(MATTHEW 27:42 **NIV**)

I read about a German Shepherd called Lucca, who worked alongside British and American military patrols in Iraq and Afghanistan, and has been awarded the Dickin Medal, the animal equivalent of the Victoria Cross. Lucca is only the sixty-seventh animal to be honoured with the medal, inscribed with the words "For Gallantry", so this is quite an award, and Lucca earned her distinction by not only alerting troops to a weapons cache hidden beneath a haystack and a 30lb pressure plate Improvized Explosive Device, but by sniffing out a bomb that exploded underneath her. One of Lucca's legs was ripped off in the blast, and she received severe burns to her chest, neck, and head. However, had Lucca not sniffed out the bomb, it is likely many soldiers would have been killed. It was said of Lucca that "Her determination to seek out explosives preserved life amid some of the world's fiercest conflicts". This courageous animal now lives in retirement in California, where she even gets to share a bed with her owner! Who would deny her that luxury?

There is a case to be made for the exclusion of animals from theatres of war, since it isn't them who repeatedly create conflicts. I sympathize with that opinion, but not so much that I agree with it. This reminds me of a robust discussion I once had, with a Muslim who maintained that Jesus didn't die on the cross, but was replaced by Judas, on account of the fact that Judas deserved to die a criminal's death and Jesus didn't (which is what the Koran teaches). Islamic logic prevents any acceptance of the fact that God should die; this is regarded as an abhorrent thought by Muslims who revere Jesus as a prophet but do not regard him as Saviour. I respect that point of view too, but I cannot agree with it. No dogs on the battlefield? No God on a cross? I thank God for his vicarious death in Christ, for therein lies my only hope of salvation.

A GOOD NIGHT'S SLEEP

Jesus replied, "Foxes have dens and birds have nests, but the Son of Man has nowhere to lay his head"
(LUKE 9:58 **NIV**)

Lucca's privilege nowadays is being allowed to sleep next to her owner, who says she is "well-spoiled" in retirement but "snores through the night".[1] The issue of allowing a canine on to the covers is controversial; guaranteed to polarize opinion because many regard it as harmless while others see it as unhygienic. I have no strong feelings either way, but I do know some people find it disgusting; they would no more allow a dog to keep them company overnight than they would sleep in a dog basket themselves. Meg and Skipper slept in our kitchen, in a bed with a collection of old blankets and towels to keep them snug. Skipper, though, longed to share our bedroom, and would often make his way upstairs in the hope of nocturnal leniency – no deal! – and only once did we allow Meg into our room, one Bonfire Night, when she was petrified by the noises of fireworks. What do you think?

God came to earth and had nowhere to lay his head; a God who made himself homeless, and would probably have given anything, some nights, weary after a day spent in the dusty heat of Palestine, for the comfort of a bed of his own. You know what it's like when you've been away – however comfortable and welcome you have been made on your travels, there is nothing like that feeling of returning to one's own bed. Quite remarkable, then, that Jesus the God-man never knew any such security, relying instead on friends and strangers for blankets and breakfast. This is staggering humility, and he asks today to be made welcome in our hearts.

1   www.dailymail.co.uk, April 2016

IT STARTED WITH A KISS

A woman of the city, who was a sinner, when she learned that he [Jesus] was reclining at table in the Pharisee's house ... kissed his feet

(LUKE 7:37–38 **ESV**)

There is (surprisingly!) heated debate on my local radio station as I write, regarding whether or not dogs should be kissed on the lips. Some regard it as a natural and harmless sign of affection, whereas others consider it disgusting. Some masters and mistresses encourage their dogs to kiss them on the lips and lick them all over their faces, while others draw the line at allowing dogs to kiss them or lick them anywhere at all. For our part, Skipper was one of the world's great lickers, and would lick hands, feet, ears, and faces endlessly – he couldn't lick enough. Meg, on the other hand, regarded such behaviour as beneath her dignity. Me? I have no tremendous enthusiasm for kissing dogs on the lips or allowing them to kiss me on mine. However, live and let lick is probably my motto on these matters! What about you?

Paul suggests Christians greet one another with a holy kiss. Judas, though, by contrast, betrayed Jesus with another type of kiss altogether. There is nothing as sinister, though, about the kiss referred to in William Rees's great hymn "Here is Love". Rees coined the beautiful line "Kissed a guilty world in love" as a way of describing God's forgiveness, and I can do no better than share the second verse of his hymn with you here, with the recommendation you look up the other verses too, for they will bring you a lovely reminder of grace:

On the mount of crucifixion,
Fountains opened deep and wide;
Through the floodgates of God's mercy
Flowed a vast and gracious tide.
Grace and love, like mighty rivers,
Poured incessant from above,
And heav'n's peace and perfect justice
Kissed a guilty world in love.[1]

1   W. Rees (1802 – 83), "Here is Love Vast as the Ocean"

GOD THE RESTORER

The Lord is my shepherd, I lack nothing. He makes me lie down in green pastures,
he leads me beside quiet waters, he refreshes my soul

(PSALM 23:1–3 **NIV**)

Friends of ours sometimes dog-sit for their family, the dog in question being a Dalmatian called Daisy. I have only met Daisy once, but she is charming and a fanatical ear-licker! Daisy wasted no time setting to on my ears when we met, so, on account of her exuberance, I tried an experiment on her, using a calming technique I had seen demonstrated on television by a lady who claimed to be able to calm any dog within twenty minutes of meeting it. I gave it a go, and it worked! Daisy the dotty Dalmatian was docile within minutes, which gave my ears a rest and seemed to go down well with her too. The technique involves massaging a dog at the base of its ears, then alternating that massage with one along the spine, searching for areas of knotted muscle. No pain, no discomfort, and Daisy enjoyed it all as I moved my thumbs around her ears and spine. The secret is to feel along the spine for lumps, then work them loose. My only problem was that Daisy then kept coming back for more! (I didn't mind, really.)

Some experts maintain that the base of a dog's ear (where it connects to the head) is sensitive because the nerves there connect directly to the brain. Therefore, to massage ears is something like massaging the brain directly, and deeply soothing. I wonder if we are a bit like Daisy at times, in that we need God to massage our souls, as it were – when we are anxious, when we can't concentrate, eat, or sleep, because we are worried. When we dread news in case it's bad, when we've done something wrong and know we will need to face the consequences. We long for peace, forgiveness, and reassurance, and the restoration of our heartbeat to a better pace. Our text today encourages us to bring all such matters to God in prayer and be still in his loving presence.

SPOTTING OPPORTUNITIES

Jesus said: "A man was going down from Jerusalem to Jericho, when he was attacked by robbers. They stripped him of his clothes, beat him and went away, leaving him half-dead ... a Samaritan, as he travelled, came where the man was; and when he saw him, he took pity on him"

(LUKE 10:30–33 **NIV**)

Mention of Daisy leads me to mention those dogs that are easily spotted, and greeted with affection and amusement. If ever we doubt God has a sense of humour, then we need look no further than his Dalmatian handiwork! These beautiful creatures originate from the Croatian region of Dalmatia, and were used as carriage dogs, trotting alongside horse-drawn carriages protecting passengers and deterring bandits. Popular in this role, they were also useful in catching vermin that might frighten the horses. Their duties kept them in great condition, and they are excellent long-distance runners. Nowadays, Dalmatians are more commonly pets, and are loyal, obedient, and outgoing, but they carry a genetic trait which means that approximately 70 per cent are deaf. Before this trait was realized, they were regarded as unintelligent, when they are anything but. You probably know this already, but are you aware that not every Dalmatian is black-spotted? Blue-eyed Dalmatians (as opposed to brown-eyed) have their spots in a chocolatey shade of brown! See if you can spot a blue-eyed one...

I live near a pub called "The Wicked Lady", named after a highwaywoman who delighted in relieving travellers of their money and jewellery, terrorizing the area. Jesus told a story about bandits like her, illustrating the Christian duty of looking after those in need – the tale of a traveller ambushed, robbed, and left to die, and commended the only passer-by (a Samaritan) who stopped to help. So what's it got to do with us? Do highway robbers still exist? People traffickers certainly do, mercilessly leaving victims cruelly exploited as they travel in search of better lives or safe havens. What can we do? Well, The Salvation Army currently holds the government contract in the United Kingdom for rescuing victims of human trafficking, so one idea might be dropping their Anti-Human Trafficking Department a line to see if you can become a "good Samaritan"? Your support might help protect travellers as they complete their frightening journeys – you might become a modern-day Dalmatian!

The Anti-Human Trafficking Officer, The Salvation Army,
101 Newington Causeway,
London
SE1 6BN

THE LAW AND THE LORD

It also forced all people, great and small, rich and poor, free and slave, to receive a mark on their right hands or on their foreheads, so that they could not buy or sell unless they had the mark, which is the name of the beast or the number of its name
(REVELATION 13:16–17 **NIV**)

A law has been announced whereby microchipping of dogs becomes compulsory in England, Scotland, and Wales from 2016. Even though the move carries the approval of the Microchipping Alliance, the British Veterinary Association, the Kennel Club, the Dogs Trust, and the Royal Society for the Prevention of Cruelty to Animals, dog owners resent having to pay for this procedure, which they regard as intrusive and unnecessary, even though some charities are offering free microchipping. Anger has been aroused by the threat of a £500 fine for any failure to comply. Personally, I'm all for it, especially if microchipping enables lost or stolen dogs to be reunited with their owners, and one of the intentions of the legislation is that dogs coming from appalling puppy farms and unregulated breeding centres will be traceable under the law; likewise, owners who abandon their dogs can be traced and brought to book. I hope this regulation means greater protection for dogs. The microchip is easily implanted, the dog hardly knows it's there, and in my opinion the benefits outweigh the protestations.

I have read around the subject of what we might call microchipping for human beings, based around the prophecies of Revelation 13, and I believe there will come a time when, in a cashless society, we will be expected to conduct financial transactions by means of an implant carrying our details. So far as I understand things, Christians are not to have any part of this as the implant/chip represents the mark of Satan, and is a sign of "the end times", so I foresee a day when Christians will need to choose, and it won't be an easy decision. (It might mean ostracization and any number of difficulties, but I also think it will represent an unprecedented opportunity for witness.) I won't stand in judgment on Christians who disagree with me or go ahead with the procedure, but I would hope to have the courage to opt out. We'll see what happens!

THE ITALIAN JOB

Peter came and said to Him, "Lord, how often shall my brother sin against me and I forgive him? Up to seven times?" Jesus said to him, "I do not say to you, up to seven times, but up to seventy times seven"

(MATTHEW 18:21–22 **NASB**)

My wife likes me to go shopping with her, but is always surprised to find a few "extras" in our bags; a bit of cheese, say, that I've sneaked into the trolley. I wonder what dogs would do if they too came shopping? Would we be similarly surprised to discover a couple of pork chops had been sneaked in, or some sausages? Well, shoppers in a supermarket in Italy might soon find out, as dogs at this particular shop can sit in special trolleys, and canine customers are most welcome! The trolleys have a compartment fitted with a solid base, enabling dogs to travel around as the shopping is done. The enterprising supermarket manager has figured out many customers now spend a lot more time – and money! – on his premises, knowing their dogs are safe and not shivering on the street outside. At present, this arrangement applies only to small dogs, given the logistics of shopping trolleys, and those trolleys, incidentally, are cleaned after each use, ready for their next passenger! I would like to be a fly on the wall if shoppers spot a few unexpected items in the baggage area – a bag of biscuits or a box of treats, maybe!

Shopping polarizes opinion. People either like it, or can't stand it! What we might all agree on, though, is the satisfaction felt when we get more than we bargained for; "buy one, get one free", for example. Even ardent anti-shoppers will take advantage of such offers! Note the market trader who is selling, say, a set of saucepans, at "Not £30! Not £20! But £15!" I've never seen such a stall without a crowd of potential customers! So what about the greatest "bargain" of all, God's forgiveness of our sins? The price has been paid, in Christ, but the offer is repeated, over and over: "Not once, not twice, but seventy times seven times!" We don't even need to queue! Instant access to instant forgiveness is instantly available.

MONEY MAKES THE WORLD GO ROUND

Not greedy of filthy lucre
(I TIMOTHY 3:3 *KJV*)

In comes news of a dreadful facility for locking up dogs in boxes outside storefronts so people can shop without needing to tie their dog to a lamppost. Under this scheme, dog owners buy or hire an upmarket wooden crate with glass doors and ventilation holes, the (ghastly) idea being that you lock your dog in, then return for it when you have finished shopping. Quite what your doggie is supposed to do when passers-by tap/bang on the glass and stare inside is anybody's guess, for a dog that is stared at is a dog that is scared. Locking your dog up like this is asking for it to be traumatized, I'm afraid. Supposing the dog panics? At best, it will feel intimidated, and this smacks of money-making with little concern for animal welfare – raking in a few dollars by exploiting a need and dressing up greed as public service.

This scheme does not involve overt exploitation insofar as customers have freedom to choose whether to use a box, but someone has sniffed out an easy way of making money without much consideration for the well-being of the dogs concerned. More sinister money-making schemes are rife, worlds away from supermarket dogs in boxes, but with the same root; that of a financial return regardless of suffering caused. Prostitution, for example, when people are sold as sex objects while pimps count their fortune and keep them shackled. Or, human trafficking, when vulnerable families are exploited or abandoned to sink unnoticed to the bottom of the ocean. Or drug-dealing, when dealers grow rich on the back of another's misery, and so on. May God preserve us from ever placing pennies above people and lucre above love.

CARLY AND CHRIST

Carrying his own cross, he went out to the place of the Skull
(JOHN 19:17 **NIV**)

The saddest story I have read for a while concerns Carly, a black and white mottled three-year-old Spaniel discovered by a cyclist at a roadside. He saw a dog nuzzling into a plastic bag and, stopping to investigate, noticed the Spaniel had tears in her eyes. The cyclist was horrified to discover the bag contained a number of dead newborn pups; Carly was desperately trying to resuscitate them and was determined to stay with them, come-what-may. They, and Carly, had been abandoned; dumped in the cold, but thankfully, Carly the Spaniel is now being cared for in an animal sanctuary, is in good health, awaiting adoption. Thank God for that kind-hearted cyclist.

Carly's puppies were found in a fish and chip bag on a grass verge, left to die among the rubbish; old tin cans, faded crisp wrappers, rotten apple cores, and empty polystyrene burger boxes; chucked out with the refuse. So too, was Jesus, the King of Glory; unwanted deity treated as junk to be thrown into a skip, left to die a painstakingly slow death without even the dignity of palliative care, or the honour of a city centre funeral, just a scrapheap "service" shared with common criminals, surrounded by people who – like the person who left Carly and her pups to perish – couldn't have cared less. What a God we serve; broken for me, broken for you. The glory of God in the garbage.

SINGING THE BLUES

We must all appear before the judgment seat of Christ
(2 CORINTHIANS 5:10 **NIV**)

On this day in 1981 I was at the FA Cup Final, watching Manchester City play Tottenham Hotspur. I wanted to go, to support City, but couldn't get a ticket, so I wrote a poem to a newspaper, pleading for that precious slip of paper. The plan worked! A reader gave me a free ticket! Unfortunately, City's plan didn't work so well and they lost, which leads me to touch on the thorny issue of whether City or United are "top dogs" in Manchester. As a lifelong "Blue" (United wear red, City blue), I have to say City, who are just about on top these days. Throughout the decades I have followed them, though, my team has been the underdog, while United have won quite a bit of silverware. Top dogs? The tide is turning! Speculation persists about the origin of the phrase "top dog", but it seems to have originated with the preparation of hunting dogs, who had to be in tip-top condition; the fitter the dog, the more tip-top its condition, the more likely it was to hunt successfully, hence the phrase we now associate with that which is most likely to succeed. (I hope it's City!)

Archbishop Michael Ramsey may or may not have been a football fan, I've no idea, but what is beyond question is his lovely influence as a churchman. I read something from his works most days, and here I share an excerpt speaking of Jesus, the supposed "underdog" who was, in fact, "top dog":

When Jesus died on the cross everyone thought he was being judged. The Sanhedrin had voted him guilty, Pilate had condemned him to death, popular opinion jeered at him, and it must have seemed as though God himself had also condemned him by letting this happen. The world had passed judgment. The truth was that Jesus dying on the cross was passing judgment on the Jews and the Roman Empire, on Caiphas, on Pilate, and on every civilisation until the end of time. They are all judged by Calvary, and it is the work of the Holy Spirit to bring the world round to the conviction that Jesus crucified is the divine judgment upon them, the divine judgment upon all of us.[1]

---

1   M. Duggan, ed., *Through the Year with Michael Ramsey* (London: Hodder & Stoughton, 1975)

DARE TO BE A DANIEL

The men went as a group to King Darius and said to him, "Remember, Your Majesty, that according to the law of the Medes and Persians no decree or edict that the king issues can be changed"

(DANIEL 6:15 **NIV**)

An English Bull Terrier called Ralph has been banned from a pub his owner had frequented for a decade because Ralph took exception to a Labrador appearing in the pub and becoming, shall we say, friendly. Ralph has form, as this is the second time he has snarled at other dogs, making as though he was going to bite them, so the landlady has had enough, and is worried Ralph might one day snap at a child. Fair point, but the ban has enraged a lot of people who sympathize with Ralph and his owner. Ralph's exclusion seems to be set in stone. The landlady is not for turning, so Ralph will need to choose another pub in which to spend his evenings. On this occasion, it seems bark was as bad as bite!

Daniel, the legendary Old Testament character, was also the victim of a legal decision that couldn't be rescinded. Prophetic interpreter of dreams, he upset the king's officials by refusing to cease his public worship of God, and those officials wasted no time reporting Daniel's breach of religious law, eagerly reminding the king that no such dictates could be overturned. The sentence of death had to be applied, with no exceptions! The king was distraught, but had to send Daniel to the lions' den. We know the rest – God sealed the lions' mouths, Daniel emerged unharmed, the king was relieved (and converted), and the zealous legislators saw all their plotting fall apart. Rules have their place, but only when they are fairly applied – often, when they are not, God will overrule! Charity and mercy must feature strongly in our law-making because the cold, naked letter of the law is rarely enough.

GOING FOR GOLD

The king then ordered Doeg, "You turn and strike down the priests." So Doeg the Edomite turned and struck them down. That day he killed eighty-five men who wore the linen ephod

(1 SAMUEL 22:18 ***NIV***)

Bonanza, the hit American TV show, featured clueless cowboys in adventures set in prospecting country, most of which were doomed to comical failure. An ancient dog sometimes appeared; part-genius, part-lazybones, part-guard dog, and, remarkably, a skilled communicator, depending on what the script required of him. His name was Walter; some kind of Bloodhound/Hound Dog, and he spent his days padding around the house or dozing on the kitchen table. In one episode, *Walter and the Outlaws*, a trio of gormless felons planned to "dog-nap" Walter in the hope of the clever canine leading them to his master's hidden stash of gold (Otis, the master, a prospector, is away on holiday and has left Walter in the care of Hoss, another of the locals, hence the optimism of the crooks, Hoss being none too bright). The dog-napping-gold-finding plan goes farcically wrong as Walter outwits the dimwitted outlaws Macie, Teague, and Willard, who wind up as broke as they were before, and twice as confused!

Macie, Teague, and Willard were labelled outlaws on account of their history of botched banditry! The Bible, though, includes stories of the people of God being treated as outlaws because of their commitment to righteousness; Jeremiah was thrown down a well, Paul whipped to within an inch of his life, prophets frequently tortured, priests attacked, and Stephen, the first Christian martyr, stoned to death. The only "crime" of which these people were guilty was speaking up for the values of the eternal Kingdom, and today we pray God's blessing upon those who are nowadays regarded as criminals, and treated with suspicion. They pay a high price for their witness; job applications are rejected when it becomes clear they are Christians, they are regarded as the lowest of the low, and they are denied legal protection as unsympathetic officials turn a blind eye to victimization. God bless these modern "outlaws".

BIRTHDAY BEAGLE!

Salvation is found in no one else, for there is no other name under heaven given to mankind by which we must be saved

(ACTS 4:12 **NIV**)

Today is my daughter's birthday! Jasmine was gifted to us some years ago, and is, like her mother, a traveller, visiting and working in places as far afield as Mexico, Uganda, and India. Jasmine's globe-trotting always includes Snoopy, her soft toy replica of the cartoon dog of the same name. Snoopy was Jasmine's first toy, given to her when she was born, and he has kept my daughter company everywhere she has ventured since, and if Snoopy was allowed to claim Air Miles, he could, by now, easily afford to take foreign holidays all by himself, though I suspect he would be reluctant to journey anywhere at all without Jasmine! Happy birthday!

Is Snoopy a Beagle, or is he not? Popular opinion seems to suggest he is a Beagle that has been anthropomorphized; given human qualities which make him a Beagle but not-really-a-Beagle. His part-Beagleness, though, deters him not one bit from living life to the full, albeit in cartoon form! This reminds me of a situation sometimes encountered by missionaries working within cultures whose efforts meet with a Snoopy-esque response, in that the natives accept Christ, but keep him as one of many idols. They have no qualms as to his divinity, but it is not uncommon for them to also retain a belief in superstition and lucky charms. We need to pray for missionaries faced with such dilemmas as they preach a unique Saviour. May God bless those with whom they share the gospel, that they too come to know life in all its fullness, in Jesus!

SKILL AND ZEAL

Simon the Zealot

(MATTHEW 10:4 ***NIV***)

Roy Keane was a famously explosive footballer, with a temper to match his considerable talent. A star for Nottingham Forest and Manchester United, Keane was as outspoken as he was gifted, and hit the headlines when he quit the Republic of Ireland squad during the 2002 World Cup Finals, following a bust-up with his manager. Keane grabbed international press attention by flying home from Japan, where the tournament was being staged. As the dust settled, he was photographed time and again in newspapers walking his dogs in the fields near his home, and those dogs became, for a while, the most photographed dogs on the planet. One of them, Triggs, even wrote an autobiography! Through good times and bad, Roy Keane could rely on his friendship with his faithful Labrador Retriever, as the chasing media pack hunted down photo opportunities. The last time I checked, *Triggs: The Autobiography* had sold almost 113,000 copies – not bad at all!

Roy Keane, great footballer, but volatile, and I can't help comparing him to Simon the Zealot, who was a marvellous asset to any team or army, but who came with a zeal that sometimes spilled over into aggression. Freedom fighter (terrorist?), political agitator, heroic action figure – Simon wasn't averse to militant action. Was he right, or was he mistaken? His enthusiasm (like Keane's) was to be applauded, especially his concern for justice. His methodology, though? If self-control is a hallmark of the Holy Spirit's influence upon our lives, then probably not. Likewise, gentleness, another telling stamp of God's ownership of our emotions. I like Keane the footballer and I admire Simon's passion, but I don't agree with either of them when it comes to the way such passion is sometimes translated. When we are riled and angry, what is our response?

FAITH FRAMED

The third time he said to him, "Simon son of John, do you love me?"
Peter was hurt because Jesus asked him the third time, "Do you love me?" He said,
"Lord, you know all things; you know that I love you." Jesus said, "Feed my sheep"

(JOHN 21:17 **NIV**)

Next to my desk, I keep a picture of Meg. She is looking straight to camera, and the photo is somewhat haunting, in that she is giving me one of the quizzical looks for which she was well known, as though she is trying to guess what I might be thinking or inviting me to figure out something about her. This snap was taken by my daughter, which is a blessing in that if it had been taken by me, no doubt something would be woefully out of focus, or missing altogether, because if I have any talents at all, they most certainly do not lie in the field of photography! A picture paints 1,000 words, apparently, which is probably true in the hands of an artist or photographer, but not in my case – not so much 1,000 words as, at best, a couple of hundred garbled efforts!

How must Peter have felt in that snapshot moment when he had just betrayed Jesus, having promised to stay loyal to the end, and Jesus looked back at him? The Bible does not come with original photography, but the written accounts of Peter's betrayal paint their own picture. Their eyes would have met; Peter's filled with guilt and remorse, and Jesus' with love and disappointment. How Peter's heart must have sunk as he "saw" his promises crumbling, but how Jesus' heart of love must have burned with compassion and distress. Many more "pictures" subsequently appeared of Peter's turbulent relationship with Christ; most gloriously, of course, his reinstatement as a living testimony to the grace of his Master. If only we had a photograph album providing us with a pictorial history of Peter's life and times, especially on the day of his restoration! They would be pictures worth preserving, to the glory of the God who lifts the fallen.

MIRACLES AND MOVIES

He told her, "For such a reply, you may go; the demon has left your daughter"
(MARK 7:29 **NIV**)

The life of Jesus was not captured in photographs, but there have been numerous attempts to detail his time on earth via the media of film. One interesting movie scenario would be his encounter with the Syrophoenician woman recorded in Mark 7, when even an experienced screenwriter would have difficulty catching the nuances with which that story is laced. The woman (a Gentile) approaches Jesus (a Jew), begging him to heal her demon-possessed daughter. Jesus – at face value – appears to dismiss her curtly, and even refers to her as a dog, at least by implication. Shocking! Whereas it was true many Jews regarded Gentiles as dogs, it seems – at first reading – that Jesus is demonstrating unkind racism, shunning her in her hour of need. Given that he came as one full of grace and truth, this film clip would jar and offend. What do we make of it?

Professor F. F. Bruce defends Jesus not by re-writing the script, but by outlining a context, without which any film would be inaccurate. He states:

What if there was a twinkle in his eye as he spoke, as much to say, "You know what we Jews are supposed to think of you Gentiles; do you think it is right for you to come and ask for a share in the healing which I have come to impart to the Jews?" The written word can preserve the spoken words; it cannot convey the tone of voice in which they were said. Maybe the tone of voice encouraged the woman to persevere ... The woman was quick-witted enough to deduce from Jesus' words the kind of reply to him that would win the granting of her request: "Sir, even the little dogs under the table eat the children's left-overs!" ... The woman's reply expresses just the kind of response that Jesus so greatly appreciated and that never failed to receive what it asked from him. Jesus was aware of a greater rapport with him on her part than he too often found among his own people. Her daughter was healed immediately. [1]

I'm with F. F. Bruce on this one! I like a Jesus who can tease and test, all in the name of love. I like a Jesus who can help and heal. I love a God with twinkling eyes! I rejoice in the fact that the daughter was healed in response to faith and humility. I find it wonderful that we – you and I – can dialogue honestly with a God who knows us, cares for us, and refuses to shun us.

1   F. F. Bruce, *The Hard Sayings of Jesus* (London: Hodder & Stoughton, 1998)

ONE OF US

Being found in appearance as a man, he humbled himself
(PHILIPPIANS 2:8 **NIV**)

One reviewer had this to say about *The Dogist: Photographic encounters with 1000 dogs*:

The Dogist is a beautiful, funny, and inspiring tribute to the beloved dogs in our lives. Every page presents dog portraits that command our attention. Whether because of the look in a dog's eyes, its innate beauty, or even the clothes its owner has dressed it in, the photos will make you ooh and aah, laugh, and fall in love ... Every portrait in the book tells a story and explores the dog's distinct character and spirit. Themed sections include Puppies, Cones of Shame, Working Dogs, and Dogs in Fancy Outfits, giving every dog lover something to pore over.[1]

Sounds good! I would consider buying it, but I have had a book-buying regime imposed (suggested) of late, and I am now obliged to dispose of a book every time I buy another, because (apparently) I have too many books on my shelves. The new rule (idea) is all well and good, but the problem is, there aren't that many tomes I am keen to part with. Unless I can find a solution, I may never know what those 1,000 dogs look like!

"[He had] no beauty that we should desire him" (ESV). Those words, tucked away in Isaiah 53, depict the physical appearance of the Suffering Servant, Jesus, prophetically described, but is Isaiah saying Jesus looked like any other man, with nothing particularly attractive about him, or is the prophet referring to the bruised and swollen face of Jesus after he had been punched and slapped, and made repulsive with bloodstains? Does it matter? To some extent, no, insofar as it makes no difference to the plan of salvation, but on the other hand, Isaiah's words are profound, in that he is describing a God who made himself ordinary in appearance, when his nature is anything but ordinary. In that description, we see a beautiful portrait of grace, and in the wounds inflicted upon Christ, we see our healing in his disfigured divinity.

---

1   www.goodreads.com

PRIDE AND PREJUDICE

When you give to the needy, do not let your left hand know what your right hand is doing

(MATTHEW 6:3 **NIV**)

A friend asked if this book would be dedicated to Skipper! I hadn't thought about a dedication, but there is a likelihood of Meg and Skipper sharing that honour. Is that odd? Shouldn't the dedication be offered to one's parents, or to people whose help has been invaluable? Author dedications used to be a means of recouping costs. Supposing this book, for example, had cost me £xxx to produce and I needed some money back to tide me over before royalties arrived, I would offer my wealthier friends the opportunity of seeing their names in print in return for their patronage. One friend might offer me £xxx on condition he is listed as a benefactor, and another might offer me a little more if his name appears right at the top of the list of patrons. I suppose it all depends on having wealthy friends in the first place, then upon their eagerness to see themselves listed for posterity as generous individuals. On balance, I think I much prefer to nominate Meg and Skipper!

Tempting, isn't it? To make sure our good deeds are acknowledged. Not many of us are content to be overlooked. It rankles, even if only slightly. Jesus, though, taught that one hand should not even be aware of what the other is doing! So, we make a large donation to charity, and that charity offers to mention our benevolence in their Annual Report. Do we decline? Or, say, we spend hours arranging something at the church – the flowers, the chairs, the costumes, only to find our efforts ignored or going without thanks. And what if that church grows from twenty members to 200 members under our leadership? Do we sense the seduction of pride fluttering in our breast, or do we quickly deflect the glory to God, unconcerned who receives the credit as long as he is exalted and praised?

DING DONG DOGS!

God will meet all your needs
(PHILIPPIANS 4:19 **NIV**)

Salvationists in the USA sometimes use "Scout Dogs" to help with their annual "Kettle Appeal" whereby volunteers raise thousands of dollars by standing outside department stores with large metal "kettles" – tins for receiving donations – and ringing handbells, and the more enterprising have a dog or two on hand to elicit goodwill and lend a paw with the effort. I have seen a video clip of a Border Collie called Lacy receiving dollar bills in her mouth, then dropping them into the kettle, and I have seen another Border Collie, Charlie, hard at work on behalf of The Salvation Army by holding a bell in his jaws and ringing it when people pass by. Many of those people find Lacy and Charlie so endearing they cough up a dollar or two which they may otherwise have kept!

Maybe we can pray for charities such as The Salvation Army who combine practical work with a Christian witness. Feeding the hungry and giving shelter to the homeless swallows up vast amounts of income, so we thank God for volunteers who give of their time, and we pray God's blessing upon professional fundraisers too, as they use their expertise to facilitate mission and social care. One of God's names is Jehovah Jireh – meaning, "He will provide", so we pray he will live up to his name by meeting daily needs – and may Lacy and Charlie continue to play their part!

GIRLS AND BOYS, COME OUT TO PLAY

Every year Jesus' parents went to Jerusalem for the Festival of the Passover. When he was twelve years old, they went up to the festival

(LUKE 2:41–42 **NIV**)

Quite a few Salvation Army dogs appear on internet auction sites – toy dogs, that is, and dogs to display as ornaments and memorabilia. On sale as I write is a bright yellow dog whose coat is embroidered with the words "God bless you" and a Salvation Army badge or a red heart. S/he is also available in shiny gold, but should that not be to your liking, you may prefer a porcelain dog bearing a similar decoration. Each to their own, I say. I've never particularly craved a Salvation Army stuffed toy of any description, but if that's your thing, then go for it. If your purchase helps The Salvation Army along just that bit more, then all the better!

Toys are emotive, aren't they! I am amazed, if ever I visit an exhibition, to see things on display that I played with as a boy! Nostalgia rises when we glimpse reminders of times gone by, and we wonder where those years went. Life seems so short at such moments. I had a Bible when I was seven – a small one with colour illustrations, and inside, I had written, "I want to be a Salvation Army officer when I grow up". Well, I managed that for a few years (being an officer, I mean, not growing up!) and I will be forever grateful to the Army for including me in its ranks for a while; that was a tremendous privilege. We think today of those whose memories of younger days include pain or difficult emotions, and we give thanks today for all those who experienced a happy upbringing. Lord, in your mercy, hear our prayers.

PUTTING THINGS RIGHT

Though he fall, he shall not be utterly cast down: for the Lord upholdeth him with his hand

(PSALM 37:24 **KJV**)

The Salvation Army's Founder, General William Booth, was photographed with his family's dog, a Collie Cross of some kind. Booth has the dog on his lap, and both look happy about the situation but, tragically, things didn't work out well. Some time after that picture was taken, Booth had his children's pet shot when it snapped at a servant and he thought it might attack one of them. He was surprised when they were heartbroken, and retrieved the carcass to have the pelt made into a rug, only to be bewildered when they received his gift with hysteria rather than gratitude! The General was a genius as an evangelist and reformer, but it seemed he was not so smart when it came to guessing the mood of his offspring and their love for their dog! In his defence, he meant well, and was trying to rectify matters – I don't believe he ever meant to be cruel, at any stage of the drama.

Can we identify with Booth's mistake? Perhaps we have made an error of judgment that has upset people and, in trying to put things right, we have only caused more distress. If only we could put the clock back and start all over again. The good news is, we can bring our calamities to God, and claim his forgiveness, finding the Redeemer graciously willing to help put things right, if we entrust our failures to his care. There is a Greek word covering such situations, which describes God's powers of recovery. Claim it for yourself today, if needs be. Mistakes and regrets may get you down, but please don't let them keep you down.

Apokathistimi: Restore back to original standing, i.e. that existed before a fall; re-establish, returning back to the ideal; restore back to full freedom; to enjoy again, i.e. what was taken away by a destructive or life-dominating power. Apokathistmi ("re-establish") emphasises separation from the former, negative influence to enjoy what is forward (the restoration).[1]

1   Biblehub.com

SEEING GOD AS HE IS

The Lord is close to the broken-hearted
(PSALM 34:18 **NIV**)

My eyesight isn't the best in the world, and I blame genetics! My maternal grandmother had poor eyesight, and was the victim of practical jokes played upon her by her own children taking advantage of her inability to see things. Likewise, my mum's eyesight is not great, and she has even been known to wear two pairs of glasses at a time! One night, I was out walking Meg quite late – about 10:30 p.m., and therefore (in my defence) dark outside. At one point, I thought I had lost Meg, that she had wandered away into a field nearby (her coat was mostly black, also in my defence). I called her and called her, all to no avail, and it wasn't until I turned around to look elsewhere that I saw her standing right behind me! She had been there all the time, wondering why I was calling her name repeatedly. Poor Meg!

Do we imagine we need to call God's name several times before he will notice us, to assume that if we bombard God with our prayers, he will pay us more attention? It's a sad spiritual error because it portrays God as uncaring, insensitive, and maybe even capricious, whereas he is much closer than we think, or than we give him credit for. He hears the whispers of our hearts long before we articulate any formal request. Do we imagine repetition to be a prerequisite in prayer; that God will respond only when we have expressed sufficient distress or volume? Repetition has its place, so too tenacity, but we err if we think God hears only the loudest and the most insistent. Our silent brokenness will do. He will find us there.

A MISSING PATCH

We fix our eyes not on what is seen, but on what is unseen, since what is seen is temporary, but what is unseen is eternal

(2 CORINTHIANS 4:18 **NIV**)

The Salvation Army produces a children's comic aimed at reaching kids with the gospel. It's full of cartoons, jokes, puzzles, facts, and so on, with the gentle introduction of Bible stories, and one of the regular cartoons details the adventures of Patch the Dog, who makes readers laugh as he tries to be good and helpful. Patch also appears in real life, not just as the work of an artist! A Patch costume is kept at Salvation Army Headquarters, and fits a grown man so that he can make "personal appearances". I once booked Patch to come and lead some children's meetings, and invited loads of children to come and meet him (and hear about Jesus). All was going well – the man who dresses up as Patch arrived, leaflets were handed out, and we looked forward to a fun day together ... until we realized the costume hadn't arrived! It had been entrusted to a courier, but something had gone wrong and it wasn't there. Well, there was nothing to be done, so we made the best of it and I like to think the kids who came along enjoyed themselves anyway.

These things happen and life goes on. In the grand scheme of things, a missing dog costume is not essential. No one died, no one was hurt, and the situation passed. St Teresa of Avila knew nothing about Patch the Dog, but she seemed to know about perspective – what is important and what isn't. Her words today might help someone realign priorities, so I leave them with you, and you with them:

Let nothing disturb thee, nothing affright thee;
All things are passing, God never changeth!
Patient endurance attaineth to all things;
Who God possesseth in nothing is wanting;
Alone God sufficeth.[1]

1   Teresa of Avila (1515–82), trs. H. W. Longfellow, *The Song Book of The Salvation Army* (London: The Salvation Army, 1986)

DRUGS AND DOCTORS, PILLS AND POTIONS

I will restore you to health
(JEREMIAH 30:17 **NIV**)

Teresa of Avila contracted malaria as a young woman, suffering seizures in a state of fever. Many of her greatest spiritual experiences came about because she was so ill and unable to rely upon her physical faculties, thus developing her mystical sensitivity. She wrote on the subject of sickness as a route to blessing, and was not as keen to dismiss illness as perhaps we are nowadays, taking an interest in natural remedies. She was anxious to discern that which God might heal in his good time, and that which might benefit from homeopathic treatment with plants and herbs, concluding that wild roses were useful in the treatment of ailments. The *rosa canina* species was thought to be effective in the treatment of rabid dog bites, hence its Roman name (*rosa canina* or dog rose). Because of its richness in tannic acid, dog rose is particularly effective in treating diarrhoea, though it can also, rather more pleasantly, be useful as a beauty aid. I have no idea which was Teresa's need of dog rose, but it seems she was ahead of her time, as *rosa canina* is now a standard homeopathic option.

We thank God for those whose ministry includes miracles as they impart the healing power of Christ, professional medics who use medical skill to offer healing through medication and/ or surgery, and caring individuals who recommend the healing power of natural remedies. We may want to pray for those in need of physical healing and relief, that they find the style of healing that suits them best, giving glory go to God for mercies bestowed one way or another. Ultimately, our complete healing arrives when we ourselves arrive in Heaven. Let us pray!

MISSING PERSONS ALERT!

The donkeys belonging to Saul's father Kish were lost, and Kish said to his son Saul,
"Take one of the servants with you and go and look for the donkeys"

(I SAMUEL 9:3 **NIV**)

My daughter lost her memory stick, so I helped her look for it, and you know how it goes when you start reaching down behind the cushions of your furniture! I didn't find the flash drive, but I did locate a £1 coin (finders, keepers!), two pens, a sock, and Skipper's collar badge. I'd bought it for him (the reverse side shows a picture of a German Shepherd), and I have to admit, it was a poignant surprise finding it all these weeks after Skipper's death. I shall keep it, as it represents some kind of tangible link with him. We never did find the memory stick, but as I do at least now have Skipper's collar tag on my desk, and it brings back memories of that daft dog! (Are you now tempted to rummage in your armchairs? Who knows what treasure may be there!)

In the New Testament, Jesus spoke about things – and people – once lost, then found; the coin, the sheep, the prodigal son, and so on. In the Old Testament, there are tales of lost livestock being found and returned to their rightful owners. With all that in mind, I encourage you to read the conversion story of John Newton, writer of the hymn "Amazing Grace", as it is a tremendous account of someone who was well and truly lost, spiritually speaking, then "found" by the grace of God. Indeed, the slave trader turned Christian minister wrote, "I once was lost, but now am found".[1] Thank God, he searches and searches in pursuit of that which is precious in his sight. Do you feel "lost" today? Be very sure, God knows exactly where you are, and how you feel. He is only too willing to return you to where he needs you to be.

---

1   J. Newton (1775–1807), "Amazing Grace"

OUT OF DATE

God is a Spirit: and they that worship him must worship him in spirit and in truth
(JOHN 4:24 **KJV**)

Following his conversion, John Newton (1725–1807) wrote a number of hymns, praising God for his deliverance. I reproduce one below, based upon Matthew 15:21–28:

Prayer an answer will obtain, though the Lord awhile delay;
None shall seek his face in vain, none be empty sent away.
When the woman came from Tyre, and for help to Jesus sought;
Though he granted her desire, yet at first he answered not.
Could she guess at his intent, when he to his follow'rs said,
I to Israel's sheep am sent, dogs must not have children's bread.
She was not of Israel's seed, but of Canaan's wretched race;
Thought herself a dog indeed; was not this a hopeless case?

Yet although from Canaan sprung, though a dog herself she styled;
She had Israel's faith and tongue, and was owned for Abraham's child.
From his words she draws a plea; though unworthy children's bread,
'Tis enough for one like me, if with crumbs I may be fed.
Jesus then his heart revealed, woman canst thou thus believe?
I to thy petition yield, all that thou canst wish, receive.
'Tis a pattern set for us, how we ought to wait and pray;
None who plead and wrestle thus, shall be empty sent away.

This hymn is not even remotely politically correct, and wouldn't have a hope of being published nowadays, but maybe that's not the point. Outdated as this ancient hymn might be, it is one of the ways in which Newton tried to express gratitude to God for a life redeemed. In that sense, aren't we all in the same boat as the former ship's captain, in that even our best notes of praise fall short of the worship we would really like to offer? When we survey the wondrous cross, we admit even our finest efforts to pay homage are inadequate. Thank God, though, he accepts our thanks. He knows we are grateful.

OUR HEAVENLY HERO

To us a child is born, to us a son is given ... he will be called ... Prince of Peace
(ISAIAH 9:6 *NIV*)

In a charity shop, I found a first edition of R. M. Ballantyne's *The Dog Crusoe and His Master: A Tale of the Western Prairies*, an adventure story involving a young man (Dick), his friends, and his dog, Crusoe. They wander the prairies hoping to broker peace between the "pale faces" (white people) and the "red men" (Native American Indians), at a time when relationships between white Americans and Native Americans were hostile. Heroic escapades appear on every page, and one beautiful colour plate shows Crusoe – a Border Collie, I think – squaring up to a grizzly bear! The Native Americans are as suspicious of Dick's intentions as that grizzly bear, and often as aggressive, but the story makes a political point under the guise of a story set in the wonderfully named Mustang Valley. Great stuff!

Ballantyne wrote books for boys featuring grizzlies, gorillas, stolen diamonds, gold prospectors, coral islands, and mysterious people from foreign lands! At the heart of *The Dog Crusoe*, though, lies a message of reconciliation between people who would normally be only too quick to kill each other with bows and arrows, axes and muskets. Behind tales of daring exploits lies bloodshed, death, fear and hatred, theft and exploitation. Is it such a leap of imagination to view Bible stories in such a way? The Scriptures are as packed as any of Ballantyne's tales with accounts of murder, skulduggery, kidnap, deception, robbery, brutality, and so on, and we even see a brave peacemaker at work as Christ steps into the pages, visiting hostile territory with his message of forgiveness and harmony. Great stuff indeed!

KING'S MESSENGERS

A greyhound; an he goat also; and a king, against whom there is no rising up
(PROVERBS 30:31 **KJV**)

George Courtauld was a Queen's Messenger, or Equerry, one of a team of people charged with the responsibility of visiting countries ahead of official visits by Queen Elizabeth II. Equerries travel to parts of the world that the monarch is to grace with her presence, checking matters such as security, arrangements for accommodation, the itinerary, and scrutinizing guest lists. Equerries also help host nations plan menus, ensuring Her Majesty's dietary preferences are catered to. Not a bad line of work, and Queen's Messengers are entitled to wear a silver Greyhound lapel badge and/or tie, whereby their authority is internationally recognized, smoothing the way for diplomatic negotiations at the highest levels. Should I take it upon myself to wear such a lapel badge or tie, I would find myself in quite a bit of trouble – they are for the privileged few only. All of the above is outlined in Courtauld's marvellous "Bulldog Trilogy"[1] – his published diaries in which he describes himself as more of a Bulldog than a Greyhound, on account of his portly shape, and where he tells no end of compelling, witty, and revealing stories about his life as one of H. M.'s trusted "Greyhounds".

Honesty compels me to admit I could never really be described as a Greyhound! I do, though, like the reference to a Greyhound in today's text, listed as it is as an animal to be admired (on account of its sleek lines and legendary speed, we assume). The writer of the proverb similarly compliments a goat (for its strength and adaptability?) and a king! Praise indeed for the Greyhound – linked here, as in George Courtauld's books, with royalty! What a wonderful truth it is that we are warmly – and repeatedly – invited into the gracious presence of the King of kings, Jesus himself. He loves us, he desires our company, he wants to work with us, and – perhaps best of all – his invitation is open to everyone; no special badge or tie is required, just a "Yes" to his gentle summons. We too can be on royal service every day.

1   George Courtauld, *The Travels of a Fat Bulldog, The Fat Bulldog Roams Again, The Last Travels of a Fat Bulldog* (London: Abacus Travel, 1999, 2001, 2002)

CHRISTENED CHRIST

She will bear a son, and you shall call his name Jesus, for he will save his people from their sins

(MATTHEW 1:21 **ESV**)

I possess a doggie – not a dog, observe, but a doggie. If he had been a dog, I would not have presumed to intrude him upon your notice. A dog is all very well in his way – one of the noblest of animals, I admit, and pre-eminently fitted to be the companion of man, for he has an affectionate nature, which man demands, and a forgiving disposition, which man needs – but a dog, with all his noble qualities, is not to be compared to a doggie. My doggie is unquestionably the most charming and, in every way, delightful doggie that ever was born. My sister has a baby, about which she raves in somewhat similar terms, but of course that is ridiculous, for her baby differs in no particular way from ordinary babies, except, perhaps, in the matter of violent weeping, of which it is fond; whereas my doggie is unique, a perfectly beautiful and singular specimen of – of well, I won't say what, because my friends usually laugh at me when I say it, and I don't like to be laughed at.

So wrote Robert Michael Ballantyne in *My Doggie and I*, detailing the differences between a doggie – a well-treated, domesticated pet – and a dog; that which a canine is before it is adopted, cleaned, brushed, and so on.[1] The clarification continues; one is a dog, the other a doggie, with more affection being given to the latter.

What's in a name? Quite a bit, according to Ballantyne! Would it therefore have mattered if God's only Son had been called something other than Jesus? Stephen, maybe, or Robert Michael? Probably not, in terms of the work of Calvary, but the fact that Jesus' name was chosen for him (and for Joseph and Mary) before his birth (when most babies are named only after they have been born) is significant, for his destiny as Saviour was wrapped up in that name. His entire identity was confirmed when his name was foretold; the name given whereby we might be saved. What's in a name? All of Heaven, in this case.

---

1   R. M. Ballantyne, *My Doggie and I* (London: James Nisbet & Co. Ltd., circa 1900)

SINNERS TO JESUS NOW CLINGING

The church of God, which he bought with his own blood
(ACTS 20:28 **NIV**)

"What is his name?" I asked. Again for one moment there was that strange, puzzled look in the man's face, but it passed, and he turned with another of his bland smiles. "His name, sir? Ah, his name? He ain't got no name, sir!"
"No name!" I exclaimed, in surprise. "No, sir; I object to givin' dogs names on principle. It's too much like treatin' them as if they wos Christians; and, you know, they couldn't be Christians if they want to ever so much. Besides, whatever name you gives 'em, there must be so many other dogs with the same name, that you stand any chance o' the wrong dog comin' to 'e ven you calls." "That's a strange reason. How then do you call him to you?" "Vy, w'en I wants 'im I shouts 'Hi,' or 'Hallo,' or I vistles."[1]

More of Ballantyne's prose, giving us the story dealing with the purchase of the dog that was to become a doggie. I like the line about dogs not being able to become Christians even if they really wanted to!

Isn't it ironic – and sad – that some people feel they can't possibly become a Christian because they are just too bad, not good enough? Given that the message of Christ is forgiveness, it stands to reason he came for sinners, those who have missed the mark of perfection. What a dreadful irony it is that so many see Christianity as out of reach, when God has already reached down, in Christ, to the depths of our human condition. None of us is good enough, and because of that, the only one who was good enough – Jesus – made everything possible. His purchase of our eternal souls is complete.

---

1   R. M. Ballantyne, *My Doggie and I* (London: James Nisbet & Co. Ltd, circa 1900)

RUNNING MAN

Ahab told Jezebel everything Elijah had done and how he had killed all the prophets with the sword. So Jezebel sent a messenger to Elijah to say, "May the gods deal with me, be it ever so severely, if by this time tomorrow I do not make your life like that of one of them." Elijah was afraid and ran for his life

(1 KINGS 19:1–3 **NIV**)

Wandering around my local market, where charities and social action groups congregate to promote their messages, I met some people collecting money for rescued Greyhounds. Many Greyhounds, you see, are abandoned when their racing days are over, when they are no longer seen as money-spinners by their owners, and need to be looked after in retirement. It's a cruel business, as these elegant, shy, gentle creatures are raced as commercial entities, then thrown out once they are past their top-speed best. The people I met rescue them, care for them, then try to rehome them, and one Greyhound in particular caught my eye – a scruffy individual with long straggly hair who certainly deserved a second chance! God bless the Greyhound rescuers!

A Greyhound in flight is a sight to see! Built for speed with an agility enabling them to corner uniquely sharply (something to do with tendons and ligaments), they fly like the wind. So too, it seems, did the prophet Elijah, on the run from Queen Jezebel, who was offended by his prophetic messages and was out to get him. We can only imagine the speeds Elijah reached as he ran, sheer panic forcing his heartbeat and his legs to accelerate. The representative of evil (Jezebel) was in hot pursuit of God's ambassador! Recognize the feeling? Evil crouching at your door, causing you to fear? The devil breathing down your neck because you've upset him by standing up for Jesus? Take heart, and read on in 1 Kings. The Lord did not abandon Elijah, and neither will he abandon his people, especially not the frightened ones.

BIBLICAL BOUNDARIES

Solomon, standing in front of the altar ...
(I KINGS 8:22 **NEB**)

A removal van was collecting the worldly goods of neighbours moving to pastures new. Nothing unusual in that, except a dog was tied to the van and was barking away while the removal men collected things from the house. He was secured at the top of the ramp lowered at the back of the van, and kept dry (it was raining) by being able to sit in the hold if he wanted to. He looked a lovely chap – as dishevelled as could be, something like a cross between an unkempt Old English Sheepdog and a shambolic Border Collie, and determined to remind his owners he would like their attention again soon! I was tempted to pop outside and share my biscuits with him, but thought better of it in case the removal men disapproved. He was still barking as I wandered back to my desk.

I have occasionally seen things in slightly odd places – where one wouldn't normally expect to see them. A dog in a removal van, for example, and I once saw a pigeon on a train (inside the carriage, I mean). What it is to be in the right place at the right time! I think of King Solomon presiding over the grand opening of the new Temple in Jerusalem – right place, right time, but it is significant he stood at the front of the altar, for even as king, he knew his place, as it was strictly priests only in certain areas of that Temple. Solomon might well have been monarch, but he understood there were no "Access All Areas" passes available, and respected the boundaries. In The Salvation Army, we sing:

Just where he needs me, my Lord has placed me,
Just where he needs me, there would I be![1]

Why would any of us want to be anywhere except where the Lord has placed us?

---

1   M. M. Richards (1911–89), "What Can I Say to Cheer a World of Sorrow?" (*The Song Book of The Salvation Army*, London, 1986)

JE REGRETTE

The Lord regretted that he had made human beings on the earth, and his heart was deeply troubled

(GENESIS 6:6 **NIV**)

Edith Piaf sang *Non, Je ne regrette rien,* which, my French-speaking wife assures me, translates as "No, I regret nothing". Good for Edith, but I can't imagine many of us share that sentiment entirely. I regret, for example, not giving a home to a mongrel I once saw wandering the streets with a piece of string around its neck, patently lost. Why I didn't take it in and make enquiries baffles (and disappoints) me to this day but, instead, I decided to take action only if he returned the following morning (which, of course, he didn't). I should have acted. I had even decided to call him Stringy if he stayed with us! However, thanks to my inaction, he was never christened thus, and I have no idea what became of him. God bless you, Stringy, wherever you might be.

I find today's text pitifully sad, that God's innocent heart of boundless love should include even one regret; sadder still that this note of regret appears because he has ventured out in creative generosity, breathing life into dust and setting humankind on its way in what was meant to be a wonderful adventure. My not homing Stringy is one thing. My stinging God the Father with my sin (for I am Adam – "human" – and therefore culpable) is quite another. My sins baffle (and disappoint) to this day, and I can but thank God for Jesus, the great sin-bearer, who didn't delay, but took decisive action to remedy my situation and bring me home – a second Adam, full of mercy.

CRIME AND PUNISHMENT

The punishment inflicted on him by the majority is sufficient. Now instead, you ought to forgive and comfort him, so that he will not be overwhelmed by excessive sorrow. I urge you, therefore, to reaffirm your love for him

(2 CORINTHIANS 2:6–8 **NIV**)

I met a chap who asked me to keep an eye on his Staffordshire Bull Terrier while he popped into the bank. I was happy to oblige, and Socks, so named because of his white feet, was delightful company. He wasn't, though, so good for my personal popularity, as people spotted him standing with me and, literally, gave him a wide berth. Maybe I'm doing Socks a disservice and it was actually me those people were avoiding, but there was no getting away from the fact a Staffie in tow resulted in an immediate sense of isolation! I didn't mind really, but it did sadden me to see people avoiding the pair of us, some walking in a wide arc away from our direction in order to do so. Oh, well!

For reasons that needn't be disclosed, I am in contact with Christians who have fallen into sin and have, as a result, been shunned or even excommunicated. Their stories are heartbreaking; I think of a church leader who sinned and left the ministry, then found former colleagues turning away from him, literally, physically, at conferences and the like. Sadly, that is not as uncommon as we may wish to think, and for all that I know what the Bible says about such matters, I can't help but think there must be more room for mercy and empathy. Being ostracized, Socks-like, is awful, and can wreck lives and futures. By the same token, my heart goes out to those in authority who exercise church discipline. Theirs is an unenviable task, and they need our prayers and understanding. God bless those in senior leadership who extend grace to transgressors. (For the record, Socks was nowhere near as bad as some people judged him to be!)

THE PARTING OF THE WAYS

He heals the broken-hearted and binds up their wounds
(PSALM 147:3 **NIV**)

I watched a television interview with a man who dresses up as a Dalmatian, asking to be called Spot. His expensive costume was custom-made, and looked detailed and authentic. "Spot" drank from a bowl (on all fours), and ate dog biscuits, explaining to his interviewers that he felt his true persona was that of a Dalmatian, and that he only really felt as though he were himself when living as Spot. His ex-fiancée was interviewed alongside him, explaining, with some sadness, that she had broken their engagement because she was unable to cope with a relationship in which her partner preferred to be treated as a dog, not a man.

Perhaps we could pray today for those struggling in relationships – those whose husbands and wives, girlfriends and boyfriends insist on behaviour that stretches love to its limit, whose demands and expectations create a strain that alters norms to such a degree that even deeply loving friendships break. Those strains can appear in all manner of ways; quirky habits, selfish routines, addictions, neglect, financial recklessness, and so on, affecting people who truly love one another but simply can't manage a "third dimension" intruding upon their devotion. Lord, have mercy.

NOW AND THEN

When you believed, you were marked in him with a seal, the promised Holy
Spirit, who is a deposit guaranteeing our inheritance
(EPHESIANS 1:13–14 **NIV**)

At this time of writing, I am reading a biography of the Reverend Dr William Sangster, a giant of Methodism in his day. He and his wife, early in their marriage, bought not a dog, but a dog collar. A strange purchase? Not really, as the Sangsters were anticipating the day when their domestic circumstances would allow them to buy a dog, and the collar was their way of reminding each other that ownership of a pet, one day, was on their agenda. I found this a delightful way of holding on to a tangible reminder of a promise made to each other. I couldn't help wondering where the collar was kept. In their hallway, perhaps, somewhere visible, or in a drawer or a cupboard? I love the idea of such a simple, ordinary object being so loaded with promise.

The gracious bestowal of the Holy Spirit is our "down payment", so to speak, of the promise of the life to come; God living in our hearts giving us glimpses of the full and complete life in the divine presence that is to be ours, one day, when this earthly existence reaches its conclusion in death. Here, we know his presence within, but it is mixed with our humanity and gold is often, therefore, mixed with dross. Nevertheless, we can at least grasp something of what Heaven will be like; full of God, but without any of our expired humanity marring our experience. Our life with God, therefore, might be described as "now, but not yet". We are to enjoy God here and now, while anticipating greater glories still to come.

DEARLY DEPARTED

Is it nothing to you, all you who pass by?
(LAMENTATIONS 1:12 **NIV**)

The collar purchased, and the marriage begun, Reverend and Mrs Sangster lived in Conwy, in North Wales. Everything was blissful, until tragedy struck:

The first love they shared in their marriage was Bruno. He was a black Retriever puppy, bought to fit the collar they had purchased in their honeymoon. In his doggy way, he chewed up everything – curtains, slippers, chair covers, and tablecloths – and they loved him. After six months he was killed on the road. Bruno was their first child and they were both heart-broken. My father hid everything that reminded them of Bruno – his feeding bowl, his lead, his chewed slippers, his biscuits. He comforted my mother, and then, that night, when he thought she was asleep, gave way to his grief and sobbed like a child.[1]

I can never understand anyone who says, when a puppy is killed or a dog dies, "Oh, well, it's only a dog." Granted, the departed pet is indeed only a puppy or a dog, but to suggest that its death is irrelevant is to misunderstand the role a beloved pet plays in family life. Having said that, I never fail to be moved by an old Salvation Army song "Is it Nothing to You?" which details the crucifixion then repeatedly asks that question. The sadness is, were I to put that enquiry to passers-by in the street on, say, Good Friday, I would almost certainly be met with a wall of apathy or maybe even rejection. The death of Christ – what love! We should pray for those to whom Jesus means little or nothing today.

1   P. Sangster, *Doctor Sangster* (London: The Epworth Press, 1969)

JUNE 6

LOSING FACE

They mocked God's messengers, despised his words and scoffed at his prophets
(2 CHRONICLES 36:16 *NIV*)

Some years later, the Sangsters gave a home to a Corgi, and I share this recollection of the world-renowned preacher and former President of the Methodist Conference, Dr Sangster, rescuing his dog from a fight:

On one occasion he was ill in bed for half a day with influenza and his Corgi dog was attacked by a Terrier which refused to let go its hold. No other help was available, and my father was summoned. He appeared in pyjamas and a yellow dressing gown, streaming with cold ... He summed up the situation, seized an umbrella from a passer-by who shrank away from the apparent maniac, prised open the dog's jaws and freed his own animal. He then gravely bowed to the passer-by, smiled at him, returned the umbrella with the words, "Thank you, my dear sir, for the loan of your umbrella", and returned to bed without another word.[1]

What a sight! Pyjamas on parade! Not much dignity there for the great man of God! And what of us? What of our dignity in the service of Christ? What of our response when the Lord calls us to lowliness? Living as, say, lowly paid people in a society where money makes the world go round, if that is what God requires us to do? Finding the courage to risk being ridiculed for the gospel's sake, or thought stupidly naïve in a culture that regards Christian belief as medieval and irrelevant? As we gaze on the naked form of Jesus languishing on the cross, mocked as a deluded idiot, may we count it an honour to endure ridicule for him, as he did for us.

---

1 P. Sangster, *Doctor Sangster* (London: The Epworth Press, 1969)

DOCTOR ELLINGHAM AND DOCTOR SANGSTER

Thou desirest truth in the inward parts
(PSALM 51:6 *KJV*)

My wife, Heather, is a fan of the *Doc Martin* TV series, featuring a grumpy and brusque Dr Martin Ellingham serving a town in Cornwall, England. The residents are set in their ways, and don't take kindly to Doc Martin's forthright manner – neither does he appreciate their slow pace of life, or the lingering presence of Buddy, a scruffy Terrier who belongs to no one in particular, but is fond of appearing in Doc Martin's waiting room. One of the longest running jokes in the series is the way in which Buddy returns to the waiting room time and time again (where he is fussed over and made welcome by everyone else), despite Dr Ellingham's volcanic fury whenever he evicts the four-legged visitor. (Needless to say, most patients take Buddy's side every time an eviction is made!)

Dr Martin Ellingham is at least being honest and open about a situation he finds intolerable – that of a wandering Terrier on his premises; there is no pretence with Ellingham, and he "tells it like it is". We may not like his blunt style, but no one could ever accuse him of deceit! Dr Sangster was concerned about such moral issues from a Christian point of view, and in his diary entry dated 18 September 1930, wrote, as part of his personal spiritual audit:

I am deceitful in that I often express private annoyance when a caller is announced and simulate pleasure when I actually greet them.[1]

Food for thought? Is honesty always paramount, or does kindness sometimes take precedence? Perhaps Sangster's idea of a personal spiritual audit is worth considering – a "check-up" with the Great Physician from time to time?

1   P. Sangster, *Doctor Sangster* (London: The Epworth Press, 1969)

RELAX

I no longer call you servants ... Instead, I have called you friends
(JOHN 15:15 **NIV**)

Away from the set of *Doc Martin*, the actor who plays him, Martin Clunes, is known for his love of dogs, and has even been nicknamed *"Dog* Martin" by colleagues. Clunes owns four dogs (one of which he found while filming in Cornwall and brought home), and is renowned for breaking off set to fuss a dog he has spotted – a complete contrast to the uptight Dr Ellingham who has no time at all for Buddy the Terrier. People who see him approaching random dogs he has never met before comment on his perfectly natural ease with them; he is not at all scared to stroke them or reluctant to play with them, and patently loves their company. Dogs, in turn, love him. They know he means them no harm, and is as pleased to see them as they are, him.

Isn't it wonderful to be at ease with God! That is, to understand him as a friend, an ally in all that is good, and a deity who wants to help us. That we may approach in order to shelter beneath his wings is quite something – to know him as a loving shepherd who has no desire to harm us, but who offers a warm embrace, forgiveness, understanding and gentle faithfulness along life's journey. He has all the time in the universe for us, to listen to our prayers, to lend his aid, and to respond in mercy to our heart's cry. This is God.

CARPE DIEM

Shout to God with cries of joy
(PSALM 47:1 **NIV**)

I spent a few hours at a National Trust Visitor Centre, poking around the gift shop, and treating myself to lunch in the company of quite a few dogs. This particular centre is dog-friendly, especially in the Outdoor Café area, where a large mural dominates half a wall, painted with a smiling Old English Sheepdog and the sign "Paws for a drink". Drinking bowls are available, and so is water, hence my canine company. One dog caught my eye, a large dark brown mop on legs; a mass of curly hair whose breed I couldn't make out. Not only was he astonishingly hirsute, but amazingly hungry (greedy?) too, sniffing under tables for scraps of food and specializing in locating long-deserted chips. What a joy to see so many happy dogs out walking, drinking, sunbathing and – in "Curly's" case – snaffling up snacks.

Sometimes, just the sheer joy of living – the rich gift of life – passes us by, doesn't it? Maybe we become so preoccupied with responsibilities that we forget to notice the blessings of the ordinary? Yet, for all our busy-ness, grass is still green, birds still sing, rivers still flow, and flowers are still brightly colourful. Maybe that's half the attraction of dogs – without an obvious care in the world, they will always scamper around a park as though it's the first time they have ever been there, savouring life itself and revelling in all that is theirs, never wasting a moment to simply enjoy it all. Might we imitate "Curly" & Co. Today, appreciating all our Creator God has given, and offering a prayer of thanks?

TEUTONIC TENACITY

Let us hold fast the profession of our faith
(HEBREWS 10:23 *KJV*)

I have finished reading about William Sangster, and moved to a biography of Pope John Paul II. My attention has been grabbed by references to Cardinal Ratzinger, who was elected as Pope Benedict XVI in 2005, but was instrumental in implementing Vatican directives while "The Polish Pope" led the Roman Catholic Church. Ratzinger was uncompromising in ensuring papal orders were obeyed, and not averse to hauling bishops and theologians before interview panels if he thought they had disobeyed! He was nicknamed "God's Rottweiler" and/or "The Church's German Shepherd" (Benedict XVI is German); nicknames meant as testament to his strength of character, hinting at the fact Cardinal Joseph Ratzinger was aggressive in his pursuit of Catholic truth. (I think the nicknames were bestowed with affection!)

We may not agree with such an approach, but no one can doubt such qualities of commitment. I can't imagine it was a barrel of laughs to be summoned to appear before an investigating panel in Rome, but no one could ever accuse Cardinal Ratzinger of being lukewarm in his defence of established doctrine. Are we, sometimes, when it comes to holding fast on points that conscience leads us to believe are non-negotiable? Is there perhaps something of a *laissez-faire* approach that creeps in when we fear disagreement? I am merely asking the question, and it's something I will need to examine in my own heart. Will you join me in doing so?

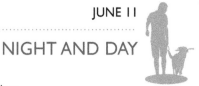

NIGHT AND DAY

The girl is not dead but asleep
(MATTHEW 9:24 **NIV**)

Driving along a country lane, I saw what I thought was a child's pyjama case or rucksack – a chocolate-brown, furry one made to look like a dog. It was lying near the gutter, as though it were a puppy, fast asleep. To my horror, I realized, as I drove nearer, it was indeed a puppy, but dead, not asleep (a Labrador, I think). How I wish it had been a pyjama case or a rucksack! It had been hit by a vehicle, but showed no obvious signs of injury; that, at least, was some consolation. Neither was there any blood pooling, so I imagine the poor little thing had taken a direct blow to the head. I can but hope death came swiftly and relatively painlessly.

I am intrigued by Jesus' description of the girl who appeared to have died, when he was summoned to help: "The girl is not dead, but asleep." The girl's father thought she had died – so too, the crowd that gathered, who laughed at Jesus when he made his remarkable statement. Was she dead? Was she in a coma? What did Jesus mean by "asleep"? We assume her family had made vigorous efforts to revive her, so she must have been a very deep "sleeper" not to have come round. Or was Jesus referring to some kind of "soul sleep" (if there is such a thing)? Frankly, I have no idea, but the point of the story is that Jesus Christ has ultimate power over comas, brain injuries, death, "soul sleep", our waking hours, and our unconsciousness. Even when we are powerless, Jesus is Lord; in our powerlessness, his power is perfectly demonstrated.

SENSITIVE SAINTS

You are miserable comforters, all of you!
(JOB 16:2 **NIV**)

Visiting an elderly gentleman, I was greeted by his ancient Cairn Terrier, who had started life with black hair but had given way to dusty grey as the years had passed. He was a lovely dog with a tiny tail that served more as propeller than tail, but I somehow managed to frighten him. As he (Whisky) sniffed around my ankles while I sat chatting to his owner, I lifted my hand to stroke him (Whisky, not his owner), and frightened him, as I hadn't realized he was partially blind and deaf. He must have seen or sensed my hand at the very last minute, and it shocked him. No harm done, and Whisky and I were soon the best of friends, but I could have kicked myself for failing to notice the dullness of his eyeballs and his unresponsiveness to commands (not that that would have helped).

I have always regarded Job's comforters as perhaps the most insensitive people in the Bible! There was poor Job, his life in ruins, through no fault of his own, experiencing utter despair, and along come his friends with ill-timed remarks and inappropriate counsel – as if he didn't have enough to cope with! They failed to notice his plight and piled in regardless with platitudes, rebukes and psychobabble. Goodness only knows why they didn't just sit with him and put an arm around his shoulder, resisting the temptation to say anything at all. May God preserve us from our insensitivities towards the needs of others.

REMEMBERING NOT TO FORGET

In remembrance of me
(LUKE 22:19 *NIV*)

Another visit brought me into contact with an elderly lady who was the most ardent fan of Bulldogs I have ever met! I like Bulldogs, but this lady put my affection in the shade. In her living room alone, I counted sixteen items of Bulldog memorabilia ranging from porcelain ornaments to cushions to stuffed toys – more mini-museum than house! She had owned two Bulldogs over the years, the latest of whom, Sandy, looked down at me from a framed picture on her wall (he died a few years ago, but his picture kept him alive in her memories). Such mutual devotion! So many reminders! Sandy and his predecessor were patently adored and remembered with a huge amount of love.

Holy Communion can be – but needn't be – a divisive issue amongst Christians. Salvationists and Quakers, for example, choose not to partake, whereas friends from other denominations feel deprived of an important spiritual experience (encounter?) if Communion is not included in a service. Well, I have no intention of entering any debate on the sacraments (that one is for braver people!), as long as we all agree the sacrificial death of Jesus should never be forgotten, by any of us – whether that is with bread and wine, a Love Feast, or in some other way. Christ died for you, and he died for me, and whichever personal reminders we prefer to adopt, and however we commemorate his sacrifice, that fact remains.

DUCKS, DOGS AND DEITY

God, the blessed and only Ruler, the King of kings
(1 TIMOTHY 6:15 **NIV**)

The curiously named Isle of Dogs, in London's East End, has, over the centuries, been marshland, port area, and, most recently, with the marshes drained, an area of urban development offering desirable properties. It is said King Edward III kept his Greyhounds there when he wasn't hunting, and that might be why it is named the Isle of Dogs, although some believe it was originally called the Isle of *Ducks* because of the numbers of wild fowl inhabiting the marshes. Personally, I go with the ducks option, on the basis they were there first, long before King Edward's Greyhounds, and because so many phrases are corrupted as language evolves. I might, though, be mistaken, and who is to say the locals of the day weren't so flattered by the presence of the king's hounds, they promoted the status-enhancing honour of royal patronage!

We have a tailor's shop in town, bearing the royal coat of arms. I've never had the courage (or the budget!) to step inside, but rumour has it the proprietor is one of the tailors retained by Queen Elizabeth II, hence the gold-painted emblem above his front door. Sometimes, I find it hard to believe the King of kings has stamped his coat of arms on my heart; I know it's true, but it takes some believing that his gracious patronage has been bestowed on such a life as mine. Do you ever struggle with that, or is it just me? It's (almost) a fact too wonderful to believe! Yet, if such grace is real (and it is), then we can but pray, "Lord, I believe; help thou mine unbelief" (Mark 9:24, KJV).

WELCOME

Anyone who welcomes me welcomes the one who sent me
(MATTHEW 10:40 **NIV**)

An unusual story emerging from official papers now released concerns President John F. Kennedy, Nikita Khrushchev, and a puppy named Pushinka. Confidential documents relating to discussions between world leaders remain under lock and key for decades, until the time comes for their declassification, but not many secret records mention puppies! One archive, though, tells how Pushinka ("Fluffy" in Russian), a "nonbreed", was gifted by Khrushchev to Kennedy as a goodwill gesture. Such were the tensions of the time, however, between the USA and USSR, that Pushinka was subjected to intimate tests, X-rays, and examinations before being allowed anywhere near the White House, as the CIA searched for hidden microphones, microchips, and bugs; anything that might relay sensitive information from Washington to Moscow!

Poor Pushinka! Offered as a gift in the hope of thawing cold war animosity, yet regarded with suspicion by her American recipients. Does this remind us of God the Father's gracious gift of God the Son to humanity? He too was offered in peace and goodwill, as the One who might reconcile humankind with a Superpower, yet was subjected to interrogations and cross-questioning as his credentials were dismissed and doubted; regarded as suspicious and insubordinate, when all he ever had to offer was transparent, vulnerable love. How will we receive him when he asks admission today?

SIGNS OF THE TIMES

We will show forth Your praise
(PSALM 79:13 **NKJV**)

One of my regular drives takes me past "The New Greyhound" public house, and curiosity has the better of me regarding its name. Why "The *New* Greyhound" instead of simply "The Greyhound"? And, was there ever an old Greyhound? Likewise, the pub sign, depicting an elderly Greyhound sitting on a lawn, being amused (tormented?) by a Greyhound pup evidently much keener to play than his aging friend seems to be ... The mystery has been solved, and I now know "The New Greyhound" came into existence when "The Greyhound", its predecessor, was refurbished – simple, really! All that remains is for me to discover why the original pub was named "The Greyhound" in the first place ...

Illustrated boards hanging outside public houses came into existence because the majority of customers in centuries gone by were illiterate. Anxious to quench their thirst, they equated a pub sign with the availability of beer! This method of distinguishing ale houses from ordinary houses was successful, hence the proliferation of such signs today. How it grieves me when churches fail to take advantage of clear signage in a way publicans recognized centuries ago! Peeling paintwork, for example, faded posters, information that is woefully out of date, leading to frustration and disappointment on the part of visitors who tend not to return. Do we really wish to convey the message that our gospel too is faded, that we have given up? Shall we begin our investment in souls by investing in a tin of paint and some attractive noticeboards? Maybe it's just a gripe of mine, or maybe it matters ...

ALL BETS ARE OFF!

They cast their silver into the streets
(EZEKIEL 7:19 **ESV**)

It transpires that "The Greyhound" was named because of its proximity to a Greyhound track that has long-since disappeared. The pub was the hub of betting rings, where those keen to place wagers on Greyhound races gathered to do so – sometimes legally, sometimes not! It was a handy location for anyone wishing to spend their time (and their money) gambling, drinking, and cheering on their favourite runner(s). "Unofficial" bookmakers would, well, "make a book" on the races without the encumbrances of inconvenient legal formalities, and nonconformist Christians in particular were up in arms against such activities, their public protests becoming part of local folklore. Why it seems to have been left mainly to the nonconformists to protest is unclear, but maybe some things are better left unknown!

General William Booth was one of many high-profile Victorians who protested against the waste of money encouraged by publicans and bookmakers in an era when it was by no means uncommon for entire wage packets (already meagre) to be gambled away long before they ever reached home, where they could be spent on essentials such as food. Good for Bill Booth, if it meant children were fed instead of bookies made richer, but what of the Church today? May it ever raise its voice wherever poverty raises its ugly head, however that poverty is brought about, and may God bless those who work to alleviate, educate, and demonstrate a better way of life. Pray for those enslaved by gambling, that they may be free.

RUNNING THE SHOW

Be transformed by the renewing of your mind. Then you will be able to test and approve what God's will is – his good, pleasing and perfect will

(ROMANS 12:2 **NIV**)

I bring to you today the story of a Black Labrador/Retriever/Rottweiler mix who actually served as Mayor of the community of Sunol, California, USA! Disenchanted with politicians, the residents of Sunol nominated Bosco Ramos to stand against two human candidates in the mayoral election of 1981. Quite astonishingly, Bosco Ramos won, and served as Town Mayor until his death in 1994, attracting international attention and being held up by one Chinese newspaper as an example of the failings of the American political process. Bosco Ramos became a local celebrity, even appearing on television, and in 2008, a statue of him was erected outside the town's post office. You have my word this is all perfectly true!

Psychiatrists advise that the human mind – the psyche – works best when the dominant element within the brain maintains control over other elements; that is to say, suppose we imagine the mind to be some kind of village, with all sorts of things going on and all kind of thoughts vying for our attention. The "village" needs a "Mayor" – someone to take charge, lest anarchy should descend and one's thoughts run amok. How wonderful it is to know, then, that God the Holy Spirit is willing to assume this crucial role for us, all for the want of being invited to do so, exercising gentle sovereignty over the battlefield of our emotions, keeping the "village" in check by bestowing order, love, and peace.

POOCHES AND POLITICS

The king's heart is in the hand of the Lord, as the rivers of water: he turneth it whithersoever he will

(PROVERBS 21:1 **KJV**)

It is not only voters in the USA who involve dogs in the democratic process! As I write, the United Kingdom is to embark on a referendum to decide whether membership of the European Union is discarded or retained, and dog owners have had their say. One "Remain" campaigner has enlisted the support of her Border Terrier under the slogan "Borders against Borders", stressing the advantages of free trade, while "Migrant Canines for Remain" features Ernie, a Hungarian Wirehaired Vizsla rescued from Hungary in 2013 and allowed to live in the UK under the EU Pet Travel Scheme. Lots more dogs, though, have been photographed simply sitting on cold, hard pavements, waiting patiently while politicians address crowds of voters; it has to be said, they look bored and fed up, hoping their walks can resume as soon as the speeches have been concluded!

This is not the place for me to comment on political matters, except to say I believe God is in control of such issues, and that he hears our prayers regarding elections and referenda. I do not, though, pretend to understand the ways of God in allowing corrupt and cruel regimes to flourish while people, including praying Christians, suffer; Ceausescu's government in Romania, for example, which brought misery to millions, and so on. Such matters are a mystery, but that does not cause me to abandon my faith in the God of nations, for his ways are not our ways. For now, I rejoice in the privilege of democracy, while praying for those living beneath the shadow of oppression.

JUNE 20

PARKING ONE'S ANGER

As far as it depends on you, live at peace with everyone
(ROMANS 12:18 **NIV**)

Have you ever been the victim of car park gazumping, whereby another driver swiftly moves in to claim the parking space you have been waiting for patiently? Has their deft driving manoeuvre left you angry? Or has a similar experience outside your house left you fuming, when someone has pinched the last remaining space, leaving you to park a distance away? One man who found himself unable to park because someone had taken up two spaces with their car drew a picture of a puppy with a black spot around its right eye, accompanied by the scribbled note, "I am giving you this dog. His name is Spot. I thought you might want him, as you seem to be trying to take as many spots as possible. I hope this helps." He left this on the windscreen of the offender. I can't help envying him such a creative response!

Is it permissible to be angry when such things happen? Should we take action, or simply shrug them off? Are Christians meant to tolerate and forgive to such an extent they allow themselves to be trampled on? Is it OK to stand up for oneself when it comes to legitimate rights? Are Christians supposed to be endlessly gracious when they have been cheated or tricked? It's something of a grey area, in that we follow One who set an example of humility, but who also resisted wrongdoing in all its forms. I'm afraid I don't know the answer! What I do know is that my grandmother always insisted "Christian" wasn't spelt M.U.G. Was she right?

KEEPING ONE'S BALANCE

Everything should be done in a fitting and orderly way
(1 CORINTHIANS 14:40 **NIV**)

My children have been asked to be unofficial photographers at my sister's wedding. A photographer has been booked to take the formal pictures, while Jasmine and Alistair are to wander around making an album of guests chatting, children playing, people eating, and so on. It's a great idea of my sister's, but she is not the first to think of it. One couple in Tennessee, USA, wanting to capture the informality of their celebrations, strapped a video camera to their dog, Ryder the Husky, and allowed him simply to follow them around throughout the preparations beforehand, the ceremony itself, and the reception, recording all that took place. The result was, apparently, quite something, especially as some present stopped Ryder to record messages of greeting. Ryder himself had a great time, by all accounts, enjoying the company of new-found friends!

It's a tricky one, isn't it – informality and spontaneity in church services. Not many of us like services to be so straitjacketed that the influence of the Holy Spirit is curtailed, but the other extreme of "anything goes" can be equally distressing. Services should reflect the nature of God – creative, expressive, warm – but there is a need for decorum too. No one is entitled to block the flow of the Spirit's leading when his people gather, but leaders have a responsibility to interpret that leading so that worshippers are edified; "heavy shepherding" is unacceptable, but so too is such an emphasis on freedom that no one seems to know what's going on. We should pray for leaders who carry such responsibilities!

DUNDEE AND DISCIPLESHIP

I will build my church
(MATTHEW 16:18 ***NIV***)

Professional dog walkers are increasingly popular, as working people are unable to walk their dog(s) and, instead, pay someone to do it for them. A problem has arisen in Dundee in Scotland, though, in that a proliferation of dog walkers threatens to take over park space! Dundee City Council has drawn up a list of conditions professional dog walkers need to agree to, in the hope others enjoying the parks can do so without feeling swamped by dogs! They are as follows:

- No more than six dogs to be exercised at any one time.
- The professional dog walking company to have relevant pet business insurance.
- Comply with all current dog related laws, regulations, and guidance.
- Keep accurate up to date records for each dog in their care.
- Dogs to be transported in a vehicle fit for purpose with dogs adequately secured.
- To have a first aid kit designed for dogs.
- Dogs to be tagged with the professional dog walking company's own company tag whilst under their authority.
- Controlling dogs at all times during exercise.
- Cleaning up any dog fouling.
- Being aware and responsible for other land use – i.e. keeping away from livestock and bird habitat areas.

Dundee City Council is to be credited for passing legislation to help manage a new problem, rather than allowing an issue to fester in the hope it disappears. They have not been content to rest on outdated statutes. Can we learn from this? Are we, as God's people, up to speed with the issues of the day, adopting modern ways of presenting the gospel? Or are we relying on dusty edicts that may no longer be fit for purpose? Might we even be guilty of hoping fresh challenges will just vanish? Today's Church is very different to the Early Church, but a timeless God will not fail his people in this generation, or any other.

FOUR BECOMES MORE!

This is the genealogy of Jesus the Messiah
(MATTHEW 1:1 **NIV**)

Remember Pushinka, the "nonbreed" whose admission into the White House was held up by CIA suspicion? I am pleased to report her subsequent assimilation into Kennedy family life, and her fruitful union with Charlie, a Welsh Terrier already resident in Washington, which produced four pups – Blackie, White Tips, Butterfly, and Streaker, nicknamed by JFK as "the pupniks" on account of their Russian ancestry. When the time came for the offspring to leave the White House, around 5,000 people wrote asking if they could adopt one; consequently, Butterfly and Streaker were given to children in the Midwest while White Tips and Blackie went to friends of the Kennedys.

We can assume those "pupniks" produced grandchildren for Pushinka and Charlie, and that those grandchildren repeated the process, and so on – which means there are probably quite a few dogs roaming America today with an illustrious heritage! Jesus' genealogy is recorded in Matthew's Gospel, and provides a fascinating insight into the bloodline of God Incarnate, not least the fact he was descended (in human terms) from all sorts of characters, including kings, farm workers, and even a prostitute. I love that about Jesus; that in some mysterious way, his DNA is much the same as mine, for all that he is God. Do I understand it? No! Does it reassure me of his innate empathy? Wonderfully, yes! This is our God; human and yet so divine.

GOLD STANDARD

To live is Christ and to die is gain
(PHILIPPIANS 1:21 **NIV**)

A newspaper advertisement encourages me to purchase a pennant featuring "over 55 coloured Swarovski crystals!" set in the shape of a dog. For "two convenient monthly instalments of just £34.50" I can own a gold-plated pendant attached to an eighteen-inch gold-plated chain. This will, apparently, serve as "a treasured reminder of a favourite companion" and I am invited to choose one of the twelve dogs available. The list is impressive. Should I wish to spend £69 on such a keepsake, I can pick either a Border Collie, a Boxer, a Dachshund, a German Shepherd, a Jack Russell, a King Charles Spaniel, a Mini Schnauzer, a Pug, a Scottish Terrier, a Shih Tzu, a Westie, or a Yorkie. I shan't be buying, but they do actually look very attractive.

Such a pendant would indeed be a treasured reminder of a beloved pet that had died. A mass-produced item of jewellery wouldn't be an exact likeness of a dog that had passed away, but it might bring some comfort; something tangible to hold on to when the actual reality is no more; rather like the way in which we keep some of the belongings of a loved one who has departed; a watch, maybe, or a particular possession that carries significance. For all that Christians believe in a life to come, we would give anything to have our dearly beloved back with us for a moment, even if only to say goodbye, hence our propensity for treasured reminders. This is no comment on the quality of our faith, simply a natural reaction to loss. Let us hold in prayer those who grieve.

SHOCKING TRUTH

God created human beings in his own image
(GENESIS 1:27 **NLT**)

The loss of a dog should not be underestimated – its impact can be severe, as television presenter Chris Packham discovered when his one-year-old black Poodle, Fish, was run over and killed by a car. Packham, who lives with Asperger's syndrome, was so attached to Fish that the sudden death spiralled him into deep depression and even thoughts of suicide, which he nearly carried out. He found the process of burying Fish particularly traumatic, especially as it rekindled memories of another pet he had lost, when he was fourteen, and it has taken him two years of psychotherapy to begin to recover. God bless Chris Packham.

Shock, like bereavement, is not to be easily dismissed. We are made, in the image of God, as holistic beings, and our bodies will often reflect our emotions. You hardly need me to tell you that, but this poses an interesting theological question; if we are indeed made in God's image, does it then follow that God experiences, say, distress, as we do? I believe so. There is of course a line of demarcation in that God would not fall prey to depression; nor would trauma ever get the better of him. Nevertheless, we have a God whose heart beats tenderly and with remarkable sensitivity. This is God. He cares, feels, and understands.

POODLES AND PRAYER

God spoke ... in various ways
(HEBREWS 1:1 ***NIV***)

Chris Packham overcame his suicidal thoughts, and I applaud him for doing so. He found the courage to continue with his career as a TV, and author, and was greatly helped in his recovery by the gift of two black Poodles, Itchy and Scratchy, bought for him by his partner, who realized Chris's Asperger's meant he was sometimes better able to respond emotionally to animals than to humans. At his lowest ebb, Itchy and Scratchy came into his life and, quite literally, saved it. Their unconditional love penetrated emotional depths psychotherapy couldn't reach, and their enthusiasm for walks in Chris's company kept him alive. God bless Itchy and Scratchy!

Who is to say God didn't provide Itchy and Scratchy at just the right time? I personally believe his mercy is so wide and his concern so immense, he is capable of delving down into our troubled hearts to bring relief, and our text today might indicate something of the variety of ways in which a loving Heavenly Father responds to our needs. How do we expect God to answer our prayers? Do we perhaps limit his ingenuity and creativity? Maybe we think he will only ever dispatch assistance in ways a), b), or c)? Can slightly daft black Poodles be messengers of his love? I don't see why not!

ACTING THE PART

God ... will never leave you nor forsake you
(DEUTERONOMY 31:6 *NIV*)

Have you heard of Pistol and Boo? Maybe not, but I expect you have heard of Johnny Depp and Amber Heard, Pistol and Boo's owners. They are Yorkshire Terriers, you see (Pistol and Boo, not Depp and Heard), smuggled into Australia under falsified travel documents, bypassing quarantine. Oops! For all Johnny Depp's skill as a thespian, he wasn't able to persuade the Australian authorities of the legality of Pistol and Boo's documentation, resulting in a Queensland court handing down a one-month good behaviour bond and some embarrassing publicity. Given the alternative was a fine equivalent to £540, a one-month good behaviour bond seems to be a reasonable option, but Pistol and Boo, meanwhile, have been photographed peering out of their travel cage looking unimpressed with proceedings!

It is to be hoped Pistol and Boo, entirely innocent Yorkshire Terriers, are free by now, and that Johnny Depp and Amber Heard are behaving in a suitably appropriate way. What of us? Are we behaving well? Do we often equate God's favour and goodwill towards us in proportion to our behaviour? If we are doing well, we think he likes us a bit more, whereas if we sin, he likes us a bit less – that sort of thinking creeps in and forms a subliminal theology. Proper Christian behaviour is to be expected from Christians, but we are mistaken if we believe God rejects us when we slip up, for grace prevails and even though he does not – cannot – approve of sin, he has no intention of turning his back on us. This is God, and this is prevailing grace.

JUST WHERE HE NEEDS ME

Whoever obeys his command will come to no harm, and the wise heart will know the proper time and procedure

(ECCLESIASTES 8:5 **NIV**)

Whatever skills I may or may not possess, it would be a stretch of the imagination to say I have a good sense of direction. Even using Satnav, I still manage to become lost, regularly! Thus it was, driving to meet a friend, I arrived in a country lane miles from anywhere. Scenic as it was, my friend was nowhere to be seen. What to do? I drove on optimistically, and to my surprise, discovered the charmingly named Dog Kennel Lane, the discovery of which made a pleasing distraction as I meandered along my unplanned detour. A little research indicates Dog Kennel Lane was so christened because in former times, the lord of the manor kennelled his dogs on the part of his land that is now surrounded by houses but was once rolling fields. Given the size of the area Dog Kennel Lane now occupies, I can only assume His Lordship owned quite a number of dogs!

I located my friend, eventually, and he had had the grace to exercise patience awaiting my arrival. Being in the right place at the right time can make all the difference – ask an airline pilot scheduled to land on a certain runway in accordance with airport schedules! Or an interviewee needing to make a good impression in order to secure a job. It's not always possible, but it's a reasonable ideal, and keeping others waiting is not great. Our text today indicates the importance of trying our best, with God's help, to be where he needs us to be, when he needs us to be there, and it seems to indicate, too, obedience on our part; a sensitivity to his will. Maybe we could pray today for those who have taken a wrong turning, that they would find their way back to God, who waits and loves?

YOU'RE WELCOME

The woman took the baby and nursed him
(EXODUS 2:9 *NIV*)

Today is my mum's birthday! I can't say she is a great dog lover, but you will remember the story of Mum's adoption of Scruffy. For all that she is not a particular fan of dogs, Mum was always willing to dog-sit Meg and Skipper whenever we needed help, even though Meg was always off-hand with Mum and didn't want her friendship. My guess is, Meg associated Mum with the fact we were going away for a few days, and would therefore sulk until we returned; Mum was cast as the villain, despite her hospitality! Nowadays, from time to time, even though Meg and Skipper are no longer with us, Mum dog-sits for a friend, enabling that friend to go here and there. Happy birthday, Mum – dog-sitter!

I don't know whether or not Moses ever owned a dog, but he benefited from the services of a sitter; his life was saved when the daughter of Pharaoh – kings of Egypt were called Pharaoh; Pharaoh means "a king" – rescued him at a time when baby boys were being killed left, right, and centre (see Exodus 2). Moses was not only rescued, but adopted and raised as the son of a princess! What a lovely ministry is exercised by those whose vocation is to foster or adopt children. Can we underestimate the impact for good a loving foster home can have upon a child who is placed for adoption? Young lives can be saved – emotionally, psychologically (and even, sometimes, literally). Thank God for those willing to open their homes and their hearts to welcome babies and youngsters in need of tender, loving care.

SHOWING ONE'S TRUE COLOURS

*Israel loved Joseph more than all his children … he made him a tunic
of many colors*

(GENESIS 37:3 **NKJV**)

A famous person has published photographs of her Maltese with its coat dyed pink to match her own dress, hair, and shoes. This is to celebrate America's National Pink Day (no, I hadn't heard of it either), but the Maltese in question can be dyed any number of colours in accordance with what her owner is wearing from one week to the next. Such human/dog colour coordination is, apparently, quite the thing in trendy circles, with each colouring lasting a few days. The dye, I am reassured, is entirely ethical – a vegan, non-irritant, specialized conditioner applied whenever doggie has a bath.

What else can we think about today, but Joseph's multicoloured coat? That particular garment – a rainbow to be worn – became the subject of a musical and the stuff of legend. Maybe what is less well known is the story behind the garment; a tale of treachery, violence, and betrayal that would leave most novelists blinking in disbelief, yet which illustrates the sovereignty of God over even our most desperate circumstances. The full account of Joseph's colourful life can be found in Genesis (in particular, chapter 37 onwards), so you may want to check out the story afresh, and see God at work in ways that should encourage us when life seems hopeless!

A GREEN GOD

God saw all that he had made, and it was very good

(GENESIS 1:31 *NIV*)

A London council is placing advertisements in the hope of hiring staff to compile DNA profiles of dogs from the mess left in public places, and on pavements. I can't imagine this council being flooded with applications for such unsavoury jobs, but I understand the frustration of the councillors who plan to, how shall I put it, pass such a motion. Apparently, it is possible to tell breed, gender, eye colour, and even the texture of the dog's coat from a stool sample, and the intention is to identify owners who leave their dog's mess lying around and issue them with a fine. I hope it works, but it's not a form of employment I would enjoy. (Oh yes, the London borough in question is ... Barking!)

Would it make sense to regard the consequences of irresponsible dog ownership as pollution? I think so, just as rubbish left lying around pollutes the environment – not only literally, but as an eyesore too. Would we regard such irresponsibility as blasphemy, in the sense that God has given us a beautiful planet to enjoy, and our lack of care for his gift – from dog mess dumped at roadsides to ton after ton of toxic waste dumped into oceans – represents ingratitude and irreverence? Would we treat any other gift in such a way? I wonder how it makes God feel.

RUSSIAN ROYALTY

The third day was Pharaoh's birthday, and he gave a feast
(GENESIS 40:20 *NIV*)

Prince George, elder child of Prince William, Duke of Cambridge, and Catherine, Duchess of Cambridge, is, as I write, preparing to celebrate his birthday, on the 22nd of this month, and "well-placed sources" report that Kate and William are planning to buy George a Bolonka Zwetna puppy as his main gift (at a mere £1,800!). I must confess – with no offence intended to the Royal Family – to never having heard of Bolonka Zwetnas, a Russian breed suitable as a pet for a little boy; small, lively, playful, and fond of sitting on laps for warmth and company. Ideal! I wonder what their Royal Highnesses will name any such acquisition. Prince, maybe? Rex?

I once had lunch with Prince George's grandfather, Prince Charles. Not because I had done anything remarkable or deserving, but because The Prince,s Trust, Prince Charles' charitable foundation, paid for my driving lessons when I was unemployed and living in the north-east of England, at a time in the political and economic climate when jobs in that part of the world were as rare as Bolonka Zwetnas. I needed a driving licence to improve my chances of employment, and The Prince's Trust came up trumps with a grant, enabling me to find work. I was, subsequently, invited to meet His Royal Highness, as one of many beneficiaries. Perhaps today we could pray for the Royal Family? They receive a mixed press, some of which is hostile, but they, like everyone else, stand in need of God's grace, Christ's comfort, and the Spirit's succour.

LUPO LOOPHOLE

The shepherds said to one another, "Let's go to Bethlehem and see this thing that has happened, which the Lord has told us about"

(LUKE 2:15 **NIV**)

Should Prince George be presented with a Bolonka Zwetna, it would need to get along with Lupo, a black Cocker Spaniel already owned by his mum and dad. Whether or not Lupo would be invited to the birthday party, though, is another matter, as the Queen once forbade his appearance at a Christmas get-together at Sandringham when he was new to the family and couldn't be relied upon to demonstrate due deference to Her Majesty's Corgis and behave appropriately. Lupo was banished to the home of the Duchess's parents for the holidays, and I can't help feeling he caught the raw end of the deal; Cocker Spaniels are sociable by nature, whereas Corgis are notoriously feisty, so perhaps the problem was theirs, not his. Well, who am I to comment on royal rigmarole! As long as Lupo is loved, that's all that counts. (*Lupo* is, incidentally, from the Latin for "wolf", in case you were wondering.)

If the Queen felt it advisable to exclude Lupo from the Sandringham celebrations, that's her privilege, and she knows enough about dogs to be trusted with her opinion. By rights, though, the shepherds featuring in the very first Christmas story shouldn't have been invited to the birthday party held not in a palace, but in a stable, for the Prince of Peace; they were regarded as unworthy invitees – a bit smelly, on account of their occupation, and only infrequent worshippers at Temple services because of their pattern of shift work (another black mark). They were seen as uncouth and irreligious, yet the Nativity story records their Christmas presence in the cattle-yard as invited guests. The least and lowly? Top of the list of invitations, it seems! Such is grace, and such is the topsy-turvy Kingdom of Heaven.

SPEAKING UP FOR JESUS

Those standing there went up to Peter and said, "Surely you are one of them; your accent gives you away"

(MATTHEW 26:73 **NIV**)

On account of the fact my parents were Salvation Army officers at a time when Salvation Army officers moved from one appointment to another every two or three years, my accent cannot be pinpointed to one location. Following Mum and Dad all over England and South Wales, I have collected snippets of accents that make me a linguistic mongrel. Unlike, it appears, dogs, who, apparently, bear regional accents, strange as that may (literally) sound. They pick up on varying levels of intonation so that a dog belonging to, say, someone from the north-east of England will demonstrate different barking patterns to a dog who hails from, say, the south-west. Given the acute sensitivity of dogs' hearing, this news isn't too surprising, and it makes sense that dogs – like children with their parents – will pick up on subtle melodies and speech patterns. As for me, I'm siding with the mongrels!

In the name "Christ Jesus", we see both his divine title ("Christ" meaning "the anointed" or "the Messiah") and his distinctly human name (Jesus was and is a very common male forename). There, in a language anyone can understand, we collect vital clues regarding his unique identity; God and man merged into one, so to speak. His names, representing the Incarnation, would have been clearly understood by everyone, regardless of accent or location. He, Jesus, had arrived as an ordinary man – flesh, blood, hair, bones, and sinews – yet he, Christ, was godly. Wherever we come from, and whichever dialect is ours, those facts remain. Jesus is Lord!

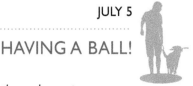

HAVING A BALL!

Rejoice with those who rejoice, weep with those who weep
(ROMANS 12:15 *ESV*)

Although I am somewhat multilingual when it comes to dialects, I am English when it comes to football, though at this time of writing, I have to admit to some embarrassment as England have just crashed to a humiliating defeat against Iceland in the Euro 2016 Championships. (Well done, Iceland!) Perhaps, though, instead of dwelling on England's collapse, I should focus on the European Pup 2016 "tournament", a match played by rescue centre puppies, set up by Dogs Trust in the hope of attracting animal lovers to give a dog a home via internet footage of the tussle. A spokesperson for Dogs Trust said, "These adorable puppies are fantastic fun and would make wonderful pets for footy-loving families" – quite right, and I hope the result of the game is lots of rehoming.[1] (In the European Pup Tournament, incidentally, England drew 1–1 with Wales!)

Football is – believe it or not – only a game. For some, it represents their livelihood, but it is a sport, and not a matter of life or death, despite the way it is sometimes portrayed as such! The beauty of sport is that played and appreciated properly, it can teach valuable lessons about picking oneself up and carrying on in the face of defeat, and embracing victory with magnanimity – not, of course, only failure and success on the playing field or the running track, but in life, generally; handling setbacks in such a way they do not overwhelm us, and holding triumphs lightly. Today's text says it all, really. Having said that, I do hope England's fortunes improve! Perhaps we should call in the pups!

1   www.dogstrust.org.uk, June 2016

NO DIGGING ALLOWED!

As far as the east is from the west, so far has he removed
our transgressions from us
(PSALM 103:12 **NIV**)

Remember Mbogo? He caused a stir when he dug up and ate a large joint of meat that had been in a neighbour's freezer for over a year. The neighbour, unsure as to whether the joint was still safe to eat, had removed it from her freezer and buried it, but Mbogo excavated it and treated himself to a very cold meal! My parents-in-law discovered him shivering as a side-effect of consuming his frozen find and, not realizing what had happened, called a vet. It wasn't until an irate neighbour called on them with a vociferous complaint that they managed to piece the story together! Let's just say the neighbour was none too pleased, and worried she might be blamed for Mbogo's demise. All was well in the end, though – the vet explained Mbogo's shivers and he went on to live another day. I have no record of what happened next in terms of the neighbourly relationship, but let's hope grace won through!

Digging up that which is buried is not necessarily a great idea! Mbogo survived his bout of the shivers, but we can do a great deal of harm if we insist on digging up the forgiven sins of our past, instead of leaving them buried in God's ocean of pardon. We fret about that which we have done which we shouldn't have done, and that which we haven't done that should have been done, instead of resting in God's mercy. Like Mbogo, we scratch away and dig until we are haunted by that we can't change anyway. By the same token, we can do damage if we dredge up the sins of those who have sinned against us, instead of letting grace win through. That which is buried is buried for a reason – as Mbogo discovered!

INDIAN SUMMER

You who are young, be happy
(ECCLESIASTES 11:9 **NIV**)

The RSPCA centre from which we rehomed Skipper is hosting a "Dog Day Afternoon". Despite that confusing title (is it a day or is it an afternoon?), the Dog Show advertised looks promising, with a nice little picture featuring an alert black Labrador, a beautiful black-and-tan German Shepherd, a Pug and a Scottish Terrier sidling up to one another, a massive dog of mixed breed who is lying on the grass looking as bored as an atheist listening to an archbishop, and a Spaniel who clearly has little interest in what is going on and has chosen to look the other way. On offer is a "Fun Dog Show", a Dog Agility Contest, and Canine Flyball, whatever that might be! I hope the fun and games raise a lot of money so that the dogs relying upon the RSPCA for shelter can continue to be looked after until they too are rehomed.

My wife, a Salvation Army officer, has just returned from India, where she inspected projects that care for those who might otherwise be left destitute; blind men, and the children of prostitutes, whom The Salvation Army feeds and shelters overnight, with breakfast thrown in, so that they aren't left alone while their mums work the streets. What has that to do with fun? You'd be surprised! The children are also treated to games, sing-songs, and activities designed to teach them of the love of God. Considering their grim start in life, you would be forgiven for thinking these kids are downbeat and inhibited – not a bit of it! They sing action choruses with gusto, and light up their dormitory with smiles as wide as the Ganges! Let's pray for The Salvation Army's work and witness in India.

SHOPPING AND SALVATION

The disciples came to him and said, "This is a remote place, and it's already getting late. Send the crowds away, so they can go to the villages and buy themselves some food." Jesus replied, "They do not need to go away. You give them something to eat."
(MATTHEW 14:15–16, **NIV**)

Heather and I wandered around some charity shops, killing time, and I was pleasantly surprised to find a framed antique print of Middlesex, my county of birth. Another pleasant surprise was the appearance of a Highland Terrier on the shop counter – actually on the glass counter, sitting there as customers paid their money and made a fuss of him. He even had a little bed on the counter-top! Well, I expect there are all sorts of health and hygiene rules preventing dogs sitting on shop counters, but I couldn't see he was doing any harm. Quite the contrary, actually – his presence was a talking point in the queue and cheered people up. Maybe the idea will catch on in other shops – though only, I suggest, with Terrier-sized canines!

I find our text today intriguing and wonderful, in that it presents a God, in Christ, who submitted himself to the ways of ordinary human life in order to reach ordinary human beings with his message; a God of groceries, price tags, shopping bills, empty stomachs, weighing scales, meal times, and so on – a deity taking the form of a servant in a bustling crowd. How marvellous this is – a God of pots and pans and recipes and shops. One of us, indeed, who queued and shopped and ate, and whose presence remains one of the biggest talking points of history.

REIGNING AND REIGNING IN!

*Do not be like the horse or the mule, which have no understanding but must be
controlled by bit and bridle*
(PSALM 32:9 *NIV*)

We live close to a park, at the centre of which is a lake, home to all sorts of bird life. It is a haven for dog walkers who, exercising suitable responsibility, may walk their dogs and give their curious canines plenty of opportunities to sniff around. The key, of course, hinges on that word "responsibility", but not every dog walker appreciates the importance of keeping their dog on a lead in a place where children play, and where geese, ducks, and swans enjoy life on and around the lake. Quite horribly, a German Shepherd (off-lead) killed a Canada Goose just days before I penned these words, shaking it by the neck until it was dead – all in sight of horrified children. It appears the owner of the GSD did nothing to appease shocked passers-by, but left the park without apologizing to those present.

This is a dreadful story, made all the worse for me because I can imagine Skipper doing the same thing, had he been allowed to walk off-lead. In defence of the German Shepherd in question, we would be naïve to think such behaviour is anything but instinctive in dogs, for however refined their training, the instinct to hunt and kill remains part of their DNA. Part of the solution is found in a strong collar and lead! Is this, though, somewhat like us in our dealings with God? I don't suggest bloodshed and murder is our intent, but who can deny our occasional need of restraint under God's good hand, when we want to do our own thing? It can be a tussle, sometimes, but how much more pleasant our pilgrimage becomes when we allow him to gently guide and, if necessary, hold us back.

MODERN MEANS

In your hearts revere Christ as Lord. Always be prepared to give an answer to everyone who asks you to give the reason for the hope that you have. But do this with gentleness and respect

(1 PETER 3:15 **NIV**)

The Canada Goose carnage in an otherwise quiet and genteel area has prompted my Town Council to dust down its bylaw regarding the control of dogs in parks. Such is the rarity of events like this in these parts that it transpires the bylaw in question dates from 1934 and hasn't been updated! Indeed, the penalty for breaking such laws carries only a £2 fine, with the slightly quaint recommendation that "dogs are put on a leash when in the vicinity of the lakes because of the presence of geese and ducks". Not exactly a fierce deterrent, but a glimpse into a bygone era of courtesy, respect, and good behaviour.

Unless you live in a cave, you will have noticed that the Church at large has been invited to consider issues of morality and behaviour that probably weren't so prominent in, say, 1934; patterns of sexual behaviour, for example, that now form societal norms but which weren't up for debate decades ago. Likewise, issues relating to doctrines and practices traditionally held whereby, for example, the once commonplace preaching of judgment and damnation is regarded as inappropriate by many, who prefer a softer approach. The modern Church is confronted with a world that regards the gospel as irrelevant, and the challenge is to respond with truth expressed lovingly and graciously, with compassion and humility. Let us pray for church leaders as they grapple with such matters.

GOD TRUST

I am gentle and humble in heart
(MATTHEW 11:29 **NIV**)

A news report tells me more than a third of children are scared of dogs. Research carried out by Dogs Trust indicates 37 per cent of children fear dogs, with 25 per cent of parents claiming such fears affect their child's daily life. The research goes on to record that 66 per cent of children have had a bad experience of dogs, and that three in ten will run and hide when a dog approaches. These are depressing statistics, and I appreciate the following "Help Points" aimed at parents and published by Dogs Trust as part of their "Managing Fear of Dogs" project:

1) Sit down and talk to your child about their worries.

2) Watch films and read books where the leading star is a dog.

3) Explain that not all dogs are the same. (Just because one dog might be badly behaved doesn't mean all are.)

4) If the fear is severe, speak to a psychologist.[1]

I find it a shame that what could be lovely friendships between dogs and children are marred by fear. What potential there is for children to love dogs, and vice versa. Good for Dogs Trust for publishing their guidelines. Is this, though, a million miles away from the way in which many people regard God; as an aggressive creature who should only ever be feared and in whose presence we are expected to tremble? I wonder if statistics exist telling us what percentage of the population is scared of God, frightened of him, walking the other way when he appears, so to speak, or even running and hiding? What a sadness this is. God bless every effort made to put the record straight. What "Help Points" can we publish today?

1   www.dogstrust.org.uk, July 2016

JESUS AND JARROW

Arise, walk about the land through its length
(GENESIS 13:17 **NASB**)

In 1936, "The Jarrow Marchers" marched from Jarrow, north-east England, to London, almost 300 miles. Theirs was a cry to the government in Westminster for work, as unemployment was rife in that region and families were starving. Stages of the march were sectioned out, and marshals blew whistles at the commencement and conclusion of each stage. Approximately five miles in, a Labrador called Paddy joined in, walking all the way to London, responding to the whistled instructions! Paddy was no fool, as the marchers were well-fed by well-wishers as they made their way to the capital, nourished with sandwiches, slices of meat, beer, and even a whole salmon as they walked through Yorkshire!

Paddy became the mascot of the march and had a great time walking the length of England! What it is to walk in harmony with friends – either literally, going for an afternoon stroll, say, or metaphorically, walking through life with those we love and care for. Even better, to walk in fellowship with God, who desires to journey with us every step of the way. Only our sin fractures such a journey, until we confess and repent, and God forgives and restores. What a walk this can be! All the way from earth to Glory!

HEATED DEBATE

Peter declared, "Even if I have to die with you, I will never disown you"

(MATTHEW 26:35 *NIV*)

I mentioned Prince George a few days ago, and he has caused a furore after being photographed offering Lupo the Cocker Spaniel a lick of his white chocolate ice cream on a hot summer's day. The photographs have divided opinion sharply, with some people seemingly only too keen to portray the young prince as an irresponsible (and even cruel) boy and others rushing to his defence, pointing out he was only trying to help Lupo keep cool. The issue is that George offered Lupo chocolate, which dogs aren't to eat, but it is obvious he meant no harm and wasn't intending to poison the dog; his was an innocent and charming gesture. Of course a dog should not be fed chocolate, but those hotheads calling for His Royal Highness to be punished may just need to cool down a bit!

Was Peter something of a hothead? It seems so, if Gospel accounts of his spontaneous outbursts are to be believed! He spoke from the heart and shot from the hip, not always thinking things through first. However, we tend to love Peter, for there is something about his openness and vulnerability that endears him to us. He could never be labelled cautious, but perhaps that is what we like – his courage, his cavalier mentality, and his willingness to speak out while others remained silent. Peter got it wrong sometimes, but who can deny the innocent authenticity of his heartfelt intentions? Maybe the Church needs a few more Peters? Are we perhaps too quiet these days?

NO KIDDING

Do not believe every spirit, but test the spirits to see whether they are from God, because many false prophets have gone out into the world

(I JOHN 4:1 **NIV**)

Scientists have concluded that goats are as intelligent and as loving as dogs, and would make excellent pets. The boffins publishing such conclusions suggest goats might rival dogs in forming emotional bonds with their owners. In their favour, apparently, is the way in which they gaze at humans in the same way dogs do when asking for treats (that may be so, but so did my children when they were younger!). The issue seems to be that money and time has been devoted to researching canine behaviour, whereas goats have been neglected in such areas, and this has upset goat people. Forgive my scepticism, but can we seriously imagine the day when people will be taking goats for a walk, instead of dogs? Can we envisage goat owners sitting, of an evening, with a goat at their feet, in front of a roaring fire? Would a goat bleat loudly enough to scare off a would-be burglar? I rest my case!

I can't see the idea of goats as pets, but if the passage of time proves me wrong, then I will stand corrected. I do not suggest the scientists studying goats are out to dupe anyone, but falling for every idea we hear is not wise. The Bible warns us against simply accepting every spiritual notion that on the surface appears to be genuine, and even from God himself. We are encouraged to employ common sense, lest malign forces of evil deceive us into beliefs that might seem well and good, but are, in fact, spurious and deceptive. Jesus will never deceive us; we can trust him entirely to lead us into truth, and only truth.

MAKING YOUR MIND UP

You also must testify
(JOHN 15:27 **NIV**)

Maybe you feel I have been unfair to goats? I have nothing against them, honestly, so in the interests of fair play, I offer below a list of goat/dog pros and cons, so you can make your mind up:

A goat costs between £50 and £250 to buy. Adopting a rescue dog is roughly the same (Skipper cost us £120), but a pedigree puppy can costs hundreds of pounds.

The average lifespan of a goat is twelve years, while most dogs live into their teens (Skipper was fourteen when he left us). Goats are notorious for wanting to escape, and a 6ft-high chain fence might cost you £5,000 to erect. A decent dog kennel will set you back, say, £300. Goats cost around £100 per year to feed. A dog eats around £400 worth of food annually. On balance, a goat will cost £10,000 to keep, over the course of its lifetime, whereas a dog will cost roughly double that, bearing in mind vaccinations, etc. Goats can be habitually destructive to fences, houses, and property. Dogs rarely are. Lactating goats need to be milked twice a day. Dogs don't!

I have set before you some basic facts – the rest is up to you, and you must decide as you prefer! Supposing we adopt a similar approach to witnessing for Jesus, hoping to persuade others to follow him? I do not suggest we compile a list of pros and cons, but there is a case for presenting the known facts about our Lord's life, then praying the Holy Spirit graciously influences our friends and neighbours as they weigh the evidence. A study course at church? A living room discussion over coffee? A pub lunch with discipleship on the menu? May God bless our every effort and lead many to salvation.

NO ANONYMITY

I have summoned you by name
(ISAIAH 43:1 **NIV**)

Through my letter box drops another collection of junk mail! Today, I can choose between buying one pizza and getting one free every Tuesday, visiting a "permanent exhibition centre for self-build, renovation and home improvements", sampling washing powder on special offer ("90 washes at less than 12p per wash"), and entering a lottery that might secure me great wealth (to spend on pizza and washing powder, presumably). I may also "prevent pesky parasites" infesting my home by investing in a course of flea treatments (for my pet, I hasten to add). Fleas can, I am told, bite up to 400 times a day, but for £144, I can protect my dog from infestation. Money well spent, except I don't own a dog at present, which leaves me wondering just how many pizzas I might be able to buy with the money I shan't be spending on banishing bugs!

I realize junk mail advertising cannot hope to be specific, and that the person paid to deliver leaflets to my house has no idea whether or not I own a dog in need of flea treatment. Companies take a grapeshot approach to such publicity, in the hope of some of their potential customers meeting demographic targets. How wonderfully different it is with God, who knows me by name and whose targeting of me with love is detailed, specific, superbly researched, and unfailingly accurate! He knows your name too!

QUICK FIX

I will watch my ways
(PSALM 39:1 ***NIV***)

I admire the People's Dispensary for Sick Animals (PDSA) because for decades, they have provided health care for animals whose owners can't afford vet's fees, and I am pleased to report their free "Wellbeing checks for dogs" scheme is doing the rounds as I type. The PDSA van is parking up in four different locations on four different days, and a vet nurse will inspect dogs in exchange for a donation. Prevention is the name of the game, as problems can be nipped in the bud simply by owners taking their dogs along for a check-up on board the PDSA van. Ear cleaning, for example – if a dog's ears aren't kept clean, infections can easily occur, or wax can accumulate, leading to expensive treatments and, possibly, some pain for doggie that could have been avoided. God bless the PDSA!

"Keeping short accounts" is a phrase I grew up with, in church circles. As a kid, I had no idea what it meant, but nowadays, five decades on, it is a sentiment I appreciate – making sure one's spiritual life, one's relationship with God, is kept in good health so that problems and issues aren't allowed to fester and grow. Maybe the PDSA approach of prevention being better than cure also relates to one's personal prayer life? A commitment to daily prayer – touching base with God, frequently – keeps sin at bay, worries in perspective, and lines of communication open.

PENGUINS AND PROTECTION

Thou shalt preserve me from trouble
(PSALM 32:7 *KJV*)

Have you ever seen a Maremma Sheepdog? I hadn't, until my wife brought home a booklet from our local cinema advertising forthcoming films, and I saw a photograph of one in there; a beautiful creature – snowy white fur and a handsome face! Cinema-going in our family, though, is never a straightforward exercise, as the four of us each like different kinds of films, and we struggle to find one movie that we will all enjoy. One option on offer in the booklet is *Oddball and the Penguins*, the true story of a chicken farmer and his dog (Oddball) saving a penguin colony. Oddball is a Maremma Sheepdog, described in the press release as "half Golden Retriever, half Polar Bear"', and trained to protect the penguins from predatory foxes who think they have located an endless source of dinners. I might go along to watch *Oddball and the Penguins*, but I can't see anyone else wanting to come with me. Interested?

A book I read mentioned people praying for God to dispatch angels to protect those in need, proclaiming a belief in the practice and giving examples of Christians testifying to the arrival of an angelic presence in their hour of need. I don't know what to make of that (forgive me if that disappoints you), but I have no hesitation in testifying to a God who rushes to the aid of the vulnerable, and answers prayer. Not every time – sometimes people who pray receive no apparent help, angelic or otherwise, and I have no belief in some kind of divine force field – but my personal understanding of God is that he is like Oddball; strong, yet gentle, and on the alert for those – like the penguins – in danger. Am I naïve? Possibly. Will God intervene personally, or rely on angels instead? I don't know. Is Oddball adorable? Yes, if his picture is anything to go by. Do I adore God? Yes.

NAME CALLING

See what great love the Father has lavished on us, that we should be called children of God!

(I JOHN 3:I **NIV**)

Are you familiar with "the Dulux dog"? For decades, an Old English Sheepdog has been used to advertise Dulux paints in one of the most successful advertising campaigns of all time. The first "Dulux dog" appeared in 1961, and the TV adverts featuring Old English Sheepdogs promoting paint consistently rank in the top fifty in terms of worldwide popularity. My grandad was a painter and decorator, so he would have known quite a bit about Dulux paints, whereas my knowledge and interest is more to do with the sheepdogs, not least the wonderful names of some of those used in the promotional campaigns; Shepton Daphnis Horsa (pet name Dash), followed by Fernville Lord Digby, then, would you believe, King Hotspur of Amblegait!

Compared with those names, I have to admit "Meg" and "Skipper" sound distinctly ordinary! Having said that, calling out "Meg" in public would certainly be a lot quicker (and less embarrassing) than yelling "King Hotspur of Amblegait" in a park! I expect King Hotspur's owners had their reasons for calling their sheepdog that, just as, in Bible times, names were bestowed with particular significance. Not, in those days, any old Tom, Dick or Harry (with great respect to Thomases, Richards, and Harolds everywhere), but christening ceremonies full of depth and meaning. What's your name? What are you called? Our text today answers those questions!

THE BIGGEST GOD IN THE WORLD

We saw the Nephilim … and we seemed to ourselves like grasshoppers, and so we seemed to them

(NUMBERS 13:33 *ESV*)

Fernville Lord Digby went from a career in advertising to one in films, starring as "Digby, the biggest dog in the world!" in 1973. A children's film of that title featured Digby as he was rescued from a dogs' home, then grew to enormous proportions after accidentally consuming a secret scientific formula for super-growth fertilizer, and whose size became such a concern that the British Army was consulted on managing the problem with bombs and artillery! All sorts of mayhem ensued in a light-hearted caper, and I particularly like a quote I read, from a little girl who was treated to a trip to the cinema to see "Digby": "I like Digby. He is a big dog. He can run fast. It was funny when the train went through his legs." Wonderful!

In the spying trip referred to in our text for today, a military reconnaissance mission was carried out, and some spies saw only the threat of giants lurking, whereas others remembered God was with them. This brings to mind a Sunday school chorus from my boyhood, which went something like: "Some saw giants, great and tall/Some saw God was in it all."[1] The moral of the story is that we each face giants at one time or another; giants of fear and worry that sap our self-confidence, and so on. We can, like most of the spies, focus on them, give up and scarper, or keep our eyes on God. Let us pray for one another, that we will have the presence of mind to choose the latter option when we are afraid or intimidated.

---

1 "Twelve Men Went to Spy Out Canaan" (childrensbiblesongs.us)

REACHING NEW HEIGHTS

Zacchaeus … wanted to see who Jesus was, but because he was short he could not see over the crowd. So he ran ahead and climbed a sycamore-fig tree to see him

(LUKE 19:2–4 **NIV**)

Large as Digby was (in the film), the title of the biggest dog in the world probably goes, at this time of writing, to Major, a Great Dane measuring more than 4ft in height! Major is three years old, and is fond of having his nails manicured! He weighs an incredible twelve stone, and will be measured and weighed by officials from the *Guinness World Records*, to see if he may lay claim to the title – a vacancy which exists, incidentally, since Giant George, the previous holder (also a Great Dane), died at home in Arizona, USA, in 2013. George measured forty-three inches from paw to shoulder and weighed seventeen stone, so Major seems something of a lightweight in comparison!

I am almost 6ft 3ins tall, which is taller than most people I meet or know. Imagine my surprise, then, when I shared a lift with a basketball team in Arkansas, USA, when I was working there with The Salvation Army (in Arkansas, I mean, not in the lift). I was the smallest man in the elevator, and empathized with Zacchaeus, who was too small to be able to see Jesus properly and had to climb a tree in order to have sight of the Saviour in a crowd. Those basketball players – the shortest one was 6ft 7ins – dwarfed me, much as the people in the crowd that day would have dwarfed Zacchaeus. Good for him for climbing a tree, and not being deterred! What a great example of determination and perseverance … all to make sure he met the Lord.

SURPRISE, SURPRISE!

Many are the plans in a person's heart, but it is the Lord's purpose that prevails
(PROVERBS 19:21 **NIV**)

Brian Clough, mentioned elsewhere, was inseparable from Del Boy, his beloved Golden Retriever. While "Cloughie" was manager of Nottingham Forest Football Club, Del Boy was a familiar sight at training sessions, regarding the City Ground (Forest's stadium) as his second home. Known for his unorthodoxy, Clough would sometimes interrupt a practice match and invite his players – professionals honing their skills and maintaining crucial fitness levels – to stroll along the banks of the nearby River Trent instead, asking them to look after Del Boy while he walked with them. Players who had only recently signed for Forest were surprised, initially, to discover they wouldn't be kicking a ball around, but had been assigned dog-walking duties instead! Del Boy loved every second, and he certainly loved Brian Clough, by all accounts.

Imagine turning up for work, expecting to carry out the usual routine of responsibilities, only to find your plans have been changed, through no fault of your own – at the whim of a boss, or through circumstances beyond anyone's control. Clough's players came to expect the unexpected, but I think most of us prefer a settled pattern of days; we like to know what will happen next. Would it be fair to say God sometimes springs surprises on us that aren't always welcome, but which are, nevertheless, activated in love, within the framework of his sovereignty? He is entitled to do so, and has our best interests at heart, but that doesn't mean we welcome his interventions, if we're honest. Can we put God in a box? I think not!

KENNEL CLUB

My Father's house has many rooms; if that were not so, would I have told you that I am going there to prepare a place for you?

(JOHN 14:2 **NIV**)

A West Ham United player called Julian Dicks was known as "Mad Dog" on account of his, erm, robust approach to the game, especially in the matter of tackling. Dicks never knowingly pulled out of a fearsome tackle, and attracted twenty-four yellow cards and one red card for his troubles. A passionate individual, Julian Dicks was once on the brink of selection for the full England team, despite his "Mad Dog" reputation, but wasn't eventually selected, and was reported as saying, "Well, I'd rather build my dog kennels than represent England" (he had a business building kennels) – a petulant remark born of frustration and said in the heat of the moment, but which attracted attention. Dicks retired from playing shortly after his outburst ... to run the "Shepherd and Dog" public house! (I wonder if his pub had kennels anywhere.)

The quality of the kennel offered to a dog depends upon the worth of that dog to its owner. Some ancient peoples thought dogs were messengers from the gods, and built top quality dog-houses. King Henry I of England had a kennel containing several hundred dogs, whereas dogs belonging to peasants sought shelter in outhouses, barns or porches. Nowadays, some kennels are bespoke, hand-crafted with lined roofs, while others are cheap plastic constructions. Isn't it something to realize that followers of Jesus will one day – thanks to his sacrificial death – inhabit what are sometimes referred to as "mansions of Glory"! That is, the finest dwelling places imaginable. I can't imagine that, but I believe it, because I believe Jesus died for me. Marvellous! My house for eternity! Handmade by God!

CANAAN COMMANDMENTS

The Lord descended to the top of Mount Sinai and called Moses to
the top of the mountain
(EXODUS 19:20 **NIV**)

A woman who moved to Israel to help preserve the Canaan Dog, an Israeli breed, risks losing her home in a legal dispute with the Israel Lands Authority. She built *Sha'ar Hagai* Kennels after renovating an abandoned building, but now faces eviction, and is worried about the future of her Canaan Dogs in terms of breeding and preservation. Superbly equipped for desert life, the breed can survive extreme heat with little water, an unusual feature in canines, and archaeological evidence indicates that Canaan Dogs were common in Bible Lands during the time of Christ. The concern is that pure-breed Canaans will become extinct if they aren't carefully preserved, as a Canaan has few genetic problems, but this might change if the kennels close and the dogs breed with urban species, negatively diluting their gene pool. What a concern! I hope this story has a happy ending.

Legend states Moses was helped up and down Mount Sinai by a Canaan Dog, and that line of thought isn't as far-fetched as it might sound. Beloved of Bedouin tribes, Canaans make excellent mountain guides; big enough to fend off would-be assailants, and at home in the terrain of the Holy Land. It is not difficult to imagine Moses relying on a Canaan to escort him back to base camp after his expedition to receive the Ten Commandments. Who knows? What really matters is that Moses did indeed make that trek and deliver God's top ten rules. Have we diluted those commandments since those days? Or do we still thank God for his advice?

CHILE DOG

These are they who have come out of the great tribulation; they have washed their
robes and made them white in the blood of the Lamb
(REVELATION 7:14 **NIV**)

A few years ago, I was out selling *The War Cry*, when along came Tottenham Hotspur and England legend, Jimmy Greaves, goalscorer extraordinaire in his heyday. I gave (not sold!) the great Mr Greaves *The War Cry*, and remembered a story about him, from 1962, when he was playing for England against Brazil in Santiago, and a dog ran on the pitch. "Greavsie" scooped the dog up in his arms and went to carry him away (much to the delight of the Chilean crowd), when the dog relieved itself all over Jimmy Greaves's pristine white shirt! (The Brazilian striker, Garrincha, enjoyed the episode so much, he took the dog home after the game.) Greaves, meanwhile, had to continue playing in the heat of Chile with a stained, wet and smelly shirt!

Jimmy Greaves had at least discovered a way of ensuring the Brazilian defenders gave him plenty of space when he ran towards them, as he had to wear his discoloured jersey with the strange odour until the final whistle! How happy are those who persevere in their Christian witness until the very end! How wonderful is the reward for those whose garments, spiritually speaking, are made – and kept – spotless by the grace of God, who pardons our sins and erases every trace of them. Sin stains, yet we are sometimes foolish enough to scoop sin up in our arms, so to speak, embracing it against our better judgment. Mercy, though, prevails, and we are washed clean every time we seek forgiveness.

OVERFLOWING WITH COMPASSION

Bring the homeless poor into your house
(ISAIAH 58:7 **ESV**)

News arrives of thirty-eight dogs that have been rescued from a house after reports from concerned neighbours about their welfare. They have, apparently, been trapped there for some time, and I can barely imagine what conditions must have been like. Thanks to the neighbours, the police and RSPCA have intervened, and the dogs removed to animal shelters. I hope they are quickly adopted, having suffered such an ordeal, but quite what the owners were thinking is beyond me. Thirty-eight dogs in one house! Goodness me – I'm one of five children and I thought our house was crowded, when I was growing up! God bless the RSPCA as they rehome the dogs; a number of different breeds who deserve tender, loving care.

From time to time, in church, I receive the weekly offering and say a prayer on behalf of the congregation. Sometimes I mention those who know nothing of the blessings I enjoy; a roof over my head, a bed, spare change in my pocket, a choice of food in the fridge, clean clothes, and so on. I am grateful for such things, but perhaps our prayers today can focus on those whose lives are truly wretched, who grind out an existence in overcrowded slums or disease-ridden makeshift tents, whose survival can sometimes be measured in hours or weeks, rather than years, and for whom malnutrition and squalor is the norm. Lord, have mercy.

STOLEN PROPERTY

When Joseph came to his brothers, they stripped him of his robe ... and they took him and threw him into the cistern

(GENESIS 37:23–24 **NIV**)

There is a growing trend for "dognapping", a crime whereby valuable dogs are stolen and whose owners face demands for ransoms. It is big business, with thousands of pounds being demanded when pedigree dogs are "dognapped". Celebrity dog owners are particularly vulnerable, as the "dognappers" assume they are wealthy enough to pay hefty ransoms for the safe return of their pets. That may be so, but what mustn't be overlooked is the trauma experienced by the dogs, whether they are pampered pooches or merely treasured family members whose owners just happen to have quite a bit of money; roughly snatched and stuffed into bags by strangers who patently don't care for them, driven away at speed (that would have panicked Skipper to the point of meltdown), then kept in grim circumstances with no opportunity to be walked in public (for fear of being spotted), pining for their owners.

Joseph suffered a similar fate to dogs who are violently removed from their homes and treated as commodities; dumped at the bottom of a pit, stripped of his identity, and left to rot until a bit of cash could be raised by his sale into slavery. There was nothing Joseph could do about his plight, just as there is nothing a stolen dog can do to resolve matters. Do we ever feel like that – as though our dreams and hopes have been ripped apart? As though our lives have been plunged into darkness? We feel helpless and hopeless. The message of the cross is that God can bring new life and new hope when all seems irreparably bleak. God brought order out of chaos, and creation from nothing. Shall we, today, bring our "nothing" to God, offering him our chaos and the bleakness of circumstances that sometimes occur?

GOD, OUR HEARING AID

Does he who fashioned the ear not hear?
(PSALM 94:9 **NIV**)

A news item featured a Guide Dog owner wanting to visit the Bug Jam Festival (no, I'm not sure what it is either) at Santa Pod Raceway. The gentleman in question was refused entry because raceway officials believed the noise and fumes would constitute animal cruelty, as the Bug Jam Festival is notoriously noisy and levels of car fumes in the air have been known to sting people's eyes. He had his Labradoodle Guide Dog with him when the Santa Pod operations manager explained his concerns. Unfortunately, this led to a furore over the rights of disabled people and accusations of discrimination. I have seen pictures of the Labradoodle concerned – a scruffy-looking grey and black character – and I have to say, she looks singularly unconcerned by all the fuss, leaving the human beings to carry on squabbling!

I support the operations manager in his decision, because his concern was for the Labradoodle to be spared ear-splitting levels of noise. Given that a dog's hearing is ultra-sensitive, I think he was within his rights to deny admission, as that dog might have ended up deaf for life. Isn't it a blessing, though, God isn't hard of hearing! Can we imagine the cacophony of prayer that reaches him without pause or interruption? My guess is, it would make the Santa Pod Bug Festival sounds seem like gentle whispers! The chambers of Heaven must daily resound with the clamour of praises and petitions, yet our Heavenly Operations Manager listens intently to everything. This is our God.

WELL DONE!

Though he may stumble, he will not fall, for the Lord upholds him with his hand
(PSALM 37:24 **NIV**)

Everyone has their moment of triumph – securing the job they have always wanted, or achieving a breakthrough of some kind; that point of satisfaction, whatever it might be for each of us personally – being picked for the football team, maybe. Why, though, do we say, at such moments, "every dog has its day"? Why not every cat, or every goldfish? The expression is used when someone lowly or unsuccessful hits their target, against the odds, signifying rejoicing and relief. I don't know why it should be a dog that has its day as opposed to any other animal, but it is an old saying: "A dogge hath a day" (*The Adages of Erasmus*), "The cat will mew, and dog will have his day" (Shakespeare's *Hamlet* Act V Scene 1), "Dogs, ye have had your day; ye fear'd no more" (Tennyson's *Ulysses*), "All dogs have their day; even rabid dogs" (Carlyle's *The French Revolution: A History*). In more modern times, the character Tony Montana, in the movie *Scarface*, says, just before shooting a corrupt police officer (and thereby getting his comeuppance, in the true nature of the phrase): "Every dog has its day, Mel."

The word "underdog" comes into its own here! Isn't it marvellous when the team that is never expected to do well claims the prize? Or when the unlikely candidate succeeds when no one really expects them to? We instinctively cheer the underdog; that person who has to struggle against multiple obstacles simply to manage what most of us take for granted; a minister I know, for example, who works daily miracles just to attend meetings or preach sermons in the face of debilitating illness. Let us pray for such heroes – those who think nothing of overcoming barriers that might prevent most of us from even trying.

NIGHT-NIGHT

My eyes stay open through the watches of the night, that I may meditate
on your promises
(PSALM 119:148 **NIV**)

Do you have trouble sleeping? Would you give almost anything for a good night's sleep? Experts reckon we need eight hours' sleep every night if we are to function properly, although Margaret Thatcher reportedly got by on only three or four hours' worth (a pattern specialists do not recommend, as it can result in errors of judgment and irritability). The Beatles famously sang the lyrics, "I should be sleeping like a dog", referring to the fact that dogs, on average, doze through thirteen of every twenty-four hours on offer, albeit lightly some of the time. Skipper, though, seemed to be the exception to that light sleeping rule, in that it was easily possible to walk into the kitchen while he was sleeping there, make a cup of tea, clatter about a bit, then leave the kitchen again, all without him stirring. Maybe that was on account of his deafness, but if his snoring was any yardstick, I am more inclined to think he had taken The Beatles' words to heart!

What do we do when we can't sleep? Count sheep? Rearrange our pillows? Make a hot drink? I went through a lovely phase once, when I would reserve time during the stillest, darkest, quietest hours of the night, for private prayer, away from the demands of the day. I used a book called *The Night Offices* and sat (in my dressing gown!) with the Saviour. I don't do it any longer, but maybe I should, for there is something special about such meditation. I found it a channel of nocturnal grace.

LOOKING FOR THE LOST

Suppose one of you has a hundred sheep and loses one of them. Doesn't he leave the ninety-nine in the open country and go after the lost sheep until he finds it?
(LUKE 15:4 **NIV**)

One day, when friends came to visit (having travelled a fair distance to do so), our front door was left off the latch, and Skipper sensed his chance to escape! While we were enjoying a cup of tea, it dawned on us that his long nose wasn't poking into the biscuits (most unusual), and that he was nowhere to be seen. A search was mobilized, with four Poxons allocated areas of the town in which to search while our friends remained at Base Camp in case the wanderer returned. We searched high and low, covering street after street, keeping in touch by mobile phone, and treating our assignment seriously in the knowledge that Skipper's road sense was nonexistent and his enthusiasm for fighting other dogs might lead to trouble ...

We searched and searched, looking in gardens, alleyways, fields, and so on, determined to find the runaway, not unlike the shepherd mentioned in our text for today, resolute in our determination to bring Skipper home. One of my college lecturers, who had been a sheep farmer before turning to lecturing, once preached on the fact that "sick and unwell sheep isolate themselves". How wonderfully reassuring it is to know that when we are far from home, spiritually speaking, the Good Shepherd goes out of his way to look for us and welcome our return. Sick and unwell? Out of fellowship with God? Lost? Come home.

A RELUCTANT RESCUEE

The more they were called, the more they went away
(HOSEA 11:1–2 **NIV**)

We spent an hour looking for Skipper, asking people if they had seen (or been licked by) a handsome German Shepherd, all to no avail until Heather spotted him in a photographer's studio, of all places! The photographer had spotted Skipper plodding along and realized he was lost – not least because he was moving in and out of traffic with his characteristic stupidity. She took him in and looked after him, despite his reluctance to receive her hospitality. Heather spied him pressing his nose against her window, planning another escape. Thanking the photographer, Heather brought our wayward dog home – by which time, our morning with our friends had been pretty much scuppered. Skipper!

Skipper was not happy to have been captured, even though he was no longer in danger of being flattened by a truck. He seemed distinctly ungrateful, and would have run away again given half a chance. Does that remind us of anyone? The Israelites, perhaps, with whom God pleaded time after time to return to the safety of his embrace? God repeatedly opened the door for them, promising forgiveness and the restoration of friendship, yet they just as repeatedly reacted with ingratitude, itching to go their own way once again, despite the dangers of their behaviour. Israelites? Skipper? Us? God is faithful and merciful. His door is always open.

MISTAKES AND MERCY

SEE PSALM 51

Not only did the photographer hold on to Skipper until Heather collected him, she went the second mile and offered us a free family portrait at her studio, featuring Skipper sitting in the middle of our smiling quartet. Much as we appreciated her offer, we declined, as we felt we had put her to quite enough trouble already! Little did we know, then, that Skipper wouldn't be alive much longer, and that, fairly soon, we would have nothing much to remember him by. I wish we had accepted her portrait; it might have helped to have it, now that he is no longer with us. We made the wrong decision.

Regrets? Mistakes? Past failures? Things we wish we had done, but didn't? Things we did do, and wish we hadn't? Scan the Scriptures and you will discover, without exception, that everyone who has ever messed up and then prayed to God for forgiveness has been pardoned, understood, and treated with divine kindness. Wrong decisions? Join the club! Take your place with Bible characters. Take your place too, in that long line of grateful, humble people approaching the Throne of Grace in the queue marked "Forgiven and Restored, Always Loved".

CONFIDENT OR CONFUSED

"I know the plans I have for you," declares the Lord
(JEREMIAH 29:11 ***NIV***)

The friends I mentioned earlier (come to our house and we'll leave you sitting by yourselves while we go out looking for our dog – those friends) lost their own dog, an adorable and ancient American Cocker Spaniel. He was a lovely old thing, and would quite happily have spent most of his life lying on his back having his tummy tickled. Harmless and charming, friendly towards everyone, and as soft as could be, he was a much-loved family pet, and his departure has left an "enormous" gap in their lives. He might not have won medals as a guard dog on account of being deaf and partially sighted, and he disguised his IQ quite well, but they wouldn't have been without him as he shuffled his way into their hearts. He fulfilled his role in the life of his pack to perfection, offering love and quiet company without limit.

Have you ever met someone who seems to know exactly what they were always supposed to do in life? Such people have grasped their sense of destiny – vocation, calling – and have no hesitation about confidently fulfilling their role on this planet. Quite honestly, I find them irritating, as I have spent most of my life not really being very sure what I am supposed to do with my three score years and ten. God bless those who know for sure what their roles should be, and God help those of us who tend to drift along hoping for the best, praying that we might be in the right place at the right time. I'm sure God has a use for each of us, and I pray he may help us all to fulfil the role that pleases him best. Pray for those seeking God's will.

PUBLICITY AND PERSUASION

He that believeth on the Son of God hath the witness in himself
(I JOHN 5:10 *KJV*)

Heather and I went out for dinner, collecting a friend en route, but arrived in our friend's town earlier than we had planned, meaning we had forty minutes to kill. We hadn't the heart to ring our friend's doorbell when she might have been busy tidying up the pile of my books she had been reading, so we wandered around a shop, taking our time to admire the fruit and veg and slowly pondering a range of shoe polishes. I picked up an advertisement for a service catering for "Pampered Pooches", and discovered a remarkable range of options on offer. This particular company, whose brochure I also collected, given that we still had thirty-nine minutes to use up, based its business upon the premise that if caring for oneself is an important "part of our beauty phenomena", then such attention should be offered to our dogs too. It pays dog owners, apparently, to "treat their animals like their children".

This company's publicity features two dogs; a Spaniel having its hair washed, and a Bull Terrier wearing a pink frill. I can't help feeling, though, that the promotional material is ever-so-slightly over the top. For example, as much as I love dogs, I do not equate them to my children. Maybe that equation is a bit much? Some might, though, lay a similar charge at the door of Christians when we proclaim that Jesus is God, that he raised the dead, healed the sick, walked on water, and so on. So be it! The proof of those claims is found in Christ himself. Ours is not to doubt, but to offer him to others, trusting him to do his own convincing, so that our friends come to realize faith in Jesus Christ is not over the top or extravagant, but real and authentic.

PREPARING TO PRAY

Our soul is dried away
(NUMBERS 11:6 *KJV*)

We were talking the other day about "sleeping like a dog", which leads me to wonder why dogs invariably sleep much better than humans. They don't have bills to pay, diaries to keep, jobs to go to, deadlines to meet, so it's fair to say a dog's stress levels, compared to ours, are low. Nevertheless, they might still have much to teach us. For example, a dog has little choice about when it eats (unless it follows Skipper's example of discovering food in bins and gutters), whereas we do, and I love nothing more than a curry late at night. Guess who sleeps better – the dog who finishes dinner at, say, 6 p.m., or the man who eats a curry at 11 p.m.? A dog will follow its routine of sorting out its bed before it settles down, while I tend to crash out without worrying about such niceties. A dog will drink (mainly) only water, whereas we humans often stock up on caffeine or alcohol before climbing into bed. The list goes on, but I think we can already see dogs have the edge when it comes to securing a good night's rest!

Some of the principles that affect our quality of sleep can also affect the quality (depth, richness) of our spiritual life. Routine, for example – do we adopt a routine of prayer and Bible reading, or are we somewhat more haphazard? Time-wise, are we wise? If I go to bed at midnight and need to be awake at 6:15 a.m., then the most I can hope for is six hours' sleep. If I use up my time watching television or overworking, then I might find I have less available to spend one-to-one with God. And so on. God is endlessly gracious and patient, but maybe we deprive ourselves of his blessings in such ways, and our souls shrink within us …

PRAGMATIC PROPHETS

Choose you this day whom ye will serve
(JOSHUA 24:15 *KJV*)

Our friend (the one for whom we arrived forty minutes too early) showed us a portrait of her Golden Retriever, her beloved pet for fifteen years until its death from throat cancer. Her Retriever had kept good health, but started to display signs of discomfort when eating and swallowing, when a tumour was diagnosed. Our friend, having been brought up on a farm, was pragmatic about life and death when it came to animals, and quickly decided upon having her dog put to sleep. For her, it was an instant decision – a "no-brainer". She loved her Golden Retriever too much to allow it to suffer, there was no hope of recovery, and she, by default, was suffering too. The injection was applied, and the deed done, with a great deal of sorrow, but no emotional regret; the facts were assessed, and a decision was made.

I wonder if such pragmatism ought to be applied to our spiritual decision-making, even when it comes to painful matters. The prophets of the Old Testament rarely left room for negotiation, proclaiming the word of God, setting out terms and conditions, and making clear the rewards of obedience and the punishments for disobedience, then leaving people to make their minds up. Stark, but effective! This approach has a certain appeal for one's own pilgrimage, does it not? How about we read the Bible and do what we feel the Holy Spirit is saying to us for that day, setting aside our emotional objections and, frankly, getting on with it? Shall we, today? Shall we invite God to make our lives beautiful portraits of uncomplicated acquiescence?

A DEFINITION OF PLENTY

I have learned to be content whatever the circumstances. I know what it is to be in need, and I know what it is to have plenty

(PHILIPPIANS 4:11–12 *NIV*)

I've been reading the beauty parlour booklet I found, and I can't help feeling Meg and Skipper were short-changed in our care! We were, I now know, supposed to treat them to shampoos followed by rub-downs with essential oils to treat their coats and skin. (Meg was treated to a tin of sardines every so often – does that count?) Likewise, it appears we deprived them of facials designed to brighten and cleanse their faces. (Sorry, Meg. Sorry, Skipper.) It might have been an idea, too, apparently, to allow them to wallow in hydro massage baths. I could go on, but a sense of failure might envelope me if I do! Here I am, writing a book about dogs, and it turns out I haven't a clue about how to look after one! Having said that, Meg really enjoyed her sardines, so maybe it wasn't all bad ...

I'm kidding! Meg and Skipper might not have received the treatments I've mentioned, but they were loved, and they knew it. One's perspective on such matters is to do with priorities, as indeed it is in church life. For example, a church in, say, England, will spend a fair bit of time discussing which chairs to buy, or which type of lectern (oak or Perspex), and will outlay thousands of pounds on the same, whereas a church in a developing country will arrange upturned large, empty, tin vegetable oil containers as "seats" when the faithful gather to worship, stacking old wooden crates (driftwood) one on top of the other in order to make a lectern. Do they feel deprived? No, not if their vibrant worship is anything to go by! They are loved, and they know it. That is enough. Isn't it?

HIDE AND SEEK

She had taken them up to the roof and hidden them under the stalks of flax she had laid out on the roof

(JOSHUA 2:6 **NIV**)

I have received an invitation to a minibus trip taking in five local pubs! Should I enlist, I can spend an entire day trundling around this quintet of hostelries – becoming, I suppose, increasingly tipsy as the hours pass. (I am assuming the minibus driver doesn't partake!) One of the public houses to be visited is the "Fox and Hounds" in a nearby village, so, intrigued by the name, I researched the history of the establishment and discovered it is named in remembrance of a fox hunt that took place nearby, during which a fox, pursued by five hounds, hid in the thatched roof of the pub, scampering up to the thatching in hope of safety. Unfortunately, I couldn't find any information regarding the outcome! Maybe the fox did indeed hide successfully, or maybe the hounds sniffed it out and caught it. Who knows? (I shan't be going on the outing, by the way – I am a teetotaller!)

That frantic fox was by no means the first object of a hunt to hide in a thatched roof! Read the story surrounding today's text, and you will see that two of Joshua's spies were hidden under flax. They were in enemy territory and – like the fox – in great danger. Thanks to a remarkable set of circumstances that would enhance any tale of espionage, God looked after the secret agents, and they evaded capture, albeit by the narrowest of margins. Let us again turn our prayer focus to those whose Christian witness marks them out as people to be hunted, chased, harried, and, in some cases, killed, for Jesus' sake. In our prayers, shall we remember Christians who are on the run in fear of their very lives? May they too find shelter and sanctuary.

GOOD HABITS

Isaac reopened the wells that had been dug in the time of his father Abraham
(GENESIS 26:18 *NIV*)

I hope those partaking in the minibus outing to the "Fox and Hounds" do not become drunk and disorderly, even if they do consume a few pints of real ale on their day out! That's up to them, but today I introduce you to Duncan Disorderly, a Petit Basset Griffon Vendeen who was known as "The Monastery Dog". Duncan lived in the Holy Trinity Monastery in Herefordshire, England, cared for by nuns until his death in June 2016. He was no ordinary dog, and even had his own web page! With the help of his adopted family, Duncan Disorderly wrote a blog describing life as a monastery mutt – the highs and lows of waiting for the nuns as they went about their prayers, duties, and services before taking him for a walk, and the joys of living in a lovely part of the world surrounded by lots of people all only too willing to make a fuss of him. Sleep well, Brother Duncan.

The monastic life – albeit, nowadays, one that is hi-tech and includes blogging, as Duncan demonstrated – is rooted in a rich history of discipline, prayer, mysticism, meditation, and the adoration of God. Times have changed, but those tenets of monasticism still have much to offer, as have teachings from ancient eras. We modern Christians might do well to (re)consider medieval classics of spiritual literature and regard them as sturdy springboards to help us navigate faith in this century. The seasoned well of mystical experience offers depths of truth relevant for every era, and we deprive ourselves if we fail to explore them.

OPTIONAL EXTRAS

David danced before the Lord with all his might
(2 SAMUEL 6:14 **ESV**)

I wish I hadn't picked up the brochure for pampered pooches! The more I read, the more I feel bewildered. I don't quite know what to make of things as I read about a Head Stylist (for dogs, this is, remember), a Bather, and a Groomer, and I wonder if I am losing touch with reality as I study details of the Blueberry Facial available, and a range of services including breed-appropriate haircuts, pedicures, eye cleansing, ear cleaning (ear plucking, if necessary), de-matting, de-shedding, and, to round things off, "a spritz of doggie cologne". Not forgetting a walk-in nail clipping treatment and the added extra of teeth cleaning, if desired. I need a cup of tea.

You are entitled to my honesty, so I'll admit I find this all a bit unnecessary. You might disagree, and that's fine, but might things have gone a bit too far? Possibly, though, it's just me, and maybe I need to embrace such ideas. Am I like that when it comes to worship, and expressing my faith? Stuck in my ways, not too keen on the fact that God might want me to consider fresh expressions of praise and service? That might well be right, actually, in that I know what I like and I like what I know – traditions and routines that have served me well and which I would be reluctant to jettison now. Am I limiting God? Might he want to show me more, and enrich my experience of him? Is my intransigence disobedience? Am I too staid?

RISKING INFECTION

Be sure your sin will find you out
(NUMBERS 32:23 *KJV*)

"Kicking something into the long grass" is a euphemism for concealing an idea that is no longer popular or feasible, which one hopes will disappear. A politician, for example, will kick an unpopular policy into the long grass in the hope it will be forgotten about; it's a way of describing that which we want to abandon or forget. Long grass, though, has an altogether different meaning for dogs and can prove fatal sometimes – foxtail grass, that is (a weed, actually), which can kill if a dog inhales or swallows a seed that lodges somewhere hard to treat. Such seeds – spikelets – have sharp tips that can burrow into a dog's body and travel to the brain, or to internal organs, resulting in infection, abscesses, and perforated lungs. The problem is, of course, that dogs love romping in long grass! Please be careful out there.

The Good Book says that our sins will, sooner or later, catch us out. Don't we just know it! Well, I do! Human nature is such that our instinctive reaction to having done something wrong is to attempt a cover-up; to hide from the truth, to conceal the evidence, to lie, to pretend. All to no avail, I'm afraid, for God is holy, and cannot turn a blind eye to that which we try to kick into the long grass. By the same token, he loves us too much to allow the consequences of hidden sin – a troubled conscience, a web of lies, and so on – to fester like a swallowed foxtail grass seed, deep within. He prefers that matters are brought into the open and nipped in the bud; not because he is spiteful or because he takes some kind of sadistic glee in watching us squirm, but because he knows how much worse matters can become otherwise. He wants us to be truthful out there.

WALKING AND WATCHING

If we confess our sins, he is faithful and just and will forgive us our sins and purify us from all unrighteousness

(I JOHN 1:9 **NIV**)

Those foxtail seeds really do mean business! Barbs that sail directly into a dog's ear canal can prove difficult to treat, resulting in no end of problems. Somewhat easier to address is the issue of spikelets sticking into a dog's fur, or getting caught between toes at the base of the paw. These can be removed with tweezers so that no lasting harm is done, but the secret is to examine your dog's fur and feet if ever he or she has been walking in overgrown, scrubby areas or meadows. A quick check can make all the difference.

The good news is, if and when our sins find us out, grace and forgiveness is available in ample measure. We serve a God who cares and understands, and our text today holds even in the face of our greatest sins. Not only is God keen to make us aware of our sins – a conviction of sin is one of the gracious ministries of the Holy Spirit in our lives – he is enthusiastic about pardoning us too. Conviction and compassion go hand in hand, and he will point us to the cross to show us – reassure us – the price has been paid. The secret is to examine one's conscience in prayer, asking God to reveal anything that needs to be removed. A quick spiritual check-up can work wonders. Our God delights in mercy.

DRIVING FORCE

The chariots storm through the streets
(NAHUM 2:4 **NIV**)

In Wayne, West Virginia, USA, a dog and his canine companion drove a car into a supermarket! I kid you not. Not deliberately, granted, but they still managed it. The owner of the dogs, you see, had left them in the car, and had kept the engine and fan running, so they would be able to keep cool. However, one of the dogs, moving around inside the vehicle, knocked the automatic gear lever out of its "park" setting, causing the car to roll slowly forward into the shop. Thankfully, the dogs were unhurt, although some damage was caused to both the car and the building! I guess it could have been a lot worse!

The Bible doesn't have a great deal to say about runaway cars or supermarkets! It does, though, refer to chariots from time to time; usually in reference to invading armies and conquering forces. Often, in Scripture, chariot drivers, fast and powerful though their vehicles might have been (the Romans favoured ones with menacingly spiked wheels, all the better for intimidating and ensuring road rage and bloodshed) are compared to God, and always come off worse in that comparison! Human might, human aggression, human technology, is as nothing compared to God's power, his anger, and his skill as the eternal engineer. It is an evaluation we do well to remember; our God is faster than the speed of light – especially when it comes to dispensing grace – and mightier than the mightiest army. He is, truly, awesome. There can be no counsel or strength against the Lord.

LOVED

Be still, and know that I am God
(PSALM 46:10 **NIV**)

When I was a boy, the children's television programme *Blue Peter* was fixed viewing for my siblings and me. It was (is) a great show, full of interesting features to keep kids occupied while tea is being prepared and homework postponed as long as possible. One major feature over the years has been the presence of *Blue Peter* dogs in the studio, usually lounging around under the hot lights as the presenters held viewers like me spellbound. I remember Shep and Petra, a Border Collie and a mongrel, respectively; lovely, placid creatures who won the hearts of a nation just by appearing on our screens once a week. Often, they would place their heads on the presenters' laps as spare coat hangers were ingeniously turned into tinselled Christmas decorations, or follow the presenters around as they created entire model villages and space stations from discarded toilet roll insides and yards of sticky-back plastic. Happy days, and delightful dogs!

When I think back, I realize Shep and Petra didn't actually do anything! They slept, snored, padded around, or sat quietly as the cameras rolled. Yet, they were very much a part of the charm of the programme as anything else – the home-made toys and decorations – and were as famous, and as loved, as the presenters. Do we sometimes feel we have to be *doing* something in order to make our mark or be of worth? Do we think we matter only because of what we do? Shep and Petra appear to have given the lie to that way of thinking! Our intrinsic value is simply in *being*; being who God made us to be, and loved by God as such, before we have done anything at all. Our work and our busy-ness is secondary; the outcome of knowing we are loved, not a way of earning divine favour.

SPEAK UP!

Let no corrupting talk come out of your mouths, but only such as is good for building up, as fits the occasion, that it may give grace to those who hear

(EPHESIANS 4:29 *ESV*)

Upon reflection (I am trying to remember TV programmes from forty years ago!), I realize Shep, the *Blue Peter* Border Collie, was more excitable than his on-screen contemporary Petra, and perhaps not as placid as I first recalled. Shep was fond of one of the presenters, John Noakes, and the feeling was mutual – they were inseparable, and Noakes sometimes had to restrain him with what became a famous catchphrase, "Get down, Shep!" which some of my friends at school repeated in games and sports sessions. Shep and John Noakes went on to star together in another programme, *Go With Noakes*, a travelogue sort of broadcast in which they explored Great Britain together – perfect "work" for a lively Border Collie!

Four decades on, I still recall John Noakes' catchphrase! I wonder if anyone will remember anything I say. My sermons, perhaps, or any counsel I might have dispensed. Part of me hopes so, if at any time I said something helpful, encouraging and edifying, but part of me dreads to think what I might have said from the pulpit when my research was sloppy or my attitude judgmental. I can but hope I haven't inflicted too much hurt over the years, or failed in my responsibility to speak truth. Maybe that could be our prayer today; that the words we speak would only ever build up other believers or point people towards the Saviour; words worth remembering.

GOD AS GUARDIAN

Stay alert! Watch out for your great enemy, the devil. He prowls around like a roaring lion, looking for someone to devour

(1 PETER 5:8 **NLT**)

Raccoon Dogs reproduce more quickly than any other canine species, which is causing problems for people in Sweden. Originally from East Asia, Raccoon Dogs represent a significant threat to Swedish wildlife. It is estimated a million are born every year, worldwide, and as they feed on amphibians and birds in wetland areas, their profligacy means some species of Swedish wildlife are threatened with extinction. Therefore, professional hunters have been employed to find and kill Raccoon Dogs – easier said than done, as these fox-like canines are skilled at hiding away – in the hope of protecting wetland habitats and restoring biodiversity. To say these dogs have outstayed their welcome would be putting it mildly, so the plan is to eradicate Raccoon Dogs altogether – which might also be easier said than done!

Ironically, perhaps, given their success at establishing entire colonies across thousands of miles, Raccoon Dogs are sluggish and lazy. These fox/badger-like creatures do the bare minimum to get by, making the least effort (except, it seems, when it comes to mating!). They are remarkably placid, and show little aggression, even when hunted. Easy prey? To be honest, I sometimes feel like that when temptation crouches at my door, failing to realize my need to rush to prayer and hide behind Jesus, lest I am caught in one of Satan's traps. Does the devil catch even God's people unawares occasionally? Yes. Are such captures inevitable? No, not if we are quick to fall to our knees the moment temptations prowl. God will help us.

JESUS AND JUDAS

The hand of him who is going to betray me is with mine on the table. The Son of Man will go as it has been decreed. But woe to that man who betrays him!

(LUKE 22:21–22 **NIV**)

Those clever Swedes, determined to eradicate Raccoon Dogs, have come up with a plan whereby, instead of exterminating every dog they see, they tag them, in the knowledge that a tagged dog will lead them to its family, as the tags can be traced. Sadly, that then leads to the entire family being wiped out, but it seems to be a necessary evil, in the interests of conservation biology. The Raccoon Dogs carrying the tags with which they inadvertently "betray" their families are known as "Judas Dogs", for obvious reasons. It's a grim business, but if the alternative is an environmental catastrophe in the Swedish wetlands, then something must be done.

The story of Judas hinges on the question of freewill. His betrayal of Jesus was treachery personified, but I wonder if Judas had any choice in the matter, given that Jesus had predicted what would happen. Could he have changed his mind and refused to sell our Lord to the authorities? Possibly, except that had he done so, Jesus would have been shown up in public as mistaken, with his prophecy left open to ridicule. Could Judas have backed out and avoided such a notorious place in history, his name tarnished for centuries? Or was perfidy his unavoidable destiny? I don't know. May God grant us the courage to stay loyal to Christ.

COUNTING ON JESUS

Jesus sent two disciples, saying to them, "Go into the village in front of you, and immediately you will find a donkey tied, and a colt with her. Untie them and bring them to me. If anyone says anything to you, you shall say, 'The Lord needs them,' and he will send them at once"

(MATTHEW 21:1–3 **ESV**)

I am a fan of a comedian by the stage name of Count Arthur Strong. Humour is, of course, subjective, and he is not to everyone's taste, but I think the Count provides moments of comedic genius. His speciality is creating surreal situations that could hardly ever occur in "real life", but which become normal in the absurd world of Count Strong. One such scenario involved him setting up a dog-walking enterprise but failing to realize the work would involve walking dogs and clearing up after them. Suffice to say, it goes wrong, culminating in Arthur, with three dogs in tow, visiting his local café carrying a bag full of dog waste, much to the disgust of customers enjoying a quiet cup of tea. The upshot of this chaotic caper is that one of Arthur's friends is left holding the dogs – a Whippet, a Chihuahua, and a Dalmatian – while the café proprietor becomes increasingly irate as another friend of Arthur's, who is blind, argues they might be Guide Dogs and, therefore, allowed in the café. In desperation, Friend No. 1 lifts the Chihuahua in the air and shouts, "Does this look like a Guide Dog?!" failing to realize the blind man can't see what is being held aloft anyway!

What do we make of the episode when Jesus instructed his disciples to approach the owner of a donkey and a colt with the directive that he would release his beasts into the care of strangers? Had Jesus made prior arrangements? Was this a prophetic miracle? Did the disciples fear causing offence with their audacity, maybe wondering if the man might charge a fee? I doubt Jesus dealt in prearranged "miracles", and reject that suggestion in favour of a belief that this deal was proof of Jesus' divinatory ability. What of our arrangements? Do we leave them in the hands of the Lord, trusting he knows every detail and is able to influence (bless) our circumstances? Or do we move hesitantly? What approach will we adopt today?

UNHASTING

Why should I not be impatient?
(JOB 21:4 **NIV**)

My sister's friend suffers from Post-Traumatic Stress Disorder (PTSD), a consequence of service as a Fire Officer and within the military. I wouldn't wish PTSD on anyone, but I am heartened to know an Alsatian is playing a part in aiding his recovery. This is good news, though I must confess my previous ignorance of such an option. I now, though, realize the employment of Certified Service Dogs to be a marvellous facility, helping the traumatized gradually reduce their dependence on medication, not least because one of the benefits of being granted a Service Dog is that it creates ties to the future, thereby alleviating some of the trauma of the past. Dogs live for the moment, possessing an innate ability to remain positive, and this influence rubs off on those who fear they might have nothing to live for, progressively creating a mindset of optimism. A dog lives for the next ball to catch, the next stick to run for, the next meal to eat, and so on, and in such ways, Certified Service Dogs encourage their owners to realize that theirs might, after all, still be a life worth living.

God rarely delivers immediate cure-alls, and the Bible promises no such things. Emotional healing takes time, God understands that better than anyone else. What we might regard as urgent, God realizes will require patience, and it is a blessing that he is willing to stay with us, loving us, helping us, and holding on to us for the long haul. This is no quick-fix deity, but a loving Father who appreciates our impatience, but asks us to trust him, moment by moment. God bless those experiencing the effects of trauma; our prayers go with them, for gentle healing.

KINGDOM STANDARDS

I have other sheep that are not of this sheepfold
(JOHN 10:16 *NIV*)

The more I hear about dogs being used to assist people affected by PTSD, the more I appreciate the service these creatures provide. Labradors, German Shepherds, and Golden Retrievers are suitable breeds to train as assistance dogs, but also (to my surprise, I have to admit) Standard Poodles, as they have a highly developed sense of wanting to please their owners. Standard Poodles, historically employed as gun dogs, thrive on receiving instructions, a throwback to the days when their hunting instinct was put to use retrieving birds. This, allied to their lightning-fast reflexes, makes them well-suited to the complexities of assisting an owner whose needs are multifaceted. I wouldn't immediately have regarded Poodles as candidates for this type of work, but I am delighted to have learnt something new!

Do you ever feel we might be surprised by some of the people we meet in Heaven, whom we might not have expected to be there? Individuals we might have judged as unlikely to be granted access through the Pearly Gates because, say, we never saw them in church, or heard much churchy language from them about their personal faith in the Lord Jesus Christ as Saviour? Our first day in Eternity might include a few "Standard Poodle" surprises; encounters with characters who might, for all we know, have developed an authentic relationship with God, albeit in a haphazard, unconventional way, responding to the light they received as best they knew how. Such, I believe, is grace. Such is the Kingdom.

MIND HOW YOU GO

His mind was troubled

(GENESIS 41:8 **NIV**)

I am interested in Psychiatric Service Dogs, trained to help those whose mental health has taken a battering, to move towards recovery. Likewise, those experiencing schizophrenia, depression, anxiety, and bipolar disorder. A Psychiatric Service Dog will, for example, lie in a handler's lap in order to provide "calming pressure", or intervene to guide its handler away from stressful situations if it senses stress levels rising. Some dogs are coached to be extra-protective of their owner if that person finds it difficult at times to mix with people; the dog deliberately keeping others at bay, creating a safety barrier, though any defensive action is controlled and appropriate so there is no threat of danger. What important work this is. What a help it must be to those whose mental faculties are in need of extra support.

I rejoice in innovative ideas such as those described above. Such progress in medical and psychological knowledge is always to be applauded, lest we continue to treat people in ways that are outdated and maybe even harmful. And the Church? Do we, like the medics, continually explore and consider new concepts in our *modus operandi*? Or are we just hoping for the best but wondering why many of the things we do never seem to work? Well, you will know the challenges of your own locale, and my prayer is that we will all embrace opportunities to present a relevant, attractive Church.

TWO THOUSAND YEARS HAVE PASSED

I will build my church

(MATTHEW 16:18 *NIV*)

Around this time in 1936, Benjamin, the world's last Thylacine, died in Hobart Zoo, Tasmania. Otherwise known as the Tasmanian Wolf, the Thyacline (Greek for "dog-headed pouched one") was a carnivorous marsupial that looked like a dog, or a wolf, but which had a kangaroo-like pouch and a striped back. Benjamin and his friends were never quite accepted as true dogs and were, I'm afraid, hunted to extinction, though the encroachment of humankind onto their natural territory also hurried the demise. I find this sad; that a creature – any creature, dog, wolf or otherwise – should be hounded and killed to such an extent that not even one survives. There have been "sightings" over the years, but it really does appear as though this unwanted dog-like creature has gone for ever.

At this time of writing, I am a few weeks short of my fifty-first birthday, and have spent most of my life, though not all, in or around the Church. The most persistent rumour circulating throughout that time has been that the Church is doomed to extinction – that is, if it isn't dead and buried already. I have heard it over and over, yet, by the grace of God, the Church is still here! I think it was Spurgeon who said, when he too was advised that God's Church would soon meet its demise, "I think they dug its grave too soon!"[1] I recall John Ellerton's lovely hymn, "The Day Thou Gavest, Lord, is Ended" with its gently triumphant note of humble confidence in God's ability to preserve his work here on earth, and I give thanks for churches around the world maintaining their witness. God is faithful.

1   www.spurgeongems.org

MY FAULT

The man said, "The woman you put here with me – she gave me some fruit from the tree, and I ate it." Then the Lord God said to the woman, "What is this you have done?" The woman said, "The snake deceived me, and I ate"
(GENESIS 3:12–13 **NIV**)

Should you wish to gauge the temperature of your town, you could do worse than peruse the pages of your local paper, especially the "Letters to the Editor" section. There, you will discover what's going on, who thinks what of whom, and what grievances are being aired! A letter in my local rag complained vociferously about a "snapping menace" in the form of an off-lead dog who bites at the ankles of joggers in a park, and whose owner takes exception when joggers complain, accusing them of running too close to her dog. One letter-writer has had enough, and wrote in to say she intends to "boot the little yapper over the field" if it happens again! I shall watch for any correspondence that appears by way of response, and if and when it does, you will be the first to know!

I can't comment on this situation as I don't visit the park in question. I do, though, smile at the way in which blame is being bounced to and fro as the joggers point the finger at the dog and its owner, and the owner retorts by holding the runners responsible. It's a scenario as old as humankind itself; Adam blamed Eve for the introduction of sin into the Garden of Eden, Eve blamed the serpent, and the serpent hadn't a leg to stand on! Has anything changed? Not much, if the letters page is anything to go by. And you and me? Do we hold our hands up and take the rap when we get it wrong, or do we try to deflect or minimize culpability? Quickest and best, methinks, to confess our misdeeds to a gracious and compassionate God, and to trust him for mercy and forgiveness!

OUR FATHER

SEE MATTHEW 6:9–13

Father Brown, G. K. Chesterton's crime-solving priest, was once embroiled in a story about a surgeon who was a bigamist and who then became a murderer, when one of his patients threatened to reveal the secret of his first – unannulled – marriage. The patient in question was being prepared for surgery, and was drowsy because of anaesthetic that had been administered, when she whispered "Mrs Weston", a reference to the surgeon's first marriage, decades earlier, which had taken place in the English seaside town of Weston-super-Mare. In her semi-conscious state, she had confused the name of the town with that of the surgeon's first bride, but she had said enough to worry him, so he killed her with an overdose of anaesthetic. To cut a long story short, Father Brown, who had married the surgeon to his second wife, investigated matters, resulting in the surgeon's arrest. Gripping fiction, all hinging on the name "Mrs Weston"! The surgeon's bigamy would never had come to light had the patient simply fallen asleep.[1] Names, though, are fascinating, and revealing – my wife's Uncle Dave, for example, christened his Labrador "Buster", we inherited dogs called Meg and Skipper, but we named "Fred" and "Scruffy" in keeping with their character or appearance. Scottish friends of ours named their Labrador "Coop" in honour of Glasgow Rangers player Davie Cooper, who died tragically young. A former colleague of mine called his Jack Russell "Kipper" after a Jack Russell cartoon dog who starred on children's TV. No doubt you are thinking of similar examples as you read …

Buster is called Buster because it seems to suit his personality – energetic, playful, strong. Scruffy is self-explanatory! The hospital patient in the Father Brown story had linked a distant memory of Weston-super-Mare with someone she met there. Likewise, we associate names with traits and perceptions – hence, "Our Father", the established prayer Jesus left, which encourages us to regard Almighty God as a loving Heavenly Father. When we begin to do so, and when we pray in such a way, our perception of him becomes clearer and clearer, so that we start to move away from foggy, anaesthetized concepts of God towards those which are much clearer, much more accurate, and more befitting his character. In approaching God as Father, we ascribe to him attributes we might otherwise miss.

Pray the words he gave us now.

1   *Father Brown*, TV episode, "The Rod of Asclepius"

ELEMENTARY

Since the creation of the world God's invisible qualities – his eternal power and divine nature – have been clearly seen, being understood from what has been made
(ROMANS 1:20 **NIV**)

To commemorate what would have been my dad's 80th birthday on this day in 2015 (he died aged 79), we took my mum for a meal at a pub/restaurant in Slingsby, North Yorkshire, England, and I was delighted to discover the venue we had chosen prides itself on being dog-friendly. Not only that, but I learnt that a Bassett Hound called Archie had won their most recent "Festive Fancy Dress (for dogs only) Competition". We raised a glass in loving memory of Dad, but if Archie's photograph was anything to go by, he seemed none too keen on joining in any celebrations whatsoever! I gather he was entered as some kind of old-fashioned sleuth, with a velvet cape, a bowler hat, and some old-fashioned spectacles giving him the hangdog expression of a world-weary detective! All that was missing was a magnifying glass! Happy birthday, Dad. We love you and miss you, every day, not just on your birthday.

A sleuth – a detective – will look for clues, Sherlock Holmes-like, and piecing together those clues to arrive at a conclusion. Not many dress in capes, bowler hats (deer stalkers?), and give the appearance of Victorian investigators which probably only ever belonged to works of fiction anyway, but the work is much the same; gathering evidence in order to establish the truth. Is that how we read the New Testament? It might be a useful exercise – picking out, or marking, certain points that lead, say, to a conviction that Jesus is indeed God; pulling the threads together in order to bolster faith and make a reasonable, logical case. No fancy dress required, just some application and dogged determination to search for proof!

A MATTER OF EXPRESSION

Deal gently
(HEBREWS 5:2 *NIV*)

True to my word, I bring you news of a letter in my local newspaper responding to the complaint about a dog spoiling the enjoyment of joggers as they indulge their pastime. To say this letter comes out in defence of dogs would be an understatement, and I shall omit the more vitriolic comments! Let's just assume the writer of Letter No. 2 isn't an enormous fan of joggers, unfairly describing them as cynophobic (cynophobia being a mental disorder whereby the sufferer is almost pathologically afraid of canines). In my humble opinion, the vitriol employed does a disservice to what might otherwise have been a carefully constructed case put forward on behalf of the rights of dogs to run around parks. To accuse people of being mentally ill, just because one happens to see things differently, is pretty awful, and offensive to those who really do labour under the weight of psychological disorders. So far, in terms of good points well made, it's 1–0 to the joggers!

The day before writing this page, I spent time with two church members who had been deeply hurt, albeit some years ago, by hard-hitting comments made in a sermon regarding homosexuals and people who cohabit before marriage. Their bruising was still tender, and honesty compels me to say it's a sermon I'm glad I didn't hear. You hardly need me to tell you that the way in which we express our feelings and convictions (be that on gay rights, sex before marriage or, come to that, the price of cheese) is often as weighty as the points themselves. A charitable expression can work wonders, even amongst those with whom we might disagree!

STAND UP FOR JESUS

Peter got down out of the boat, walked on the water and came towards Jesus. But when he saw the wind, he was afraid and, beginning to sink, cried out, "Lord, save me!" Immediately Jesus reached out his hand and caught him

(MATTHEW 14:29–31 **NIV**)

A woman in Devon, England, has taken up Stand Up Paddle Boarding. I hadn't heard of it either, but it is something like surfboarding, except that paddlers, well, stand up and paddle. Races are held for those who want to do those things at competition level, and this woman has adapted her board so it has rubber at the front, upon which stands Tally, her Jack Russell, who insists on travelling along. (Tally even accompanied her owner on an eight-mile race, wearing her own little lifejacket.) I can't honestly see myself Stand Up Paddle Boarding, but I understand why it would appeal; exercise in the fresh air combined with beautiful scenery and the camaraderie of fellow paddle boarders. Splash!

Impetuous Peter! Climbing out of the boat and walking on water – impressively obedient to Jesus, who had encouraged him to try and, for a short while, standing up and striding the sea! Even though he sunk when his faith gave way, we admire Peter for at least trying (especially when there was no record of anyone else prepared to take Jesus at his word that day). It's why we love him, and why we identify with his successes and failures. May Jesus himself enable us whenever we step out in obedience to his call – and may Jesus help us, as he helped Peter, if and when we too find ourselves in deep water for our efforts!

BEST FOOT FORWARD

I praise you because I am fearfully and wonderfully made; your works are wonderful
(PSALM 139:14 **NIV**)

A television programme featured surgery being carried out on two dogs; Molly, a boggle-eyed Cavalier with a tumour on her skull, and Archie, a Norfolk Terrier hobbling about on a wonky leg. Nothing remarkable about that, in that operations on dogs are performed all the time, but this broadcast focused on the ever-increasing use of bionic limbs. Archie, for example, was diagnosed with a malformed elbow, and was prescribed a bespoke titanium joint that was 3D-printed in Belgium and ordered by post. Quite astonishing! The levels of technology now at play in what will soon become routine veterinary work are amazing – not that Archie cared too much about being at the forefront of technological progress as he ran across a field on his state-of-the-art newly jointed leg!

I know next to nothing about technology, science, or anything like that (I wish I did). From time to time, though, I hear about remarkable scientific and technological breakthroughs (such as Archie's 3D-printed limb), and I marvel at the intelligence behind such matters. We human beings are indeed fearfully made, and the centuries bear witness to the fact that the advancement of knowledge moves at lightning speed – leaving some of us feeling left behind! God has granted such acumen to his creation – our brains, common sense, wit, swiftness of thought, intellect – and we can but praise him and thank him for doing so. May God the Creator bless those who employ their skills and gifts for the benefit of humankind – and animalkind!

LAWNS AND LORDSHIP

The grass withers and the flowers fall
(ISAIAH 40:8 **NIV**)

A caller to the consumer programme on my local radio station was upset because the plastic grass "lawn" she ordered and paid to have installed is, according to her, substandard. Fair enough, and I hope the matter is amicably resolved ... especially as a staggering £31,000 has been spent thus far! The caller explained that she owns two Labradoodles, and was tired of mud being splattered all over her kitchen floor and living room carpet whenever her dogs came indoors from the garden. I had to smile when the radio presenter asked if it wouldn't have been considerably less expensive simply to wipe the Labradoodles' feet before they set foot in the house, mud and grime being pretty much unavoidable. No – the woman was adamant; £15,000 expended on each Labradoodle was money well-spent!

Should I find myself with £31,000 burning a hole in my pocket, it is unlikely I would spend it on plastic grass. However, each to their own, and the oxymoron known as plastic grass is, apparently, durable, clean, and attractive. I wonder what the people of Bible times would have thought of it? Our text today has its origins in the flat-roofed Holy Land dwellings of the time, where little shoots of grass would spring up, and sometimes flowers too, but wouldn't last long because of the burning heat of the Middle East and the absence of soil. The psalmist employs the analogy of our brief existence here on earth being similar – here today, gone tomorrow, so to speak. That being so, how shall we use our years? Our time is short, but God will help us to leave behind a Christ-like influence that will last, and will even bear fruit in eternity.

A SERMON FOR THE STREET

Suppose one of you has a hundred sheep and loses one of them. Doesn't he leave the ninety-nine in the open country and go after the lost sheep until he finds it? And when he finds it, he joyfully puts it on his shoulder and goes home. Then he calls his friends and neighbours together and says, "Rejoice with me; I have found my lost sheep." I tell you that in the same way there will be more rejoicing in heaven over one sinner who repents than over ninety-nine righteous persons who do not need to repent

(LUKE 15:4–7 **NIV**)

In August 2006, staff at a rescue centre in Lincolnshire, England, were trying to rehome a stray Wire-Haired Deerhound that had been found wandering the streets of Gainsborough. I do hope the staff were successful, but I can't help wondering how the Deerhound became lost in the first place, as the average height of Deerhounds, standing on their hind legs, is roughly 5ft – difficult to lose! There could of course have been all sorts of reasons behind its need for rehoming, but they are such beautiful, dignified creatures, with quiet natures, that I can't imagine the rescue centre lacking in applications. Here's hoping the misplaced gentle giant was quickly found by someone willing to offer it spacious accommodation!

Are you ever "grabbed" by the title of a sermon? I was, when I once heard a Baptist minister preaching on Luke 15, under the heading "If you are lost, he is looking for you. If you are found, start looking for the lost!" The message was pretty good, too, emphasizing the endlessly searching heart of God on behalf of those who have wandered astray, and the responsibility Christians have of playing their part in bringing the lost home. I needn't add any more to that, really, so I shan't.

A WORD IN EDGEWAYS

Your word is a lamp for my feet, a light on my path
(PSALM 119:105 *NIV*)

Dogs, we know, are intelligent creatures, but exactly how intelligent varies from breed to breed, research indicating that many breeds are roughly as intelligent as a two-year-old human being, in terms of their ability to understand words. Border Collies can cope with about 200 words or phrases, followed by Poodles, German Shepherds, Golden Retrievers, and Dobermans, though there is not much to choose between them. Impressive, but if rumours of "the terrible twos" are correct and human beings at that particular age display "terrible" behaviour (tantrums and the like), we can but hope canines and people don't also have that in common!

Experts at crossword puzzles and word games inevitably possess a larger vocabulary than people who rarely indulge in such pastimes. Likewise, those who read widely are likely to develop a stronger grasp of the English language than those who don't. (No criticism is implied there, as that is simply a factual observation.) It's not dissimilar with God's word, the Bible, in that the more we read it, study it, and feed on it, the more our fluency with the ways of God develops; we become more familiar with his mercies and graces, and our relationship with him matures and deepens. Two hundred words? One hundred and fifty psalms, for starters (one a day?) provide an enriching overview of a loving deity's dealings with his people.

A ONE-OFF!

Your hands made me and formed me
(PSALM 119:73 *NIV*)

Aren't fingerprints remarkable? To think we can be uniquely identified by a combination of ridges and creases on our fingers and thumbs is amazing. We are indeed "fearfully and wonderfully made" (Psalm 139:14). Did you know, though, that dogs have nose prints? It's true! The folds and shallow crumples on a dog's nose are so distinctive, they can be used to identify individual animals, and each nose has its own print. Indeed, the Canadian Kennel Club has accepted nose prints as proof of identity since 1938, enabling the relocation of lost dogs found without collar tags.

What a tragedy it is, as someone once observed, to be born an original, yet die a copy. God the Creator has made each of us in a unique manner, intending us to lead lives of individuality according to our God-given talents and temperaments. Our essential Id is ours alone, and dilutes when we feel the need to be like someone else. There is nothing wrong in aspiring to emulate our heroes, but that should only ever apply to admiring their achievements or characteristics; we should draw the line at trying to live our lives vicariously. Each of us is who we are for a reason, made to an exclusive design. You are you and I am me!

DON AND HIS DOGS

The Lord God had planted a garden
(GENESIS 2:8 **NIV**)

Are you a gardener? Heather and I have an agreement whereby I look after the flowers in our little garden, while she tends the vegetables. We get along well, and the garden seems to be coping with our joint attentions. Although I am by no means an expert, I am a fan of Monty Don, whose television gardening programmes bring their own combination of relaxed expertise and practical advice. I like Monty not only because he presents in a down-to-earth way, but because he is a dog lover too, having owned several over the years. He currently looks after two Golden Retrievers, Nigel and Nellie, who patently adore him as they accompany him in the garden and the greenhouse. Monty's first dog was a Labrador, Gretel, though he grew up around his grandmother's Corgi, Meg, and previously cared for Eric, half-Jack Russell, half-Fox Terrier.

Do you garden? I dabble with flower-growing, but that's about it. I am, though, fascinated by research extolling the virtues of gardening as an aid to a healthier frame of mind. Soil, apparently, when it is disturbed, releases a natural chemical that has definite psychological benefits, even helping to alleviate some symptoms of depression and anxiety. My grandparents had an engraved stone in their garden for years, displaying an excerpt from a poem that I share with you today, praying good mental health for you and God's blessings:

The kiss of the sun for pardon,
The song of the birds for mirth,
One is nearer God's heart in a garden
Than anywhere else on earth.

(Dorothy Frances Gurney, 1858–1932)

PETER MAKES HIS POINT

Peter, who had a sword, drew it and struck the high priest's servant, cutting off his right ear

(JOHN 18:10 **NIV**)

Eric was, by all accounts, nowhere near as calm as Monty Don himself, and had a penchant (*à la* Skipper!) for attacking dogs several times his size, repeatedly and routinely challenging Dobermans and German Shepherds to fights and repeatedly and routinely coming off a painful second best! Such playful aggression was part and parcel of his nature, and Eric took defeat and injury in his stride, bearing no grudges. Ultimately, though, Eric's behaviour led to him being put to sleep aged ten, as he was such a threat to other dogs in the area. The feisty little warrior failed to distinguish between fun-fights and fearful fury, hastening his own demise.

Eric's exploits remind me of Peter's! A band of Roman soldiers and Jewish Temple Police were deployed to arrest Jesus, yet Peter was so incensed by their presence, he pulled out a sword and chopped off an ear belonging to the servant of the high priest. No doubt about it, the party assigned to the arrest that evening would have been armed and, in the case of the soldiers, protected by military-grade armour; professional warriors trained for combat. Their order was to make an arrest, and to use brute force if necessary. Peter, though, ignored such niceties (and odds!), striking out with his blade! Fearless? Foolish? I can't recommend his rapier antics as a method of evangelism, but his commitment to protecting Jesus (*à la* Peter!) is to be admired; brave and undaunted for his Lord.

THINGS WORTH KNOWING

Avoid foolish controversies and genealogies and arguments and quarrels about the law, because these are unprofitable and useless
(TITUS 3:9 *NIV*)

In comes news of a report claiming to have discovered that dogs are not really, after all, "man's best friend". Researchers from the University of Portsmouth, England, have concluded that dogs are selfish creatures who are happy to play with their owners, but not so keen to help them. Given a choice between searching for a lost toy or an item of interest to the owners (a notebook, say), the twenty-four family dogs tested opted to look for the toy, leading scientists to the conclusion that dogs are not as altruistic as we think. Shall you tell them, or shall I? The fact that a dog doesn't show much enthusiasm for searching for a lost notebook is simply because dogs, generally speaking, don't have much use for notebooks, whereas they do for toys. It has nothing to do with being unhelpful! The result of the study was clear-cut: dogs only like objects that dogs like. I wonder if the boffins at work should be awarded with medals for stating the obvious!

Part of me wonders what this study was meant to confirm. Another part of me wonders how much money was spent on this research. Was it, I have to ask, worth it, if all we have discovered is that dogs like toys? Some questions are worth asking, and some are not, perhaps especially when it comes to matters of faith and belief. We can, if we aren't careful, tie ourselves in knots getting nowhere fast with queries and pursuits that are somewhat pointless, whereas there are plenty of enquiries worth pursuing. Are we making the right enquiries today?

HITTING HOME

I do not fight like a boxer beating the air
(1 CORINTHIANS 9:26 **NIV**)

British gold medallist Nicola Adams, only the second Briton to retain an Olympic boxing title since 1924, flew to the 2016 Rio Olympics safe in the knowledge that her dog, Dexter (a Doberman, not a Boxer!), was being looked after by her mum. Nicola's mother prefers to tune in to Nicola's bouts on TV in her living room, rather than travelling to watch her daughter box live, and unapologetically gives priority to caring for Dexter! We can therefore only imagine the scene back home in England whenever Nicola's televized bouts are screened, with Dexter the Doberman and Denver, Nicola's mum, glued to the screen! (Let's just hope stay-at-home Mum is not in the doghouse!)

Nicola Adams patently knows her sport well – two Olympic golds speak for themselves. Honed and skilled, she is able to land punches that matter and emerge as a champion bantamweight. Paul would have been familiar with the Isthmian Games of Corinth, and therefore used a sporting analogy when writing to Christians in that area. He may even have been a spectator at a few Isthmian boxing bouts – who knows! Had he been, he would have seen boxers as talented as Nicola, but also boxers who took something of a more optimistic approach by flailing their arms around in the hope of at least hitting something! And you and I? Have we a focus in our ministries? Targets? Objectives? Let us pray that God will help us too to strike gold, as it were, as we work for him until the final bell rings.

RENEWAL

Renew our days as of old
(LAMENTATIONS 5:21 **NIV**)

Not long ago, at this time of writing, I had the privilege of giving my sister away at her wedding, working with her chief bridesmaid as we tried (hard!) to keep my sister calm on her big day! All went well, and I hope it did, too, for two devoted pensioners from Somerset, England I read about, who renewed their wedding vows with Suki, a four-year-old Lurcher cross, as bridesmaid! The groom, at the grand age of ninety-two, collared Suki from a friend and even kitted her out with a handmade flower garland. By all accounts, Suki the Lurcher/bridesmaid cross did a great job, and was rewarded with a slice of wedding cake! Quite right, too!

The prolific Salvationist poet Will J. Brand (1899–1977) composed over 350 songs and 150 sonnets. One of his poignant songs of consecration includes the following words, which I keep on a card next to my desk. I share them with you today, as a prayer:

By the love that never ceased to hold me,
By the blood which thou didst shed for me,
While thy presence and thy power enfold me,
I renew my covenant with thee.

LISTS AND LOVE

In every situation, by prayer and petition, with thanksgiving, present your requests to God

(PHILIPPIANS 4:6 **NIV**)

One of my weaknesses is nice pens. Sad, I know, but I am no fan of cheap plastic efforts, preferring steel ones or fountain pens. To that end, I was buying a refill for one of my better pens and, at the till, was handed my receipt and a picture of a Bichon Frise with an invitation to "feed my dog's individuality with a free trial of dog food made just for them". Overleaf, I was encouraged to tell this particular company all about my dog so that they could then set to on making up a batch of food that would take into account breed, age, condition, amount of exercise, and even taste preferences! This set me thinking; how would I have completed such a questionnaire for Skipper ...

Breed: German Shepherd/Border Collie cross with a sprinkling of clown.
Age: Thirteen (we think). (Behavioural Age: Four.)
Condition: Remarkably strong, slightly odd, cantankerous, handsome.
Amount of exercise: As much as possible in all weathers, including chasing other dogs, pulling people along, and fighting.
Taste preferences: Preferably, food that has been abandoned beneath hedges and in doorways but, generally, pretty much anything in vast quantities.

It would be interesting to see what the dog food company would do with Skipper's order! Might we liken this to our text for today? Isn't it wonderful that we are invited – encouraged – to list our prayer requests, safe in the knowledge that a loving Heavenly Father will always consider everything we bring to the Throne of Grace? Wonderful, too, to remember that our every need is known to him and that he is more than able to take into account all we present before him. This is our God.

LOVE AND LAUGHTER

A cheerful heart is good medicine
(PROVERBS 17:22 *NIV*)

On this day in 1925, the great comic actor, Peter Sellers, was born. I love his *Pink Panther* films, in which he played the permanently clueless Inspector Clouseau, so, in order commemorate his birthday, I reproduce below what I regard as one of the funniest – silliest – jokes from *The Pink Panther Strikes Again*:

Clouseau: Does your dog bite?
Hotel Clerk: No.
Clouseau (bowing down to pet the dog): Nice doggie.
(Dog barks and bites Clouseau in the hand.)
Clouseau: I thought you said your dog did not bite!
Hotel Clerk: That is not my dog.

Wonderful! I like jokes; the cornier, the better, and I like humour. Does God? Well, if we are made in his image, and if we are created with the ability to laugh, then logic tells us he does. Humour that is never cruel, that is, or vindictive, unkind or crude, but that which can make light of troubles, slights, and discouragements, and which keeps irritations in perspective. Do we laugh often? I have a feeling God does.

A PATTERN OF WORSHIP

God demonstrates his own love for us in this: while we were still sinners,
Christ died for us
(ROMANS 5:8 **NIV**)

As I write, England is experiencing distinctly unusual weather patterns. The meteorological norms of August and September seem to be non-existent. For example, we Brits have enjoyed some days (consecutive days!) of golden sunshine, but as I type these very words, cold rain is pouring down as hard as it can be and the day is something of a washout – good for my lawn, but not much fun otherwise! Weather forecasters are having trouble trying to predict what English weather might include from one day to the next, from temperatures suitable for sunbathing one day to chilly moments shortly afterwards. Quite possibly, Englishmen of ancient times, especially those who came under any Roman influence, would have referred to these unpredictable weeks as "the dog days" or, more accurately, dies caniculares (which translates, literally, as "the puppy days"), a reference to the Dog Star of the Orion constellation, which was said to be responsible for erratic weather and, in some cases, even the appearance of mad dogs! Thankfully, I haven't (yet) seen any mad dogs strolling across the wet grass outside my window, but I can't help wondering what might happen next – weather-wise, that is!

Much of life is, when we come to think of it, entirely unpredictable. Forasmuch as we like to plan ahead, we only need to look at ever-fluctuating weather forecasts (not only in England!) to realize that we don't actually have much control over anything at all! What is predictable, though, is that each of us will, at some time or another, sin, and that God will, in turn, forgive those who confess and repent. In a world of ever-changing ideals, events, standards, and norms, those two facts won't ever alter; our sins and God's mercies. "The God days" – of grace and mercy, that is – are here to stay, all over the world!

GOD IS IN THE DETAIL

The very hairs of your head are all numbered
(LUKE 12:7 **NIV**)

According to BBC Radio Four's *Gardeners' Question Time,* an excellent way of preventing slugs destroying one's beloved blooms and cultivated cucumbers is to brush your dog, then scatter the hair collected around the soil in which you are growing your fruit, flowers, and vegetables. Slugs dislike the way in which hair sticks to their bodies and tangles around them, and will therefore avoid any such covered areas. Does this actually work? I've no idea, but the suggestion is humane, eco-friendly, and cheap! I can't vouch for its success, but perhaps gardeners reading this might want to give it a try? If nothing else, at least your dog will look well-groomed!

On average, men grow 80,000 hairs on their head over the course of a lifetime (some are more blessed than others!), whereas women produce approximately 100,000. Some men are, shall we say, follicly challenged, whereas others are more hirsute. Whatever our lot, Jesus himself taught that God knows every single hair on our heads! That is, his love for us is so immense and so intense that not one solitary detail of our lives escapes his attention or loving awareness. We may have 80,000, 100,000, issues, worries, and concerns, yet the wonderful fact is that each of them has a place in the heart of God. He knows. He cares. He would rather die than belittle or dismiss one single matter that troubles us.

SHOWING OUR CARDS

Will not the Judge of all the earth do right?
(GENESIS 18:25 *NIV*)

With a few notable exceptions, most footballers pick up a yellow card or two during their careers. Ordinarily, though, they are penalized for fouls or some other kind of misconduct, and usually once the game is underway. In Argentina, though, San Lorenzo captain Pablo Alvarado received the quickest yellow card ever to be shown when he was booked by the referee several minutes *before* kick-off – for time-wasting as a result of walking his dog out onto the pitch as the teams were limbering up! Apparently, Alvarado felt San Lorenzo could use a mascot and that his dog, some kind of Collie cross, would be the ideal candidate. The referee, however, disagreed and quickly reached into his pocket for a card!

I watch a fair amount of football, and one of the standard talking points amongst fans and pundits alike is the variation in refereeing standards. Granted, football referees have a tough job, but what frustrates many supporters (and players) is the way in which some refs are yellow-and-red-card-happy and seemingly eager to dish out punishments, while others are more lenient. Thankfully, there is no such disparity with God, who dispenses justice, mercy, discipline, and compassion with equanimity; he is always fair, never fickle or capricious. We might well be guilty of all sorts of misdemeanours, but every offence on our part is met with grace on his.

JUST GOD

Keep me safe from the traps set by evildoers, from the snares they have laid for me

(PSALM 141:9 **NIV**)

On the subject of justice being meted out, three men in Scotland were taken to court for their involvement in the horror known as hare coursing, in which dogs are used to hunt hares (the hares are trapped into enclosures) while spectators film the chase and the kill. In this case, convictions were secured when samples taken from the hare killed in the incident were analyzed and DNA of one of the dogs used was found on the corpse. Police also found footage of the coursing in the men's van, but it was the crucial DNA evidence that secured jail sentences and fines. I am delighted to report that the guilty trio were banned from owning dogs for a year.

King David knew what it was to be hunted! His reign was littered with accounts of battles, encounters with enemies, and bloodthirsty chases as he was pursued time and time again by political and military rivals and adversaries – with no hope of securing DNA evidence against those keen to slay him. His hope, though, lay not in forensic science or legal options, but in God alone, as our text today demonstrates. This was the prayer of a man on the run, fearing for his life, and I can but recommend a reading of the entire psalm; it will embolden you, reassure you, and bring a reminder of God's strong protection towards the vulnerable and frightened.

ME, MYSELF, I

You are my Lord; apart from you I have no good thing
(PSALM 16:2 **NIV**)

The law swung into action when it came to convicting hare coursers in Scotland, but offered little protection to King David in Jerusalem. In Italy, though, a law has been passed making it easier for supermarkets to donate food to charities by changing the rules on sell-by dates. Likewise, farmers are to be encouraged to donate surplus produce to charity, which was previously illegal. One side-effect of the relaxation of such laws is that restaurant customers will be urged to use "doggie bags" in order to decrease amounts of food waste. So as to protect Italian cultural sensitivities, these will be rebranded as "family bags", but "doggie bags" they are, really, the euphemism discreetly covering the embarrassment of diners keen to hang on to their leftovers under the flimsy pretence of taking some titbits home for their dog!

Aren't euphemisms funny? The way in which we cover up our foibles with phrases and descriptions we think somehow improve or enhance that which we find embarrassing. There is nothing wrong with appropriate discretion, but airs and graces designed to give a false impression are not only transparent, but vaguely ridiculous if they mean we are trying to be someone we aren't. God loves us exactly as we are, and there is absolutely no need to hide anything from him, or to disguise our truest feelings. Dare we risk it? We do not worry about offending God's sensitivities by presenting ourselves at the Throne of Grace without pretence! A radical step? Rest assured, it will be met by radical grace.

WHAT'S DONE IS DONE

I repent in dust and ashes
(JOB 42:6 **NASB**)

Speaking of Scotland, we were visiting Heather's parents, who live there, when I was handed a leaflet promoting the PDSA Vet Care range. I repeat my admiration for the PDSA, but I can't help feeling, yet again, that Skipper and Meg were badly done by under my ownership! I think (hope!) they were well cared for, exercised, fed, and watered, and so on, but when I read about the range of PDSA products available (Salmon Oil, Borage Oil, Golden Flaxseed Oil, Liquid Formula Vitamin E, Triple-Strength Green Lipped Mussel, Hyaluronic Acid, Pure Glucosamine, Raspberry Scent, and Crunchy Biscuit Bites), I am left wondering where I went wrong! Skipper and Meg were generously treated to biscuit bites, but that, I'm afraid, is as far as it went! (By the way, what exactly is a Green Lipped Mussel?)

I could, I suppose, spend the rest of my life in sackcloth lamenting my incompetence as a dog owner! I shan't, though, because I did my (albeit imperfect) best. Only yesterday, at this time of writing, I was reading from the Church of England's *Book of Common Prayer*, and appreciated the words of the General Confession. Do you too feel like I do with Skipper and Meg, but with life, generally? If so, treat yourself to a portion of available grace today, with this prayer:

Almighty and most merciful Father; We have erred, and strayed from thy ways like lost sheep. We have followed too much the devices and desires of our own hearts. We have offended against thy holy laws. We have left undone those things which we ought to have done; And we have done those things which we ought not to have done; And there is no health in us. But thou, O Lord, have mercy upon us, miserable offenders. Spare thou those, O God, who confess their faults. Restore thou those who are penitent; According to thy promises declared unto mankind In Christ Jesus our Lord. And grant, O most merciful Father, for his sake; That we may hereafter live a godly, righteous, and sober life, To the glory of thy holy Name. Amen.[1]

---

1   *The 1928 Book of Common Prayer* (New York: Oxford University Press, 2007)

RESEARCH SECRETS

I will praise the Lord, who counsels me
(PSALM 16:7 **NIV**)

The children's author Katherine Rundell wanted to research wolves and wolf behaviour for one of her novels, set against a backdrop of the Russian Revolution. In order to understand how wolves think and operate, Rundell read an astonishing twenty books, learning about wolf anatomy and the way in which they hunt. She also watched documentaries and visited a wolf sanctuary in Wales, where she observed wolves playing together so as to learn their habits, enabling her to set accurate scenes and descriptions when it came to writing what I hope became a best-seller. Her attention to detail is to be applauded!

Understanding the conduct of wolves is one thing, and Katherine Rundell's examination of pack behaviour would no doubt have been beneficial. Likewise, in a way, studies in human behaviour, when psychologists and counsellors share their expertise in order to help those in need of therapy, having made a studious analysis of problems and mind-patterns. Not everyone benefits from counselling, despite the best efforts of psychotherapists, but it is a source of reassurance to know that when we pray, we come before a God who not only created us – our brains, our nervous systems – but cares deeply about any distress we may experience as a result of painful mental health issues. This is our God.

GREAT IS HIS FAITHFULNESS

He remains faithful forever
(PSALM 146:6 **NIV**)

I am very pleased to report that a website promoting the virtues of my beloved Northumberland not only includes information regarding holiday accommodation and hostelries, but a series of "dog symbols" too – paw prints dotted along the coastline indicating beaches, pubs, campsites, and restaurants where dogs would be welcome. What a great idea! (Some owners of self-catering cottages even include welcome packs for dogs!) As well as providing pointers to local attractions and beauty spots, the website features a line of paw prints starting at Seaton Sluice at the south of the county, and rising north up to Berwick-upon-Tweed.

One of my ambitions is to research and write a book highlighting the rich history of Christianity in Northumberland and the north-east of England, ranging from the days of Bede and Cuthbert to the most modern expressions of Christian faith in that region. Whether or not I will ever actually get around to fulfilling that ambition remains to be seen, but any such study would clearly highlight the faithfulness of God towards his people over the centuries, through good times, perils, blessings, and trials; times of joy and celebration, and periods of tribulation; I would be able to track the "God prints" at every stage. At no time, be it in Northumberland or elsewhere, has God ever once abandoned his own. Nor will he.

OFFENCES AND OFFENDERS

Love … keeps no record of wrongs
(1 CORINTHIANS 13:4–5 **NIV**)

Should I stumble in my research regarding Christianity in the north-east of England, I could, I suppose, while away a bit of time filling in forms reporting dog fouling in Stockton-on-Tees. The Borough Council there has had enough of dog fouling going undetected, and is encouraging residents to complete a questionnaire, should they see offences being committed, and submit it to the council offices, which may result in legal action being taken. It's worth a try, and the questionnaire, under the campaign headline "Pick Up Or Pay Up" requests the following information:

Date
Time
Location
Description of Owner and Dog
Dog Owner's Name
What You Saw

On balance, I shall probably stick to writing books, but I applaud Stockton-on-Tees Borough Council for at least making an effort to clean up the streets. What, though, if God enlisted the assistance of volunteers to inform him of the misdemeanours of others; a sort of secret spy service whereby Holy Snoopers list their complaints in the hope God will take action against miscreants? How absurd! For one thing, God knows it all already, and for another, is not interested in keeping any such lists of wrongs. His omniscience is matched only by his capacity to forgive and forget.

THE LIVES OF WIVES

Strength and dignity are her clothing, And she smiles at the future
(PROVERBS 31:25 **NASB**)

Would you mind if we stayed in the north-east of England a little longer? I'd like to tell you about a photographic competition held by *The Northern Echo*, a regional newspaper produced in Darlington, County Durham. This paper ran the competition under the heading "Winning Smile" and among the usual entries of children smiling and grandparents grinning was a marvellous picture of an unnamed Terrier being held in its owner's arms and looking for all the world as though it was laughing. It's a great shot, and the photographer has managed to catch the Terrier at just the right moment, with its teeth showing and its tongue poking out, giving the impression it is remembering a particularly funny event, or, perhaps, looking forward to tea-time!

Proverbs 31 makes fascinating reading, extolling the virtues of a good wife. Such a wife can, apparently, afford to be optimistic as her faith in God and her virtuous lifestyle combine to give her confidence. That's quite something, and the ideals of Proverbs 31 are to be held up as exemplary. What, though, today, of wives whose lives are loaded more in favour of fear than faith? I am thinking of the scourge of young girls being taken as wives (or, more accurately, sexual slaves) in countries where such barbaric practices are tolerated and even encouraged. Those "wives" need our prayers, so that they can be rescued and, maybe, one day, are able to smile again. Lord, have mercy. May they too find something to look forward to as you hear our prayers.

IN A CLASS OF HIS OWN

What did you go out to see? A man dressed in fine clothes?
(MATTHEW 11:8 **NIV**)

The actor Tom Hiddleston has taken part in a promotional campaign for the fashion designer Gucci, modelling shoes available for a mere £515, trousers costing £570, and a suit that would set you back £2,128 – I think I'll order two of everything! The ads also feature a glossy-haired Afghan Hound, who sits and stares at Hiddleston as he loafs about in his loafers, and I find the choice of an Afghan Hound interesting as the photoshoot is designed to promote opulence, and the Afghan fits the bill perfectly. Meg, for example, was well-bred with impeccable manners, but wouldn't have looked anywhere near as at home in this promotion, whereas the unnamed Afghan Hound, all elegance and silky locks, looks tailor-made to model for Gucci, every inch the classic example of sophistication.

I shan't actually be ordering two of everything (or even one of anything!), but what intrigues me is the way in which we associate wealth – high-end price tags – with success and breeding. Can we imagine, for example, a scruffy little Terrier or a manky old mongrel being considered for the Tom Hiddleston photoshoot? We are inclined to link refinement and class with accomplishment, whereas that isn't necessarily the case! Did Jesus wear fine clothes? Did he amass a wardrobe-full of designer label apparel? Was he known for frequenting only the homes of the rich and famous? Yet, he was God! He came full of grace and truth, yet was definitely "working class". What a paradox, and what a challenge to many of our assumptions! What a God!

WE'RE ALL GOING ON A SUMMER HOLIDAY!

One rests content

(PROVERBS 19:23 *NIV*)

I have been invited to give a dog a holiday by visiting that dog as part of my holiday! A business has opened up whereby people who want to go away on holiday but don't want to, or can't, take their dog(s) with them invite the likes of me to move into their house for a week or two, keeping Fido company. The idea is that dogs, although they will of course miss their owners, will feel comfortable in familiar surroundings and might even enjoy a little extra attention than they normally receive. Reasonable expenses are paid in respect of the fact that the dog-sitter also enjoys a holiday of sorts, making this arrangement a win-win!

General Wilfred Kitching CBE was international leader of The Salvation Army from 1954 to 1963, and an extremely busy man, head of an entire Christian denomination. Despite that, General Kitching adopted a rule whereby, unless he was travelling overseas, he refused to work past 8 p.m. He knew the benefits of rest and relaxation – recreation – realizing there was more to life than earning a living or even exercising one's ministry as General of an international movement. More to the point, Kitching balanced his life in such a way that he regarded overwork as detrimental to his relationship with God. Holidays? Relaxing evenings? Time to recharge our batteries, so to speak? All gifts of the God who made us and who knows how best we function.

HE GAVE US EYES TO SEE THEM

Lift up your eyes on high and see: who created these
(ISAIAH 40:26 **ESV**)

How often do we walk our dogs without fully appreciating the experience? I realize it's not always easy to savour one's surroundings – if it's pouring down with rain, for example, or your dog is fascinated by a muddy puddle you can't avoid stepping into, or if you have set out in biting winds! Ordinarily, though, there is much to see that maybe, if we are concentrating on our dog's behaviour or a particular route, we inadvertently overlook. Walking Meg and Skipper, I would occasionally see Kingfishers by the river or, more commonly, Red Kites flying overhead – a wonderful sight. Sometimes, a Heron would silently keep us in his gaze as we wandered by, and, once or twice, a White Egret. There is a lot to enjoy, as well as the actual pleasure of walking one's dog. Whoever would have thought that walking Meg and Skipper would offer so much more besides!

What is this life if, full of care,
We have no time to stand and stare?

(From "Leisure" by William Henry Davies, 1871–1940)

RESTLESS

There is anxiety by the sea, It cannot be calmed
(JEREMIAH 49:23 **NASB**)

Dear old Meg was, 99 per cent of the time, delightful company. One on occasion, though, we took her with us for a family holiday, staying in a pod in Seahouses, on the Northumberland coast. The design of the pod was based on an upturned rowing boat, if you can imagine that (though quite a bit larger!), and we settled down for our first night in our new accommodation. Meg, though, was having none of it (I still don't know why), and was as restless as could be, pacing up and down, making all sorts of noises, and depriving us of sleep. Eventually, I'd had enough, so I tied her up outside so that she could sleep on the veranda (please don't worry – it was a very warm night), but even there, she wasn't entirely happy, and wouldn't be calmed. We did at least, though, manage a decent night. I have no idea what was troubling her, but it sticks in my memory because it was very rare indeed for Meg to annoy me.

Have we trials and temptations?
Is there trouble anywhere?
We should never be discouraged,
Take it to the Lord in prayer.
Can we find a friend so faithful
Who will all our sorrows share?
Jesus knows our every weakness,
Take it to the Lord in prayer.

(Joseph Medlicott Scriven, 1819–86)

SNIFFING OUT GRACE

Jesus wept

(JOHN 11:35 **NIV**)

On that particular holiday, we visited "The Amaize-ing Maze" – a maze in a maize field! Paths had been constructed through a vast area of high-grown maize and, for a small fee, we were challenged to find our way from one end to the other. Needless to say, the maze of maize outwitted us as we ran into one dead end after another, until we eventually decided to abandon the project and retrace our footsteps back to the entrance. That, too, was easier said than done, until we noticed Meg sniffing her way through every twist and turn and, without one single mistake, leading us back whence we came. Her marvellous sense of smell proved ultra-reliable, and within a much shorter space of time than would otherwise have been the case, we followed Meg's nose and made it out! Amazing Meg!

Being lost, or feeling lost, not knowing which way to turn, can be frustrating, and it can be frightening. Losing one's bearings in a maze is neither here nor there, especially with a dog on hand to lead the way, but doing so in life is another matter altogether. Here's a poem I wrote about a man I saw who appeared not to know where to go next. As I share it with you, perhaps we can pray for any such who are known to us, that the Holy Spirit will guide them gently back to where they belong?

I saw a floppy sock today,
With a man attached, who had lost his way;
Crossing the road, bemused, alone,
Coat far too small; no comfort zone.
The sock, you see, was soaking wet
With rain, and hadn't sandal met
For quite some time.
Its owner stumbled; someone's son,
And Jesus wept for threads unspun.

A SILENT AND COMPLEX WOE

The Father of compassion and the God of all comfort
(2 CORINTHIANS 1:3 **NIV**)

Isn't the silence of loss difficult to explain? When a loved one leaves us, for example, but also when a beloved dog reaches the end of its days and the sense of absence is almost palpable? Those noises which perhaps we took for granted, the background sounds of everyday life, are suddenly silenced, and the sheer presence of a departed pet is no more. It's hard to take, and how much we would give for one more walk in the rain! Clean floors, dry coats, and uninterrupted evenings are unwanted if it means one's canine companion is around no longer, and lives only in memories.

Grief, we find – even grief for a beloved family dog – has its own rhythm. It is a phenomenon that cannot be hurried, bargained with, or even properly explained and understood. We say goodbye with our mouths, and with our intellects, but the heart (the soul?) takes so much longer to come to terms with the sorrow of parting. It is as though such slowness is part and parcel of the healing process, and may even be a blessing in disguise. With that in mind, you may care to locate a copy of "The Sunset Poem" from Dylan Thomas's *Under Milk Wood*. It's an odd little ditty in many ways, and is also known as the "Prayer of the Reverend Eli Jenkins", but it goes some way towards capturing at least the pathos at play when a pet dies. I warmly commend the poem to you, but do be warned – it can be a tear-jerker! For those experiencing loss right now – of a loved one, of a dog – there is tremendous comfort in knowing that God knows our hearts better than we know them ourselves; our slow-healing hearts, our torn hearts, our distressed hearts. Ours is the God of silence.

THE DAY AHEAD

*All these blessings will come on you and accompany you if you obey the
Lord your God*
(DEUTERONOMY 28:2 **NIV**)

As I type, I am looking at a replica of a seventeenth-century woodcut depicting a hunter and his dog setting out for the day. It's not a great work, and even an expert would be hard-pressed to identify which breed of dog is featured, but what catches the eye is the hound's stance, and the woodcutter is to be congratulated on capturing exactly the right mingling of the dog's submission to its owner and eager expectation. For that reason, I warm to this otherwise unimpressive woodcut!

Submission and expectation! Would we regard that as a fair description of obedience and belief, spiritually speaking? All we receive from God is due entirely to his grace, I realize that, for we have no merit of our own, but any reading of Scripture indicates a secondary relationship within our primary relationship with the Father; the correlation between our submission and our expectation. That is, if we are exercising due submission to God's will, then we can afford to expect his blessings (not least, unbroken fellowship). On the other hand, if we are living in rebellion, then I am not so sure blessings will follow. God's love remains the same, but we find our greatest happiness when we obey. Conversely, we find unrest and disquiet of soul when we persist in disobedience, though we remain dearly loved. How will we set out for this day? With a submissive heart and (therefore) an expectant demeanour? With God's help, may that be so for us all.

NOT LOST. NOT FORGOTTEN.

Deep calls to deep
(PSALM 42:7 **NIV**)

Do you remember my mention of PAT Dogs (Pets As Therapy)? A heart-warming story emerges from the John Coupland Hospital in Gainsborough, Lincolnshire, England, of Alfie, an eight-year-old Bichon Frise who has completed his training to visit elderly patients on the wards. The healing power of a visit from a PAT dog was summed up in this quote from a member of staff:

You could see the positive impact that Alfie was having on particular patients, especially those with dementia. They were more animated and chatty than usual and it definitely brightened the day.

Heather showed me an internet clip of an elderly lady living with dementia, and whose days were spent, by and large, sitting motionless, seemingly oblivious to most of what was happening around her, and apparently incapable of conversation. A visitor called to see this lady, and sang to her; words from well-known hymns. The transformation was remarkable, as something in her tortured brain picked up on lyrics she would have sung hundreds of times over the years, before dementia took its cruel toll. Her cognitive abilities will probably never recover, and will almost certainly deteriorate. There, though, in that internet clip, was a glimpse of grace at work, deep in the human heart. Love never fails.

HOME COMFORTS

I was sick and you visited me
(MATTHEW 25:36 **ESV**)

Alfie the Bichon Frise fulfils a marvellous role for people who have had pets over the years at home but are no longer capable of looking after an animal. Hospital patients, for example, and those living in residential homes, who will miss the affection and physical contact a dog provides, are able to meet a friendly dog who can be stroked, and will sit on their lap for a while. Such visits are a tremendous boost to morale as those whose days can be lonely enjoy talking to their PAT visitor. Good for Alfie!

A friend of mine, a retired Salvation Army officer, spends hours and hours of her retirement voluntarily visiting hospital wards. I really do take my hat off to her, as it's a demanding ministry and not one I think I could sustain for very long. (I do not, incidentally, compare her to a Bichon Frise!) Perhaps today we could spare a thought, and a prayer, for those in need of long-term care, who may never again see the homes they have lived in for years. Likewise, maybe we could pray God's blessing on those whose ministry is to faithfully visit such people? Theirs is a wonderfully selfless work.

GOOD FOR THE SOUL

When I refused to confess my sin, my body wasted away, and I groaned all day long
(PSALM 32:3 **NLT**)

So, what difference does a visit from Alfie actually make? Well, generally speaking, research indicates that stroking a dog tends to reduce blood pressure, and has a calming effect. Indeed, one website lists the following benefits in which dogs can improve the health of us mere humans:

1) Lower blood pressure.

2) Stress reduction.

3) Lower risk for heart attacks.

4) Lower risk for strokes.

5) Help with alleviating depression.

6) Walking a dog keeps you physically fit.

7) Dog owners develop fewer allergies.

8) Strengthening of the immune system.

9) Benefits to mental health.

10) Stronger bones.[1]

Not bad!

The psalmist listed some of his ailments and troubles, which he felt had befallen him as a result of his failure to confess his sins. Whether or not he owned a dog, I can't say, and it might have helped him a little if he had, but he felt a great deal better once he had made a clean breast of it by confessing; not necessarily to a priest, or to anyone else for that matter, but to God – to God, that is, who longs to forgive and restore. Spiritual well-being? With or without a dog, mercy is available, should we feel the need to come clean today.

---

1   Adapted from www.dogstrust.org.uk

THERE'S WORK TO BE DONE

We are God's handiwork, created in Christ Jesus to do good works, which God
prepared in advance for us to do
(EPHESIANS 2:10 **NIV**)

Did you know ancient Egyptians bred three different types of dog – a guard dog, a hunting dog, and a decorative friendly one? Cubs were identified for character traits, and allocated their life's work according to whichever characteristics were to the fore. Dogs who looked to be particularly brave and loyal were trained as guard dogs, cubs who showed an aptitude for harrying and cornering quarry were taught how to hunt, while those demonstrating no great amount of bravery or specific intelligence were kept as show dogs to be decorated and pampered. A good system, do you think? It seems to have served the ancient Egyptians well enough, so who am I to argue!

In the service of Jesus, there's a place for all. It goes without saying we can't all do the same job or have the same ministry, but none need ever feel excluded. Jesus knows, more than anyone, which skills, gifts, and graces we possess, and has a work and a sphere of service available for everyone, whatever – and wherever – that might be. Have you found and enjoyed your vocation? If so, thank God. Are you still hoping to do so? Place everything in the hands of the Lord. He will not fail you.

THE ROCK OF ALL AGES

Christ Jesus came into the world to save sinners
(I TIMOTHY 1:15 **NIV**)

The ancient Romans, on the other hand, were much more interested in breeding fighting dogs for the circus, and to that end, Mastiffs were sought and prized. I do not condone the appalling treatment of dogs being used to fight in circuses, but have a look at pictures of Mastiffs and you will at least understand why the Romans used them in such ways. They (Mastiffs, not Romans) derive from Molosser Dogs; solidly built breeds that descend from the same common ancestor. (Molossia was an area of ancient Epirus, where large Shepherd Dogs were known as Molussus.) Some of them are enormous, and all the more beautiful because of that; gentle giants, I should imagine, which makes their being forced into circus fighting all the sadder. The word *dogo*, incidentally, is a Spanish word meaning "Molosser". I mention that in case you weren't aware of it!

The Incarnation took place when the Romans were at the height of their powers. If we think about it, Christ could have come to earth at any time, yet he chose to make his appearance at a moment in history when a ruthless and hostile regime held sway. Was he making a point? Was his arrival timed to align with prophecies concerning his birth? I don't pretend to know, but what I do know is that he came, and did so in the full awareness of what awaited him in the form of Roman brutality, thuggery, and execution. Perhaps, then, *when* he came is not the question, so much as *why* he came. The answer – for all ages – lies in today's text. Hallelujah!

LIFE, DEATH AND TAXES

Jesus said to him [Zacchaeus], "Today salvation has come to this house"
(LUKE 19:9 **NIV**)

I have just discovered that Doberman Pinchers are named after a German gentleman called Karl Friedrich Louis Dobermann, who kept himself busy by working as a night watchman, tax collector, and dog pound keeper and who, in the 1890s, needed a guard dog to keep him safe on his rounds. Apparently, Herr Dobermann looked at the dogs in his charge, which included a Great Dane, a Greyhound, and a Rottweiler, and came up with the Doberman Pinscher, or Terrier. (A Pinscher, by the way, was most commonly used in ratting.) Whoever would have thought that a tax collector in need of better protection would have given us such a sleek and impressive breed!

Let's face it – tax collectors are never going to win popularity contests! With great respect, their job marks them out as people who will, with state permission, organize the legal removal of hard-earned money from our bank accounts, something hardly likely to endear them to the general population! What do we make, then, of Jesus' encounter with Zacchaeus, who was not only a tax collector, but the chief tax collector! Corrupt, dishonest, greedy, exploitative, yet, for all that, the object of Jesus' full attention. This tells me so much about grace, as we see Christ making his way to the house of the most unpopular man in town. An easy visit? Unlikely. A popular move? Not a bit of it. Tough love? Too right! This is our God.

BE CAREFUL

Beware of false prophets who come disguised as harmless sheep but are really vicious wolves

(MATTHEW 7:15 **NLT**)

As you know by now, we Poxons head to Scotland from time to time, paying our family dues and enjoying the Perthshire scenery. It is nigh on impossible to visit any tourist shop in that part of the world without seeing all manner of West Highland Terrier souvenirs on sale – replica toys, embroidered scarves, lapel badges, postcards, and so on. West Highland Terriers are hugely popular as a symbol of Scottish identity and kept nowadays, by and large, as pets. In days gone by, though, they were bred as hunting dogs, their famous white coats distinguishing them from foxes and otters against dark, heathery Scottish backgrounds. Maybe their modern-day domestication disguises a feisty, tenacious temperament (they are renowned for being bossy!), but wildlife such as rabbits and rats will soon find out, should they come too close, that a hunter's instincts never quite disappear!

Personally, I have always found Westies friendly and not particularly aggressive – but then I'm not an otter or a hare! Their fluffy white coats lend them an air of cuteness, hence the abundance of keepsakes. Does that remind you of anything? What was it Jesus said about wolves in sheep's clothing? He warned, didn't he, that sometimes, that which can appear harmless and innocuous – what is more harmless than a sheep! – can emerge as dangerous and ferocious. Jesus was warning his followers – you and me – against gullibility, especially in spiritual terms; against that which presents itself as acceptable, yet can prove as deadly as a wolf, which can easily tear to shreds without a flicker of mercy. Let us be on our guard out there! Jesus will help us.

LOCKED IN TO LOVE

I desire mercy

(HOSEA 6:6 **NIV**)

Speaking of Scotland, an idea piloted in America is making its way across the Scottish penal system, whereby violent and unstable prisoners are brought into regular contact with therapy dogs, and the signs are encouraging, with fewer disturbances being reported, and improved relationships between prison officers and convicts. American studies demonstrated that the feeling of unconditional love and acceptance experienced by prisoners who may not ever have been loved in their entire lives triggered the production of interferon, a protein that strengthens the immune system. Likewise, the stimulation of endorphins, which act as a natural anaesthetic. The psychology behind the therapy is that offering prisoners the opportunity to look after creatures weaker than themselves – small dogs, say, that trust them and depend on them – boosts self-esteem and self-respect, providing a purpose in what might otherwise be a bleak life behind bars.

I wrote a poem about a man whose tattoo suggested he had abandoned any notion of mercy. I'll share it with you, but not without first thanking God for the mercy represented in the dog prison therapy programmes towards those who may feel – mistakenly – they have exhausted God's store.

Maybe, my Lord, it made you sad too?
The man in the pub, I mean (well, his tattoo);
"No Fear" and "No Mercy" inked blue into skin;
No mercy? None given? None taken, for sin?
Sweet Jesus, forgive him, and then, at the last,
Ignore that tattoo as a thing of the past.
Have mercy, dear Saviour, and heed not that ink;
A parlour once visited, too young to think.
For, Lord, you love mercy; it oils pearly gates,
The queen of all graces our great need translates.

LOVE SO AMAZING

The fragrance of your breath like apples
(SONG OF SONGS 7:8 *NIV*)

I told you the story about Meg leading us safely out of the Maze of Maize. Bright as she was, I wonder how her sense of smell would have compared to that of a wolf, or a coyote, or other wild dogs. Wolves, for example, passing downwind of potential prey, turn to scent upwind, and can detect the smell of their victims from up to roughly 1.5 miles (2.5 km) away. Quite remarkable, but dogs (including wolves and coyotes, jackals and dingoes, etc.), have a sensory surface area within their noses considerably larger than that found in a human nose. Roughly speaking, our nasal sensory area, unfolded and spread out, would be approximately the size of a postage stamp, whereas Meg's, say, would be about the size of a postcard, resulting in a sensitivity that can be up to a million times greater than yours or mine.

King Solomon didn't hold back when it came to his sensuously poetic description of his beloved. Whether he was writing with a literal woman in mind (one of his wives or concubines, maybe), or a fantasy female who filled his thoughts, we don't know. Maybe, he was referring to his love for his much-loved nation. Possibly, he was waxing eloquent about the love of God. (My guess is, his poem was always meant to be overtly sexual and unambiguous.) Either way, he gave full vent to his feelings, penning a love letter of high sensitivity and potency. My British reserve notwithstanding, I can't help but admire such abandon; a love that gives itself completely, unashamedly, and wholeheartedly; a foreshadowing of a love that gave its all on Calvary and which, in turn, demands my all in response. Love, indeed, so divine.

BOSS

Those who live according to the flesh have their minds set on what the flesh desires; but those who live in accordance with the Spirit have their minds set on what the Spirit desires

(ROMANS 8:5 *NIV*)

That highly developed sense of smell means dogs are happiest when they are sniffing – ask any dog walker out in the rain who can't understand what their dog finds so fascinating about a bin! To that end, it is mostly smell that dominates a dog's entire life. A dog will instinctively smell people, other dogs, familiar objects, routes, furniture, and so on, building up a library of information and exploring new smells with every outing. All manner of primeval reasons contribute to this state of mind, and this obsession with smelling is put to good use when dogs are employed to sniff out drugs and explosives, but there is no disputing the fact that the wet nose runs the show! Everything else, it seems, is secondary.

I once heard a preacher preach on the question of who was pulling the strings. He spoke well from the story of Job, inviting his listeners to explore the various scenarios at play as though the characters were puppets, then asking the congregation to decide whether God or Satan was in charge of their actions and words – pulling their strings, so to speak. Some of what he said was light-hearted, but it made for an excellent approach not only to that particular narrative, but to life in general; that is to say, who is the boss? What dominates? What instincts do we obey? I've thought about that sermon often. Who is running the show?

GAME FOR THE GOSPEL

The city shall be full of boys and girls playing in its streets
(ZECHARIAH 8:5 **ESV**)

Not that it matters nowadays, but when I was a teenager, my cousin came to stay with us, and dented my juvenile pride by treating my brother to a night out while I was left at home! I must confess to indulging in some kind of pity party while I rather sulkily watched TV and thought of he and she cavorting. We lived beside the seaside at the time, leading them to indulge in a spot of Bingo on the promenade, and I can't recall having been quite so jealous of Bingo players either before or since that memorable evening! Such distant memories came flooding back when I saw a board game on sale – Dog Bingo! I kid you not! The game works on the same principles as the Bingo my cousin and brother enjoyed without me (not that I bear a grudge all these years later, you understand), except sixty-four assorted dogs are listed instead of numbers. I like it. Do you think I should invite my cousin over for a game of Dog Bingo, but not invite my brother? (I'm only kidding – honestly!)

Most Sundays, I preach somewhere or other, and am encouraged to "bring a word" for the children and young people present. I try to make it fun; introducing reminders of the love of God within what I hope is an interesting presentation. "Bible Bingo" is one of my attempts at being entertaining, enthralling, and evangelical all at the same time, whereby I use not Bingo numbers or the names of sixty-four dogs, but Bible verses, with chocolates as prizes. Granted, it's not something Billy Graham ever felt the need to consider doing, and I realize there are those who will be horrified at the thought of Bingo in church, but if one youngster comes to know that God loves him or her, then it's all worth it … Incidentally, God loves my brother and my cousin too!

PUTTING ON A SHOW!

*Since the creation of the world God's invisible qualities – his eternal power
and divine nature – have been clearly seen, being understood from what
has been made*

(ROMANS 1:20 **NIV**)

The multimillionaire music mogul and TV personality, Simon Cowell, celebrates his birthday today – happy birthday, Simon! On-screen, Simon Cowell portrays an image of cool efficiency bordering on arrogance, and is sometimes abrupt in his comments about the musical acts he judges live on television. Personally, I think quite a bit of it is an act in itself, because what I regard as the "real" Simon Cowell peeks through whenever he is confronted with dogs – dogs, say, who are performing as part of an audition, or, more noticeably, whenever he is seen with his own pets, two Yorkshire Terriers (brother and sister) christened Squiddly and Diddly. Suddenly, the "hard" appearance melts, and a much softer side of Mr Cowell emerges. Those two Terriers manage to do what many people fail to do in bringing out the nicer side of the powerful presenter!

Simon Cowell is a showman to his fingertips, and knows full well viewers tune in to listen to his controversial put-downs and caustic comments. On one level, it's a game; he has a product to sell, and viewing figures are the lifeblood of his industry, though it's horrible to see people being hurt. Cowell knows the value of an audience – and so does God! Look around you ... towering trees, foaming seas, intimidating mountains, swaying fields, gigantic icebergs, running rivers, floating clouds, painted rainbows, delicate flowers, and so on. The list is endless, almost, representing the glorious craftsmanship of the Master Showman ... all for us to enjoy and appreciate.

THIS IS OUR CHURCH AND YOU ARE WELCOME TO IT!

Treat the stranger who sojourns with you as the native among you
(LEVITICUS 19:34 **ESV**)

I received a leaflet from the Guide Dogs service, listing ways in which I might be able to support their work, and I make no apology for relisting those ways here, in case you might be interested. Please don't feel obliged to respond, as we shall remain friends even if this is not for you, but Guide Dogs would be delighted to hear from you at www.guidedogs.org.uk/supportus.

These volunteering opportunities are set before me:

Helping out with walkies
Fundraising
Raising Guide Dog awareness at work, school or university
Organising sponsorship
Arranging "Challenge Events"
Distributing "Dogalogues" (catalogues selling doggie items!)
Heading up publicity campaigns

Taking my daughter back to university after a visit, I popped in to the parish church close to where she studies, and was so pleased to receive a warm welcome, especially as this was mid-afternoon, when it might be expected no one would be around the church. A delightful team of Welcomers greeted me at various stages as I nosed around, and one asked me if I was OK. They were all volunteers. What wonderful opportunities exist for those who have a bit of time on their hands, and whose gifts are suited to making visitors welcome and even offering a cup of tea. Who knows what impression this may make on a stranger? Interested?

THERE IS GOD

Are you not from everlasting, O Lord my God
(HABAKKUK 1:12 **ESV**)

Our son, Alistair, is celebrating his birthday today! Happy birthday, Alistair! While his sister, Jasmine, is a creative sort, Alistair is a scientist, and likes nothing more than applying scientific logic to life's issues. Thus it was that he found himself determined to teach Skipper some basic fetch and retrieve tricks (before we discovered Skipper's senility, that is). Alistair's approach was to apply fundamental, logical principles, and to some extent, he succeeded, even though Skipper's attempts at catching a ball were nearly always more hilarious than helpful. Despite Alistair's impressively patient efforts at teaching Skipper what to do next, logically, Skipper's grasp of matters improved little, though he seemed to enjoy what he obviously regarded as just a bit of fun, endearingly failing to comprehend what he was supposed to be learning. Alistair gave up in the end, swallowing the hard lesson (for a scientist) that there is not always an exact formula for success!

The parent of an autistic child once pointed out that "nature knows nothing of straight lines". I like that phrase, for it reminds me that life, even the Christian life, doesn't always pan out as we think and hope it might. Our best-laid plans have a nasty habit of backfiring or collapsing, sometimes in ways that are calamitous (inoperable cancer), and sometimes in ways that don't matter much (teaching Skipper to fetch a ball). Our only constant is God. When all else fails, there is God. Through every changing scene, there is God. When life goes wrong, there is God.

LOOKING AFTER BABY

I gave you milk, not solid food, for you were not yet ready for it
(1 CORINTHIANS 3:2 **NIV**)

As I write, news is emerging of the undiagnosed illness from which the late, great Robin Williams was suffering at the time of his tragic suicide in 2014. Williams knew something was wrong with his brain, and wanted to "reboot it", but only now do we realize he was a victim of Lewy body disease (LBD), a strain of dementia with symptoms including paranoia, delusions, insomnia, tremors, and memory problems. Robin Williams was afflicted with a severe form of LBD. That is indeed sad, but we remember this genius of the acting profession best by recalling his films, not least *Old Dogs*, in which he and John Travolta starred as two bachelors who become the unexpected caretakers of twin children. Successful businessmen, Williams and Travolta find their lives, and their careers, turned thoroughly upside down as they encounter one mishap after another in their efforts to combine professional and parental responsibilities. These two "old dogs" – entrenched in their routines and lifestyles – soon come to realize they will need to learn new tricks if they are to keep their heads above water!

Can we imagine the "new tricks" the first disciples would have had to learn after encountering Jesus? One minute, they were fishermen, businessmen, publicans, and so on – the next, they were called upon to be evangelists and missionaries! Quite a steep learning curve for those guys! Steeper still, we might imagine, the new set of religious beliefs they were expected to absorb as they stepped into a radical culture of as-yet-unexplored faith. Let us pray today for new converts to Christianity. As Williams and Travolta discovered, pitfalls are plentiful in any new experience! All the more reason, then, for us to support spiritual "babes" in prayer.

CAVEMEN AND CHRIST

When Gentiles, who do not have the law, do by nature things required by the law, they are a law for themselves, even though they do not have the law. They show that the requirements of the law are written on their hearts, their consciences also bearing witness, and their thoughts sometimes accusing them and at other times even defending them

(ROMANS 2:14–15 **NIV**)

An exciting discovery has revealed evidence of what could be the earliest known journey in British history, a trip of roughly 250 miles from Wiltshire to Yorkshire, England, said to have taken place approximately 7,000 years ago by a Mesolithic hunter-gatherer and his dog. Scientific investigation of a dog's tooth found close to the historic site of Stonehenge suggests the pair made the trek on foot. Examination of the unearthed tooth is said to demonstrate that Mesolithic man was keeping company with domesticated dogs in that era, probably using them for hunting, and that such dogs fed on salmon, trout, wildfowl, and deer, drinking river water. Scientists and archaeologists speculate that the dog who originally owned the tooth was some kind of Alsatian, judging by its shape, size, and the make-up of tooth enamel.

What a find! One solitary tooth that, thanks to the expertise of those who are examining it, can tell us so much. Ancient history has been made to come alive! The man who walked his dog all those centuries ago – 5,000 years before Jesus – knew nothing of the gospel, yet grace spans the aeons, and there is every possibility he made his peace with God – as he understood God – in his primitive way. I am a great believer in God's grace being sufficient for those who responded, BC, to the light they were shown, and who lived accordingly, following the dictates of conscience, even though they had no sight of Calvary and redemption as we know it. This is grace. This is our eternal God.

KEEPING WATCH

Thou God seest me
(GENESIS 16:13 **KJV**)

Dog expert Dr Roger Mugford, mentioned previously in these pages, has suggested the use of cameras left recording dogs while their owners are out of the house. The good doctor is interested in finding out more about what pets do, and how they are, when they are left alone; whether they pine and sulk, misbehave, or are perfectly alright, the idea being to show owners what goes on and whether they might need to consider changing working patterns if their dogs are suffering because of their absence. That, of course, might not be possible or practical, but I like the suggestion as it might highlight evidence of a dog struggling to cope, whose owners are unaware of any problems.

There is an old TV sitcom in which a framed tapestry hangs from the wall of a dreary living room, featuring the embroidered text, "Thou, God, seest me". The placing of the verse so that it can be seen in the background whenever the camera pans that way is clearly meant to convey the impression that God is stern, anti-enjoyment, generally angry, and a killjoy of the first order, and that those in his view had better watch their step, lest he strike them dead. God does of course watch us, day and night, so the embroidery is quite correct, but only ever out of deep concern for our well-being, longing for us to keep well by keeping close to him. His watchful eye is benevolent, and in that, we should rejoice, for his attentive nature means that he knows, immediately, if we are struggling. This is God.

MAY I HAVE YOUR ATTENTION, PLEASE

I have revealed ... and proclaimed
(ISAIAH 43:12 *NIV*)

I expect you, like me, have worked with all sorts of ministers over the years; some with lovely skills in pastoral matters, others with a gift for teaching, and those with a flair for evangelism (though none of those need be mutually exclusive). It has been my privilege to work alongside evangelists from Counties, a charity devoted to outreach within the United Kingdom. Theirs is a great ministry, and one of their missioners visits lunch clubs, groups, and gatherings with his Springer Spaniel, Tango, plus various others of his four working gun dogs. They have a great time, he and Tango performing a dog-handling routine and a demonstration of dog-training and communication – including plenty of jokes and action! – before the evangelist talks to those whose attention he has gained about the various ways in which God wants to communicate with us. So much for never working with children or animals!

Wouldn't it be interesting to actually list the ways in which we notice God communicating with us over, say, the next twenty-four hours? My guess is, we would be pleasantly surprised (and reassured) as the list grew; God grabbing our attention through, maybe, the weather, then continuing to speak to us by way of nature and scenery, his word, his abiding presence, the sight of a bird in flight, a conversation, a hymn, a radio broadcast, and so on ... all because of love, as he endeavours to walk with us and talk with us ... do you have pen and paper ready?

BOUNDLESS

He saved us through the washing of rebirth and renewal by the Holy Spirit, whom he poured out on us generously

(TITUS 3:5–6 **NIV**)

I have seen pictures of Tango at work, and he has that endearing mix beloved of Springer Spaniels, of giving every appearance of being as daft as a brush, yet in reality, being highly intelligent. It comes as no surprise that Counties are only too happy to "employ" him in outreach evangelism, for Tango appears to have a charm that transcends age groups, appealing to men, women, and children alike in a way that most evangelists would love to! God bless Tango and his owner as they travel around presenting the good news of God's love for one and all.

There, in Tango's enthusiastic, tail-wagging way, is the grace of God in a nutshell; abounding, impartial, generous, and not easily discouraged! Tango the Springer Spaniel will run and run, as will an indefatigable God in his pursuit of the lost and the hurting. Tango barely recognizes age or gender; he doesn't distinguish between rich and poor, clever or not; his giant heart only ever wants to love. The love of God is freely available, charming and endearing. It has neither limit nor measure.

NEVER ALONE

I will ask the Father, and he will give you another Helper, who will stay with you
(JOHN 14:16 **GNT**)

You will remember Dr Roger Mugford's idea of cameras around the house recording the behaviour of domesticated dogs when they are left alone. He might be on to something, as it seems there are important guidelines to bear in mind when considering the "home alone" syndrome from a canine point of view. Broadly speaking, they are as follows:

- Never show guilt when you are leaving the house. (Your dog will sense it, become anxious, and possibly wreak havoc.)
- Check to see if your dog sleeps contentedly, or if separation anxiety is leaving your pet exhausted (quite a different kind of sleep).
- Teach your dog to stay calm, using techniques any vet would be happy to suggest.
- Tire your dog out before you leave for work! (Easier said than done!)
- Keep your dog occupied while you are away (toys, chews, even video gadgets).
- Consider doggie day care (a neighbour popping in, or a professional visitor/ walker).
- Consider a partner dog, on the basis that two dogs are sometimes better than one.

These guidelines need to be taken seriously, as no dog owner wants their pet to suffer. Yet, their implementation would undoubtedly require patience, application, repetition, and diligence. Similarly, following Christ as a lifestyle choice calls for such qualities in prayer, behaviour, and Bible reading. The good news is, we aren't expected to meet the high standards of holiness and discipleship by ourselves. We are never left alone in our pursuit of Christ-likeness. The Holy Spirit will help, support, and guide, day in and day out.

HOME IS WHERE THE HEART IS

I will live among the people
(EXODUS 29:45 **NLT**)

As I write, my birthday is approaching, and I am toying with the idea of asking for a dog as a present – a rehomed "oldie" would be my preference, and I have been browsing websites, searching for a rescue dog to adopt. It may or may not happen – there are so many factors to consider – but I have my eye on an eleven-year-old Dalmatian called Diamond, currently being cared for by the National Animal Welfare Trust. Diamond the Dalmatian looks suitably forlorn in her photographs, and certainly makes a good case for adoption, but what a dilemma! To adopt, or not to adopt? Now that I have spotted Diamond, my heart is torn. There is no question I would love to give her a home, but I have to ask if my circumstances allow for that …

Isn't it a good thing God doesn't hesitate in deciding to adopt us into his family? Regarding Diamond, I need to weigh up practical considerations, yet God has no need to procrastinate; his mind is made up, his heart is set on adoption, and he is immediately capable of arranging a spiritual home for us within his being and presence. Moreover, he longs not only to provide a new home for us, but to live within us too, by the gracious indwelling of his Spirit, so that we live with him and he lives within. What could be more secure? What better expressions of welfare and trust could we ever hope for? This is God, our Father. We are rehomed in love.

DIVINE DISTRACTIONS

He performs wonders that cannot be fathomed
(JOB 5:9 **NIV**)

One concern regarding Diamond would be leaving her indoors, without me, should I need to be away for a few hours. Granted, there are enough comings and goings in our house for that not to be a massive problem, but it would prey on my mind, for all that. The option of a companion dog is a non-starter, as Diamond can't cope well with canine company, and I don't fancy the responsibility or expense of a pair of pooches. Doggie day care might work, but recruiting professional help is expensive, and my budget might not stretch far enough. How about, then, Dalmatian distraction tactics in the form of chewy toys and so on, including a popular range of indestructible cones filled with treats that can, apparently, occupy dogs for hours as the treats are difficult to extract? I like this idea! Diamond would be kept busy and happy, extricating snacks, then enjoying them, and I would have peace of mind knowing she wasn't bored or distressed.

The older I become, and the more I read of the Bible, the more I realize what I don't actually know! The longer I walk with Christ, the more I sense my ignorance of his ways, as it seems there is always something new to learn, even though we might assume the opposite to be true. This paradox is a rich blessing, in that the beauty of pilgrimage is that the more we learn (of Christ, of God), the more we discover there is to unearth; the deeper we dig, the more precious the spiritual gems we extricate. A boring faith? Not by that reckoning! A faith – a relationship – worth gnawing at, in the hope of finding a hidden glimpse of truth? Definitely!

PEOPLE AT PEACE

The earth is at rest and quiet
(ISAIAH 14:7 **NLT**)

If and when I left Meg and Skipper home alone (Meg took it in her stride, while Skipper was a nightmare), I made sure the radio was on before I went out. BBC Radio Four was my station of choice, as it features people talking all day and hardly ever offers music. I thought a range of voices – presenters and guests chatting – would provide some sort of company, and as both Meg and Skipper were hard of hearing, I wondered, too, if the radio turned up loud might act as some kind of security, would-be burglars (not that we have much worth stealing!) being deterred by what they might think was an unusually noisy but well-spoken family. Did it help? I don't know, but it did at least break what might have been an unbearable silence for those two old mutts.

My wife, Heather, works best in silence, and can't easily cope with distractions of noise. (Best to leave her in peace if she has a project to think about or emails to write!) I, on the other hand, love to have the radio on while I type. Without it, I am quickly distracted. What a lovely surprise I had, then, when we went together on a Silent Retreat Day. I hadn't thought I would enjoy it, whereas I knew Heather would. How wrong could I have been! It was marvellous! It was a privilege, despite my reservations, to spent hours in silence. I chose to sit in a chapel most of the time, but the option of wandering in beautiful grounds was also available. May I recommend such an experience? Time out, with God, in quietness. Would you be as reluctant as I was? Allow me to encourage you to explore the idea!

UP AND OVER

As your days, so shall your strength be
(DEUTERONOMY 33:25 **ESV**)

Should the cone of treats fail, I think I would probably opt for some kind of doggie therapy; gently teaching Diamond coping techniques based on reassurance – lessons in separation that would enable her to realize I will always return, and that my care of her is on my terms. She would learn that I couldn't always be with her, but there was no need for panic. I tried such things with Skipper, having read books by experts, but I'm afraid they were all to no avail. Skipper would go into stressed mode as soon as I left the house, and would sit by the door until the moment of my return. Sadly, he also took to gnawing his paws, such were his levels of anxiety. Poor old Skipper. We never did hit upon a real solution.

I'm not a great fan of any theology presenting the Christian faith as the cure-all for every difficulty known to humankind. I love the Catholic phrase "the cure of souls", but I am yet to be convinced of teaching equating the Christian pathway to a bed of roses – largely because I have yet to encounter a Christian without at least one problem, including the man I meet in the mirror every morning! My experience of pilgrimage is that God, far from removing or dissolving the obstacles life puts in our way, helps us through them, or over them. No magic wand exists, but God promises to provide strength for the journey, and all we require to be overcomers. What hurdles are you facing today? Ask the Saviour to help you. He will.

PRAY OR PREY

The mind governed by the Spirit is life and peace
(ROMANS 8:6 *NIV*)

Skipper would always be fast asleep by the time I returned, which I somewhat naively ascribed to old age. Quite possibly, that was the case, but now that I am a little older and wiser, I am inclined to think he slept because he had first endured an exhausting period of frantic desperation triggered by my departure. Apparently, some dogs find the first fifteen minutes of separation from their owners intolerable, and are beside themselves with worry. They salivate, pant rapidly, pace up and down, and leap at the door; all with an increased heartrate. This frenzy leads to exhaustion – hence, maybe, the sleeping Skipper I always found lying across the threshold, poor old boy.

I hesitate to mention this, as I am no expert, but I am interested in worry and how it relates to those professing faith in Christ. I have, though, read around the subject, and am intrigued by what sometimes appears to be a contradiction between Jesus' counsel not to worry and the increasing tendency of human beings – including believers – to do quite the opposite, hence the modern proliferation of counsellors, therapists, and so on. Likewise, the increasing use of medication such as antidepressants, as we gaze at a troubled world and find ourselves to have troubled lives. Prayer – meditation – is a tremendous therapy, creating, as it does, perspective and peace. Without it, we are vulnerable, and prey to a range of worries. Prayer changes things. We cope best on our knees.

ON GUARD

The letter that he took to the king of Israel read: "With this letter I am sending my servant Naaman to you so that you may cure him of his leprosy." As soon as the king of Israel read the letter, he tore his robes and said, "Am I God? Can I kill and bring back to life? Why does this fellow send someone to me to be cured of his leprosy? See how he is trying to pick a quarrel with me!"

(2 KINGS 5:6–7 **NIV**)

I have been reading about 2nd Lieutenant David Render, a British soldier who served in France during World War Two. He was assigned to a tank division, and was on patrol one day when he spotted a stray German Shepherd, an enemy animal trained to sniff out mines. Taking pity on the GSD, Lieutenant Render and his comrades adopted it and even made it an honorary crew member! Unfazed by the din of fierce battle raging all around, their new mascot slept contentedly in the body of the tank – grateful, no doubt, to be cared for, fed, and sheltered after a time wandering in fear and hunger, exposed to the elements and in great danger.

There is no such thing as an enemy dog! Dogs know nothing of nationality, even in times of international conflict, and I have always been astonished and saddened by tales of absurd hostility dished out to German Shepherds and Dachshunds when Britain was at war with Germany. We do, though, sometimes treat equally innocent foreigners with suspicion, as witnessed by the influx of immigrants to Europe in these days, many of whom are homeless, frightened, defenceless, and hungry yet, still, regarded with fear and caution, and sometimes treated appallingly, when the majority are victims of warfare with little choice but to wander in hope of finding kindness. Read around today's text, then consider how mistrust can all too easily lead to aggression, when compassion should be the order of the day.

NO TURNING BACK

Jesus replied, "No one who puts a hand to the plough and looks back is fit for service in the kingdom of God"

(LUKE 9:62 **NIV**)

The writer, India Knight, proud owner of Brodie, her Wheaten Terrier, has declared that "most people shouldn't get a dog".[1] As I am thinking of doing just that, my ears pricked up like Skipper's used to, when I noticed her statement. India is adamant in her opinion that the majority of potential dog owners fail to realize the extent to which ownership will impact their lives, maintaining that such lives really do need to be rearranged around the presence of a pet. I don't think I agree with such a blanket statement as "most people shouldn't get a dog", but I endorse her caution that adopting or buying a dog will inevitably mean permanent adjustments to one's routine, and her warning that such adjustments need to be carefully considered.

I have always felt a twinge of sympathy for those willing volunteers who had seen Jesus at work and volunteered to follow him, only for their enthusiasm to be dampened, if not squashed altogether. Granted, Jesus was at pains to flag up the terms and conditions of discipleship – all or nothing, in a nutshell – but I can't help feeling sorry for those who were keen to support his revolution but were then quickly made aware of some of Christ's reservations. Fair enough – Jesus didn't want to hoodwink anyone, and he played a straight bat, but I would hate anyone to be discouraged. How about we pray today for new converts, say, or candidates for ministry, that they would make their commitments with their eyes wide open, but would also discover the fortitude to stick with their resolve?

---

1   India Knight, *The Goodness of Dogs* (London: Penguin, 2016)

TO LOVE WHERE LOVE IS NOT RETURNED

These three remain: faith, hope and love. But the greatest of these is love
(1 CORINTHIANS 13:13 *NIV*)

My search for a worthy successor to Meg and Skipper leads me to look at websites offering dogs for rehoming. Plenty of possibilities present themselves, but one in particular has caught my attention; a mixed-breed Collie-type dog who has been badly treated and is now in need of tender, loving care. This poor creature was left outside most of the time by his previous owner, in all weathers, including freezing temperatures and, for good measure, has had one ear cut off at the top, and his tail chopped in half. Remarkably, he remains friendly towards human beings, despite being the victim of such horrific brutality. I might adopt him, but if I don't, or can't, then I hope someone else gives him the loving home he deserves.

Why anyone should want to treat any dog like this is beyond me, but let's hope for a happy ending. Whether or not this Collie bears emotional scars remains to be seen, but we know how quick dogs are to forgive and continue to love. Friends of mine, Zimbabwean Salvationists whose lives were disrupted/disturbed/ruined by the insane antics of Robert Mugabe, and who would be entitled to bear grudges and harbour thoughts of revenge, only ever spoke of Mugabe in terms of concern for his soul. They prayed for him, wanting his salvation, in a way that taught me much about grace and mercy. People with every reason to be vengeful were filled with love and disquiet for a brutal man and his eternal destiny.

A COLOURLESS CANVAS

Why, my soul, are you downcast? ... Put your hope in God
(PSALM 42:11 **NIV**)

Speaking of politicians, though I hesitate to group President Robert Mugabe with Sir Winston Churchill, I mention the great English statesman in regard to the problems he faced with clinical depression – what he called his "black dog", a phrase coined by Dr Samuel Johnson. When in the grip of the "black dog", Churchill was so paralyzed by despair that he daren't stand close to the edge of a railway platform (for fear of killing himself), nor could he attend sessions of Parliament. His famed appetite disappeared, so too his legendary energy, until he eventually emerged from such periods to be his normal self again. Winston Churchill, a gifted watercolour artist, described the "black dog" as "coming" and "going" (visiting) and its welcome absences as times when "all the colours came back into the picture".[1]

Depression, like any other illness, is indiscriminate, plaguing prime ministers and peasants alike. The chemical make-up of the human brain is complex, and whereas external factors can be influential, the unpleasant reality is that any of us is vulnerable – even someone as otherwise resilient as Sir Winston. If we know anything about God, we know he draws close to those who suffer. He never promised to explain everything to us – the dark mystery of suffering in particular, maybe – but he has promised, repeatedly, to stand alongside us if and when the "black dog" comes calling. Our healing may not appear (though it may), but our great hope this side of Heaven (Paradise restored) lies in his abiding presence. Even on our darkest, most colourless days, we are not abandoned.

1   www.theconversation.com

NO KIDDING

Rachel saw that she was not bearing Jacob any children
(GENESIS 30:1 ***NIV***)

More from India Knight, who skates on thin ice by slamming the idea of dogs as surrogate children. She has little time for what she refers to as "fur babies", defending the right of dogs to only ever be regarded as dogs, and not as children for owners who for one reason or other aren't able to have children or no longer have their own offspring living at home.[1] Whether we agree with her, or couldn't disagree more, India Knight is to be applauded for stating her case clearly and unequivocally, and her opinion is of course to be respected.

God has blessed me with children, and for that I am grateful – they are an endless source of love, fun, good company, and education (they teach me much!). I do, though, have friends whose marriage cannot, for biological reasons, include such a blessing, and it just so happens they have a beautiful dog upon whom they shower affection and attention. Have they settled for owning a dog instead of having children? I don't think so, as their dog, for all that it brings them great joy, is not regarded as a substitute for a child; they do not afford it that status, but their pet enables them to express feelings of devotion that might otherwise remain stifled. Is that wrong? I think not, as we are designed to love and be loved. Theirs is no "fur baby"! Today, we might want to pray for those who would dearly love to become parents, but can't.

---

1   India Knight, *The Goodness of Dogs* (London: Penguin, 2016)

COMING HOME

We have this treasure in jars of clay
(2 CORINTHIANS 4:7 ***NIV***)

As you may have gathered, my sympathies lean towards rescue centres when it comes to adopting a dog. I realize some people prefer to shop for a pedigree pooch, and I respect that, but my personal preference is to adopt, not shop, largely because of the number of dogs put to sleep every year because they can't be rehomed. Likewise, my abhorrence of puppy farms, where puppies are often kept in cramped, filthy cages but advertised as "living at home" and presented to potential buyers as well cared for, when the reverse is the case. Such unfortunate puppies are often riddled with disease. Hence, my recommendation to opt for adoption! Plenty of charities exist who do their best but would welcome the opportunity to release their charges to good homes. (Is my bias obvious?!)

Rehoming is not always easy. Checks and balances exist for good reason; in this case, the welfare of dogs. I wonder, though, if we Christians sometimes need to "rehome" some issues we may inadvertently have misplaced; laughter, for example, which in some churches (as I know from personal experience!) is frowned upon as silly, frivolous, and unbecoming of God's serious and solemn children, especially during a sermon. Might this gift of God need to be rehomed so that it is heard ringing along the pews and up to the rafters? The ability to see ourselves – the Church at large – as flawed (but loved), a bit weird, sometimes (but treasured), and occasionally not fit for purpose (but still God's own); might the gift of perspective need to be rehomed? And so on, and so forth. It's just a thought …

EVICTION

I will dwell in them
(2 CORINTHIANS 6:16 *KJV*)

On this day in 1858, President Theodore ("Teddy") Roosevelt was born (though he wasn't actually President at the moment of his birth – that came later!). An avid hunter, Roosevelt was nearly always in the company of what became known as a Rat Terrier, made famous by its ability to catch rats at the White House after Roosevelt's elevation to the office of President. He liked Rat Terriers, both for their ability to keep rodents out of American politics and as company, and so keenly did the populace identify one with the other, Rat Terriers were eventually called Teddy Roosevelt Terriers. The name persists to this day for a breed closer in appearance to a Jack Russell than anything else.

The President's favourite Rat Terrier was Skip, who is credited with having killed over 2,000 rats in or around the White House, keeping the residence fit for the first family. Do Skip's actions remind us of a story Jesus told, about a man who rid his house, so to speak, of demonic presences, but then neglected to fill that empty house with anything better, which meant more demons subsequently took up residence? Point being, when we rid our lives, Skip-like, of sin and its besetting influences, it is important we then invite the Holy Spirit to indwell us with his gracious presence; our minds, our hearts, and so on. God the Holy Spirit longs to live within, and to keep us clean from sin. All he needs is our invitation.

ONLY THE LONELY

The grinders cease because they are few
(ECCLESIASTES 12:3 **NIV**)

I am writing in the afternoon, but spent part of this morning in the company of Penny, a lovely little Whippet Dalmatian cross belonging to a clergyman friend and his wife. Penny is a skinny creature, but perfectly happy and quite obviously doted upon. The only snag is, age has done her teeth few favours, which means eating can sometimes be tricky, in that bits of food that haven't been properly chewed are sometimes then swallowed and don't go down easily or properly. (Not, it has to be said, that Penny's appetite has diminished correspondingly!) What a smashing dog – slowly chewing her way through whatever years she might have left (she's getting on a bit), her spotty Dalmatian ears winning her friends everywhere she goes!

What can be done for a dog whose grinders are few? My friends will look after Penny and help her to feed, but the signs of age are evident! A church I know organized a drop-in for people who might otherwise be alone for days at a time – elderly people, mainly, whose families have moved away. What a wonderful project this has become; not particularly evangelical, but an expression of God's love to those in need of friendship and company. Tea, cake, chatter, and natter, that's about it – not rocket science, yet it really has transformed the lives of those whose latter years were destined to be spent largely in isolation. An idea worth considering for your church? I have a feeling God hates the idea of loneliness, when he has created us to socialize. Fancy giving it a try, for his sake?

ONE THING AT A TIME

"Come now, let us reason together," says the Lord
(ISAIAH 1:18 *ESV*)

When I am writing, I listen to the radio, lest I find the silence distracting and never get any work done. Thus it was I heard the story of a lady calling in to the consumer hour with a complaint about her shower. It wasn't working properly, and she was trying to negotiate a refund. Fair enough, until it emerged – on air – that she was in the habit of sharing her daily shower with her dog (who, by all accounts, thoroughly enjoyed it)! Her dog was, she said, a "small breed", but the problem with her shower was caused – or, at least, wasn't helped – by the amount of dog hair going down her plughole every morning. Not altogether surprisingly, the shower company were reluctant to accept liability, leaving the radio presenter having to tactfully explain to the woman with what must by now be the cleanest dog in England that she should consider showering alone! I wonder if she followed his advice ...

Some say cleanliness is next to godliness! William Booth, Founder of The Salvation Army, preached a gospel of "soup, soap and salvation", maintaining that if someone was hungry (soup), or flea-infested (soap), they were hardly likely to be interested in a sermon (salvation), however captivating the preacher. In that sense, Booth understood that cleanliness was at least a route to salvation, even if it doesn't actually have much to do with godliness! Personally, I think God understands that sometimes, practical matters hinder our spiritual progress or intent. Furthermore, I believe he is willing to help us deal with such matters if it means, say, our prayer life can then improve, or our church attendance become more frequent. God is reasonable! He knows our lives, and he will work with us as we approach him.

DOGGIE DOMESTICANA

She looketh well to the ways of her household
(PROVERBS 31:27 *KJV*)

Speaking of such matters, I watched a television programme about a woman who was so obsessed with cleaning that not only did she spend several hours every day dusting, polishing, and bleaching her house, but she vacuumed her dog too! Her obsession with her home remaining spotless had left her with a fear of dog hair ever once appearing on her furniture, so out would come the vacuum cleaner in order for her to prevent that possibility. Exactly what her dog – a perfectly ordinary Jack Russell with very little surplus fur – thought about it is anybody's guess, but he seemed quite content and may even have enjoyed being kept in such good order!

The Salvation Army runs a ladies' group called Home League. Established decades ago to help and support wives and mums as they ran homes and looked after families, its function has changed somewhat nowadays. Instead of offering advice on matters of housekeeping, it is now more of a social gathering with a Christian flavour. The motto of Home League, though, remains the same, and I have chosen it as our text for today. This motto is emblazoned on Home League materials worldwide, underneath a picture of a house sitting on top of an open Bible. It might be a bit dated, but it remains a powerful image, and a reminder that home life – family, cooking, cleaning, washing, getting on together – is blessed and enhanced when Bible teaching is adopted and followed; that remains a timeless truth.

THE LIGHT SHINES

Where, O death, is your victory? Where, O death, is your sting?
(1 CORINTHIANS 15:55 *NIV*)

This date represents Halloween, when all things ghoulish are celebrated. I don't condone the celebration, but as this is a book about dogs, allow me just to focus today on a few tips for when people might come knocking on your door in search of treats. Perhaps the following pointers could be considered, as many dogs will be confused or disturbed by visitors in strange costumes and by lots of people coming to the door, but never being invited in:

1) Secure your dog behind a closed door or in a room away from the front door.

2) Play music or leave a TV/radio playing in the dog's room to mask the sounds of the activity at the front door.

3) Close curtains so that your dog does not see people coming and going.

4) If your dog barks at the sound of the doorbell, disconnect it or watch for trick-or-treaters so that they do not have to ring or knock.

5) Puppies and dogs that like to chase can get overly excited by costumes with dangly bits or streaming material. Supervise your dog if it is with you as you answer the door.

6) Keep your dog indoors around Halloween time. Pets have been stolen, injured or poisoned as part of Halloween pranks or other rituals.

7) Dogs don't like to be dressed up! It makes them anxious and uncomfortable.

Far better, in my humble opinion, to celebrate today the lives of saints who have gone to Glory, thanking God for the promise of eternal life secured by the death of Christ – loved ones, maybe, who have gone before, and whose souls are safe in his embrace. This is the Christian focus and meditation; the victory of light and life over death. Amen! Hallelujah!

WHERE WE ARE TREADING IS WHERE THE SAINTS HAVE TROD

Since we are surrounded by such a great cloud of witnesses, let us throw off everything that hinders and the sin that so easily entangles. And let us run with perseverance the race marked out for us

(HEBREWS 12:1 *NIV*)

I prefer All Saints' Day to Halloween, observed by many Christians today, when those who have departed to eternal rest are commemorated. Reflections are shared on their lives, as an encouragement and a spur to those of us who remain this side of Paradise. I like the inclusivity of All Saints' Day, in that the great and the famous are recalled, but so too the ordinary and anonymous; all those who trusted Christ for salvation. One such was St Anselm, a medieval monk who became Archbishop of Canterbury and spent time meditating on the moral and theological obligations of all creatures; human beings, oxen, and even dogs, wondering what responsibilities accompanied the gifts and graces bestowed upon them. Anselm maintained dogs had been given tasks to fulfil, and these were nothing less than divine ordinations; to protect, for example, to hunt, or to demonstrate loyalty and obedience.

Whatever we might think of Anselm's speculations, we give thanks today for all such gifts and graces, and for lives well lived in the service of Jesus.

For all the saints who from their labours rest,
Who Thee by faith before the world confessed,
Thy name, O Jesus, be forever blest,
Alleluia! Alleluia!

(William W. How, 1823–97)

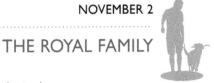

THE ROYAL FAMILY

I have loved you with an everlasting love
(JEREMIAH 31:3 **NIV**)

Foo Foo the Poodle was a favourite pet of Crown Prince Maha Vajiralongkorn of Thailand, before he succeeded his father and became king. Nothing unusual about that, except Foo Foo was made an Air Chief Marshal in the Royal Thai Air Force and often accompanied the prince on royal engagements, being introduced to the US Ambassador to Thailand in formal evening attire including paw mitts. (The Ambassador cabled back home to Washington, expressing his surprise at meeting Air Chief Marshall Foo Foo!) The privileged Poodle once even jumped up onto the head table during an official function and drank from the guests' water glasses, but such is the reverence for Thai monarchy, no one dared complain. The bizarre antics came to an end in 2015, when Foo Foo died and was cremated with full Buddhist funeral rites.

A dog being treated as a dignitary! We can only imagine what the American Ambassador thought at the time! To be honest, I don't know what to think – is it amusing that a Poodle is installed as an Air Chief Marshal, or sad and worrying? Human nature really shouldn't surprise me any longer, yet it continues to do so, and I can therefore only marvel at the way in which God continues to love and bless, whether that love is bestowed upon a Crown Prince whose behaviour raises eyebrows or, for that matter, on any of us. Yet, such is grace. We are loved unconditionally, even though some points of our conduct sometimes defy explanation. We may not indulge in eccentricities or atrocities (most people don't), but that fact remains – grace prevails, and includes Thai princes, peasants, and people of all nations. This is God.

DIOS BENDIGA A MÉXICO

Some wandered in the wilderness, lost and homeless
(PSALM 107:4 **NLT**)

Eccentric behaviour appears in all kinds of ways, and is of course subjective. What one person may regard as eccentric, another may regard as normal. I do, though, think it is at least unusual to spend £4,000 on a birthday party for a dog, but that is exactly what one Chihuahua devotee did to celebrate her Chihuahuas' joint first birthday! The Mexican-themed party (Chihuahuas originate from Mexico) included a clown, face painting, three doggie cakes, and a dwarf (no, I don't understand either), as Salvador and Purdy were cheered and toasted with their siblings and pooch pals. Their devoted owner, explaining the idea of a Mexican party (guests were invited to wear sombreros and ponchos – not that Salvador and Purdy would have cared too much what anyone wore) said she chose the theme because she wanted to take the Chihuahuas back to their roots ...

I worked briefly for The Salvation Army in America, and once enjoyed a Mexican meal in a restaurant just a short distance from the Mexican border. To this day, I regret not making any effort to actually visit Mexico, but my daughter made up for my failure by visiting Mexico to work on a project building houses for families who live and work, by and large, on rubbish tips, scavenging what they can in order to survive. Mexican law dictates that children whose parents can't provide a home for them are put up for adoption – a legal nightmare for destitute loving parents unable to offer their children a roof and four walls to live within, hence the project. Families living under the threat of losing their beloved children are given a house, and the dreadful threat of separation is removed. They still scrimp a living – of sorts – from the tips, but they can at least stay together. Maybe we could pray for such people today, asking God to bless and help the rubbish tip dwellers of Mexico.

DINNER TIME

They broke bread in their homes and ate together with glad and sincere hearts, praising God

(ACTS 2:46–47 **NIV**)

Speaking of dining out, TV chef Rick Stein has opened his first London restaurant after years offering excellent cuisine in Cornwall, England. I've always liked Rick Stein's programmes, and really felt for him when his dog, Chalky, died a few years ago, as Chalky and Stein were inseparable. The Rough-Haired Jack Russell was as much a part of broadcasts as the famous chef, his fiery temperament providing the perfect complement to Stein's phlegmatic nature. For a while, the Jack Russell became part of television culture – so much so that a Member of Parliament even tabled a motion in the House of Commons lamenting his death! I wish Mr Stein success with his capital venture, but it won't be quite the same without Chalky on the scene.

No doubt about it – food played an important part in the life of Jesus' disciples. Food to eat daily, of course, but if we scan the Gospels we find numerous examples of meals providing opportunities for socializing and bonding. Can we imagine what they talked about as they shared meals together? That must have been fascinating! They would have touched base over bread and cheese, and fish suppers, comparing notes on what their new way of life was like, following Jesus. What interesting conversations those would have been! I love this concept; the people of God talking about Jesus as they munch their lunch! What a lovely, edifying thought.

REMEMBER, REMEMBER, THE FIFTH OF NOVEMBER

If it is possible, as far as it depends on you, live at peace with everyone
(ROMANS 12:18 **NIV**)

I have little choice, on this date, but to refer to Bonfire Night, or Guy Fawkes Night, when here in the UK bonfires are lit and fireworks exploded to commemorate the day in 1605 when Guy (Guido) Fawkes failed in his attempt to assassinate King James I by blowing up the House of Lords. I am not opposed to bonfires or fireworks, and I am certainly not opposed to the tradition of treacle toffee that often accompanies the commemorations, but I need to issue a plea for dogs to be kept safely indoors while explosions and bangs take place outside – preferably, with the television or radio volume turned up and, ideally, with human company for reassurance. Most dogs hate Bonfire Night. The noises scare them, and I remember Meg literally shaking with fear when the blasts started. Have fun, please, but look after your dogs too!

Thanks to the good auspices of a friend who works in the Palace of Westminster, I once hid in the very spot Guy Fawkes hid in as he guarded the explosives he planned to use, prior to his discovery and arrest! That was a bit of fun, but there was nothing remotely funny about his plans. Saddest of all, perhaps, was that Fawkes' murderous intent had its origins in religious disputes between his English Catholics and the reigning Protestant monarch. Fawkes and his fellow plotters wanted to restore a Catholic throne to England, and saw murder as the way to proceed. How sad and ironic that such hatred should exist between people all naming the name of Christ as Saviour, albeit from different theological perspectives. Lord, forgive your people and teach us ways of peace, even – especially – when we disagree.

A SPOTLIGHT ON LOVE

The Lord smelled the pleasing aroma and said in his heart: "Never again will I curse the ground because of humans, even though every inclination of the human heart is evil from childhood. And never again will I destroy all living creatures, as I have done"

(GENESIS 8:21 *NIV*)

The rented storeroom used by Guy Fawkes and his fellow conspirators was a dark place, deep in the bowels of Westminster Palace – ideal for hiding away the thirty-six barrels of gunpowder found in their possession. Guards searching for their hideaway did a great job of tracking it down, given that no such things as battery-operated torches or flashlights existed in 1605. Undoubtedly, they could have made good use of the latest gadget designed to detect dog urine on surfaces (carpets, for example) where it can be smelled, but not necessarily seen. The device, a UV flashlight Pet Urine Detector, is meant to help puppy trainers and breeders who want to keep their premises clean, but can't always see where spillages and accidents might have occurred, and may even come in useful for domestic owners as they train their puppy. Mysterious odours can now be located and cleaned away!

Towards the end of her days, dear old Meg lost control of her bladder from time to time. Not her fault at all, and I suppose the blessing was that we were left in no doubt at all where she had urinated! The twin gifts of sight and smell served us well! Not to worry – no harm was done, and a more pleasant aroma was soon in place ... comparable, maybe, to the aroma mentioned in today's text, when Noah made a burnt offering after leaving the ark; God was pleased with the sacrifice – representing atonement and propitiation – and promised never again to destroy every living creature with a flood. God was satisfied. His wrath was appeased. As the old Sunday school chorus puts it: when you see a rainbow, remember God is love.[1] Read around our text for today as a reminder of God's pardon and faithfulness.

---

1   This is how I personally remember the chorus. So too, it seems, does Kevin Holdsworth, Provost of St Mary's Cathedral, Glasgow, if his blog is anything to go by: thurible.net 10.2.14

SHEPHERD OF OUR SOULS

Who knows whether the ... spirit of the beast goes down into the earth?
(ECCLESIASTES 3:21 **ESV**)

It's possible no one has reached more people with the gospel of Christ than Billy Graham, who was born on this day in 1918 and whose reputation as a preacher and a man of integrity has brought him worldwide respect and affection. Years ago, when I was working in the States, I found Billy Graham Boulevard and drove close to where the great preacher lives, but didn't quite have the courage to ring his doorbell! Probably just as well, for not only would an unannounced visit have been discourteous, I might have put myself in the way of Dr Graham's pair of German Shepherds, which I believe he bought in order to protect his wife, Ruth, whenever he was away from home on a mission tour. Had those dogs done their job properly if I had called, that might have been a visit to regret! I like to think those German Shepherds looked after Ruth and kept Billy company when he wasn't travelling the world preaching.

I think God will have prepared everything for our perfect happiness. If it takes my dog being there [in Heaven], I believe he'll be there.[1]

(Billy Graham)

Perhaps our prayers this day could include thanks for the way in which God has used Billy Graham over the years. We might also pray for the ongoing ministry of the Billy Graham Evangelistic Association.

---

1 cheezburger.com

ALL SHALL BE WELL

He rules

(PSALM 22:28 **NIV**)

Julian of Norwich, born on this day in 1342, was an interesting woman; a devout Christian mystic, gifted writer, theologian, counsellor, advisor, and someone still revered in both Roman Catholic and Anglican circles, Julian (her name derives from the fact that her monastic cell was attached to St Julian's Church in Norwich, England) claimed to have been visited more than once by the devil, or, at least demonic forces. Her prayers were, apparently, disrupted by visitations organized to distract her, or to tempt her to sin, but I am saddened to read, in her writings, that such characters sometimes appeared as dogs. Granted, I can imagine foul beasts of Hell appearing as, say, fiery dragons or grotesque gremlins, that sort of thing, but it seems to me unfortunate that dogs – which are, by and large, kindly disposed towards human beings and not particularly frightening or malign – should receive such a bad press in her works. I wonder what sort of things she saw. Snarling creatures, maybe, or fierce dog-like monsters. I do not doubt her testimony, but I struggle to place dogs in any category of evil.

One of Julian's works is said to be the oldest surviving book written in the English language by a woman. So, she was a trailblazer for female authors too! Without doubt, her witness has stood the test of time, and the Catechism of the Catholic Church quotes her in regard to the sometimes unfathomable plans of Divine Providence. Julian of Norwich taught that "all manner of things shall be well", believing our Lord himself had taught her such. Whatever her opinion of dogs, Julian's teaching comes as reassurance when we encounter situations we cannot understand. Her words echo through the ages into our lives today.

MONEY MADE THEIR WORLD GO ROUND

God has been gracious to me and I have all I need
(GENESIS 33:11 ***NIV***)

Speaking of dragons, I enjoy watching the television programme *Dragons' Den*, in which budding entrepreneurs pit their wits against a team of multimillionaire "dragons" (successful businessmen and women) in the hope of securing investments for their business ideas. One entrepreneur, an engineering graduate, asked for £150,000 to be invested in his invention, an activity monitor that can be attached to a dog's collar to monitor and record movement. The data of activities such as walking and running (and even sleeping) is then transferred to an app so that owners can seek informed advice on their dog's specific health and nutritional needs, and all the better care for their pet. A good idea, but unfortunately for the would-be tycoon, his pitch was rejected and he left *Dragon's Den* with his tail between his legs.

Those who know about such things tell me the kings and pharaohs of Old Testament days were eye-wateringly wealthy. Apparently, their wealth would have made that of the "dragons" – well-off though they are – seem almost paltry, and they weren't only cash-rich. Vast property empires were theirs, and treasure troves of precious gemstones, not to mention livestock and – as a recognized symbol of prosperity in Old Testament times – several wives and servants. Good for them, but what we might care to study is how often such people ascribed their affluence to God, readily crediting him as the generous source of their blessings. We might not be as rich as they were – not many are! – but that principle applies to us all; God has blessed us, and sent every good and perfect gift. Ours is to give thanks.

MAKE NO BONES ABOUT IT

The entire law is fulfilled in keeping this one command: "Love your neighbour as yourself"

(GALATIANS 5:14 **NIV**)

I have no idea whether or not Sir Norman Wisdom was wealthy, but he was immensely rich in terms of God-given talent. Not only was Sir Norman a clown of the highest order, but he was also a multitalented musician who could play numerous instruments at will. For all that, he was probably best known for the pathos he brought to television and cinema screens in his role as Norman Pitkin, playing the perpetual underdog in pursuit of some hopeless romantic ideal or other. Have you seen him in *A Stitch in Time*, made in 1963? He wins the audience over early on in the picture, engaging hearts and cleverly establishing character by covertly feeding two dogs who wander into the butcher's shop where he works. Taking it in turns, and knowing Pitkin to be as soft-hearted as marrow, the dogs – a Cocker Spaniel and what looks like a scruffy Norfolk Terrier – come to the counter when the boss isn't looking and are fed scraps and bones before running away with their booty.

Strictly speaking, according to the precise letter of the law, Norman Pitkin was guilty of theft, in that those spare bones in the butcher's shop weren't his to give away, even though they would only have ended up in the rubbish otherwise, thrown out as garbage when those sneaky dogs could have made good use of them. There is no wisdom in thieving, but is there a great deal in strict legalism? What about supermarkets throwing away entire skip-loads of perfectly edible food while hundreds go hungry every evening, just because sell-by dates have expired? Can that be right? It is, I know, a complex moral maze, but I think I know what Norman Pitkin would have done. What of you and me? Lord, move us at the impulse of love.

DOGS OF WAR

The Lord will go forth like a warrior
(ISAIAH 42:13 **NASB**)

Today we remember Remembrance Day, and commemorate the formal cessation of hostilities of World War One at the 11th hour of the 11th day of the 11th month in 1918. We recall the sacrifice made by those who gave their lives, but we should not overlook the massive part dogs played in that conflict, when 20,000+ were trained for specific roles; Sentry Dogs trained to protect barracks, Scout Dogs skilled at moving ahead of patrols and issuing warnings, Messenger Dogs employed to carry vital messages (faster than human runners), and so on. Their involvement is not forgotten as they shared the appalling conditions of the trenches, dodging bullets and facing terrifying explosions. Canine contributions such as those listed above, and others, would have made more difference to the war effort than is perhaps always recognized.

God of our fathers, whose almighty hand
Leads forth in beauty all the starry band
Of shining worlds in splendour through the skies:
Our grateful songs before your throne arise.

Your love divine has led us in the past;
In this free land by you our lot is cast;
Oh, be our ruler, guardian, guide, and stay;
Your Word our law, your paths our chosen way.

From war's alarms, from deadly pestilence
Make your strong arm our ever sure defence.
Your true religion in our hearts increase;
Your bounteous goodness nourish us in peace.

Refresh your people on their toilsome way;
Lead us from night to never ending day;
Fill all our lives with heaven-born love and grace
Until at last we meet before your face.

(Daniel C. Roberts, 1841–1907)

TREE TREATS

Grey hair is a crown of glory; it is gained in a righteous life
(PROVERBS 16:31 *ESV*)

Remember Mbogo, the Elkhound cross who liked going round in circles? It seems he was quite proud of his fur coat, which was, I am told, super-shiny and luxurious, a condition he encouraged and maintained by ... eating avocados! Please don't worry – he wasn't ever actually fed the exotic fruit, but helped himself to large amounts of windfalls from the tree that grew on my in-laws' land, running to the tree every morning to see what free beauty treatments were available. His scavenging wasn't noticed at first, until his coat started to take on an impressively glossy sheen, when matters were investigated and Mbogo's love of avocados detected! (I wonder if my parents-in-law ever considered going into business with African avocado treatments for dogs!)

I take great pleasure in today's text! As my hair continues to turn from brown to grey to silver, I am delighted to learn that such turning is a good thing, and a sign of God's blessing! To be honest, though, it makes little difference to me what colour my hair is, as I do not look to external signs and visible evidences of God's goodness towards me. For sure, they can be useful, reassuring, and encouraging reminders, but no more than that, as my belief in the love and mercy of God runs much deeper than anything I can see, or even anything tangible; it is a matter of faith and trust, not dependent upon symbols which, rather like my greying hair, are here today and gone tomorrow. My witness to a gracious God lies deep within. It is found in his word and experienced in my spirit. Anything else is a bonus!

BLOODHOUNDS AND BLACKBURN, MOSES AND MURDER

[Moses] killed the Egyptian and hid him in the sand
(EXODUS 2:12 **NIV**)

My parents-in-law are to be congratulated on quickly solving the mystery of Mbogo's increasingly lustrous coat. The clues were pieced together, the main protagonist followed, and the evidence gathered – in this case, fallen fruit. I wonder if they might have appreciated the help of the Bloodhound from Blackburn, Lancashire, England, who is said to be the first dog used by British police to solve a crime. In 1876, a murder had been committed, but detectives were having trouble pinning down the evidence in order to press charges until a Mrs White, noticing a dog constantly running to and from a paper parcel in a field, investigated the wrapped bundle and discovered gruesome human remains that would otherwise have remained undetected. To cut a long and barbarous story short, it transpired the murderer had thrown the package over a wall and, without its discovery, would have escaped charges. Further evidence was unearthed when a man volunteered the services of his two dogs to the Chief Constable who, when they were let loose in a suspect's house, sniffed out calcined bones hidden in a chimney. From that point on, after a successful prosecution, the use of dogs as detectives was regarded as a good idea!

Murder most foul! Search the pages of Scripture, though, and before long you will find numerous cases of such bloodshed and skulduggery, even amongst the people of God. Indeed, the revered leader Moses was guilty of such a crime, yet went on to become one of the great leaders of Biblical history. No one condones murder, yet if even a murderer can find forgiveness, restoration, and a place in God's service, should we ever doubt the saving power of a gracious Redeemer? Such extravagant redeeming grace shatters many of our preconceptions about God's willingness to reach out to even the vilest offender, but his love has no measure and his power no boundaries. This is God.

VIVE LA DIFFERENCE!

Each departed to his home
(JUDGES 9:55 **NASB**)

From those modest beginnings in 1876, the deployment of dogs in crime-solving has spread internationally, to become an accepted part of forensic and investigative work. What is interesting is the preferences given by different nations as to which breeds of dog their police force will use, as follows:

In Australia, Australian Shepherds are used on account of their high intelligence, whereas in Belgium, Belgian Malinois are popular with the police because of their tremendous ability to sniff out the trail of a suspect. The Calgary Police Department, in Canada, on the other hand, mainly uses German Shepherds, while Danish police officers enjoy having Doberman Pinschers with them on patrol. In Hong Kong, Malinois (also known as Belgian Shepherds) are recruited, while the Dutch Police Dog Service gives preference to Dutch Shepherds. Indian police, though, keep law and order with the assistance of Indian Pariahs, known to be good and loyal guard dogs, but their counterparts in Russia much prefer Rottweilers on patrol. And finally, but remarkably, the first police dog used in Sweden, in 1910, was a somewhat unlikely Airedale Terrier!

Is it just me, or do you ever wonder what nationality we will be in Heaven? Silly speculation, I know, but I have to admit it crosses my mind occasionally! Will Africans still be Africans, and will the English still be English? A friend of mine, a French Salvation Army officer who served in Northern Ireland, was disappointed, in one meeting, to find French and Northern Irish flags displayed in his honour, as a mark of affection. He would, he explained, have preferred only the Salvation Army flag, stating that his only true homeland is in God's Kingdom and that he desired no other allegiance. It's certainly an interesting – and challenging – point of view! What do you think? Where are we most at home?

A LONELY LORD

As they approached the village to which they were going, Jesus continued on as if
he were going further. But they urged him strongly, "Stay with us"

(LUKE 24:28–29 **NIV**)

Just when you think you have heard it all ... A radio report informs me of a craze for "People Walkers". I kid you not. Apparently, some people find walking a dog a lonely experience and, in the absence of any other company, pay someone to walk with them. As part-time work goes, it's not bad – Fido gets his or her exercise, while the owner, albeit a few pounds out of pocket, does at least have someone to talk to. I can't honestly decide whether to applaud such ingenuity – an out-of-work actor, for example, who offers his services as a People Walker, between jobs – or to feel sad that anyone has to actually pay a relative stranger simply to avoid that lonesome feeling. I shouldn't think the dogs mind too much, as they are walked and, in a way, doubly cared for, but there is a sense of poignancy attached to the idea, is there not?

The question is sometimes posed: If God knows everything anyway, why should I pray? The implication is, what's the point of ever asking God for anything, if he knows my needs anyhow? Sadly, that misses one of the main points of prayer, in that God is no divine vending machine who exists simply to dish out provisions, but a friendly deity who longs to walk with us through life, in fellowship. When that fellowship is fractured – by sin, or neglect – then God's heart is fractured too, and there is a dreadful sense of poignancy surrounding a loving God who wants to be the Divine People Walker, yet is ignored or forgotten. Of course he already knows everything, but that's hardly the point; God desires our daily company, and is delighted to offer us his.

MAKING YOUR MIND UP

Leave these men alone! Let them go! For if their purpose or activity is of human origin, it will fail. But if it is from God, you will not be able to stop these men
(ACTS 5:38–39 ***NIV***)

All things considered, I think I have almost certainly probably abandoned my idea of adopting another dog, despite perusing the claims of some excellent applicants. Without doubt, a vacancy exists, as the gaps left by the departures of Meg and Skipper have never been filled, but practicalities prevail and I need to balance my ongoing desire for a new friend against what is right and fair for the dog in question. I cannot honestly claim to be a suitable dog owner, despite my best efforts at persuading myself otherwise; what happens if and when I go away, for example, or my working day means I am out of the house most of the time (as it sometimes does)? No, I think the answer, for now, has to be a reluctant no, maybe ...

Did you spot the indecision there? Even as I type, I can picture Diamond the Dalmatian looking out at me from my computer screen, tugging at my heartstrings and asking for a home. Most of my mind is made up, but I can't honestly say the matter is cut and dried. What does that make me? An agonizing agnostic? One of the great unsure undecided? I sometimes wonder about the eternal destiny of those who died without ever having quite made their minds up about Jesus. They never claimed him as Saviour and Lord, yet neither did they specifically reject him; theirs was no atheism, but it wasn't a statement of faith either. Lord, have mercy on those who can't decide. Nudge them into belief. Minister to their doubts.

CANINE CHRISTENING

He knows my name

(PSALM 91:14 **ESV**)

What do you think of this idea? There is a suggestion doing the rounds, promoting the idea that potential dog owners should rehearse calling out, loudly, in public, the name they plan to bestow upon their dog when it comes to live with them. Meg and Skipper were already christened – as is Diamond – but supposing you plan to adopt or buy a puppy who has yet to learn a name. In order to test the suitability of your name ideas, it is suggested you stroll around a park, say, shouting out options in order to see which best fits. Hmm. What if, for example, you fancied calling your puppy Whisky – would it really be such a great plan to spend an evening walking around outdoors shouting "Whisky!" "Whisky!" I think not. Some appellations would be perfectly alright, I suppose, but I can't pretend to be entirely convinced ...

Over the years, I suppose I have spent a fair amount of time proclaiming the name of Jesus in public – not shouting, which is rather pointless, but sharing a gospel message with the help of a microphone, in Salvation Army "open-air meetings". I have always been quite happy to share a brief message, even though no one has ever come to faith through my efforts (not to my knowledge, anyway), in the hope that at least naming the name above all names will impact someone, somehow. Am I mistaken? Possibly. Am I outdated? Maybe. Will I dust down the microphone again at some point in the future? Almost certainly! God bless Salvation Army street preachers speaking of the Saviour as the crowds go by.

JUST BECAUSE OF LOVE

He first loved us

(1 JOHN 4:19 **NIV**)

I picked up a second-hand biography of Samuel Pepys, which has led me to dip briefly into Pepys' famous *Diary*, where I came across this fascinating footnote:

Charles II.'s love of dogs is well known, but it is not so well known that his dogs were continually being stolen from him. In the "Mercurius Publicus," June 28–July 5, 1660, is the following advertisement, apparently drawn up by the King himself: "We must call upon you again for a Black Dog between a greyhound and a spaniel, no white about him, onely a streak on his brest, and his tayl a little bobbed. It is His Majesties own Dog, and doubtless was stoln, for the dog was not born nor bred in England, and would never forsake His master. Whosoever finds him may acquaint any at Whitehal for the Dog was better known at Court, than those who stole him. Will they never leave robbing his Majesty! Must he not keep a Dog? This dog's place (though better than some imagine) is the only place which nobody offers to bed [sic].[1]

King Charles II was often the victim of dog theft. To what end his dogs were stolen, I'm not sure, but a point to ponder today is that Charles's dogs would have loved him entirely regardless of his position as King of England. They would have had no idea that their master was a monarch, and would simply have done what dogs do in their hierarchical structure. Their devotion to him was based not upon his royal status, but simply because dogs tend to love anyway; they don't have ulterior motives, possessing little guile, and I cannot help linking the dedication of the king's dogs to the commitment shown to us by the King of kings, described in a hymn by Arthur Smith Armott (1870–1941):

Tell them of the baby in the manger laid,
Sent from Heaven above;
Tell them how for them he was a ransom paid,
Just because of love.

1   www.pepysdiary.com

FOUND AND LOST

God's kindness is intended to lead you to repentance
(ROMANS 2:4 **NIV**)

Part of my daily lot – and privilege – is to collect Heather from the railway station, when she has completed another day's hard labour for The Salvation Army. On dry days, I walk to the station and we wander home together. On rainy days, I use the car. The vagaries of railway timetables being what they are, I keep a paperback in the car in case Heather's train is delayed, to read while I wait. One such book is *The Stranger* by Albert Camus, featuring Old Salamano, a curmudgeonly malcontent who lives with his ancient, scabby, disease-ridden dog, whom Salamano pulls around on its lead, often violently, cursing it and spitting at it. He appears to despise the creature because it is old and useless, yet when the dog goes missing one evening, during a parade, Old Salamano is heartbroken and tearfully pleads for help in finding it. His true feelings emerge only once he realizes what he has lost.

How do you pray? When do you pray? If you are anything like me, you wonder if you might do better! Speaking personally, I try to reserve a quiet time most days and, most days, I succeed; time alone with God to pray and read from the Bible. Other days, though, somewhat inexplicably, I neglect those times of fellowship; through laziness, because of sin, or due to misplaced priorities, until the Lord gently woos me back again. Those days "away" from God carry a sense of something missing, something not quite right and, somewhat like Old Salamano, I come to appreciate afresh that which I have lost, albeit temporarily. Thankfully, God is faithful and abounding in steadfast love, but how much better it would be if I treasured my communion with him in the first place.

GOD AND GENEALOGY

David was the son of Jesse. Jesse was the son of Obed. Obed was the son of Boaz.
Boaz was the son of Salmon
(LUKE 3:32 **NLT**)

Not rocket science, this one, but pet nutritionists have concluded that dogs fed on so-called superfoods such as salmon, peas, and sweet potato have greater brainpower in terms of long-term memory and the ability to respond to commands (we were, then, clearly, by that token, feeding Skipper all the wrong things!). Ordinarily, a dog's long-term memory decreases with age, but such a decline can be slowed down with improvements in diet. Docosahexaenoic acid, for example, found in salmon, improves mental development, while the beta carotene and chlorogenic acid in sweet potato can assist cognitive ability. Personally, I'm not altogether sure where peas come into the mental mix (an aid to memory, apparently), but I can't see any harm in putting this theory to the test. (I have to say, though, Meg and Skipper would have been very surprised to find helpings of top quality salmon in their bowls!)

Should you find yourself in the Sistine Chapel, cast your eyes around for a lunette (a "half-moon" recess in architecture) naming (but not depicting) three characters: Salmon, Boaz, and Obed. Salmon married Rahab, by whom he had a son, Boaz, who subsequently married Ruth, which union produced Obed, and some art critics suggest Michelangelo's family snapshot portrays Boaz, Obed, and Ruth. Keep digging and you will come to see that Salmon was the great-great-grandfather of David, meaning Jesus was born of his line. A relatively obscure figure, Salmon nonetheless therefore has his rightful place in the lineage of Christ. Today, we give thanks for the marvellous ways in which God slowly outworks his purposes down through the generations, sculpting providential ideas as the centuries pass. This is God, who was and is, and is to come; eternal, patient, and unresting.

THAT SINKING FEELING

They took Jeremiah and put him into the cistern of Malkijah, the king's son …
it had no water in it, only mud, and Jeremiah sank down
(JEREMIAH 38:6 **NIV**)

Sheep worrying is a cause of concern for many shepherds, as a dog let loose in a flock of sheep, especially when lambs and pregnant ewes are present, can be a killer. Even a trusted family Labrador can pose a threat, hence the insistence of many farmers that dogs on their land remain on a lead, and their legal entitlement to shoot dogs that are not controlled. Furthermore, the owner or person in charge of a dog that is dangerously out of control in public commits an offence under the Dangerous Dogs Act 1991, for which the sentence can be up to two years imprisonment and destruction of the dog. Serious stuff, then, and one idea in the air that might help is the use of a noxious substance that could be sprayed on sheep, which dogs would find offensive. Given dogs' remarkable sense of smell, this could work, but I can't help wondering how the sheep might feel about smelling repulsive all the time, even if they are kept safe – or, for that matter, how farmers will cope with the preventative but prevailing stench!

Poor Jeremiah! Rejected because of his prophetic witness to a sinful community, he was dumped down a well which would have stunk, to, well, high Heaven. Caked in filth and left to rot, he must have wondered what he had done to deserve such a smelly fate. He had, after all, only carried out God's instructions to preach repentance, yet his reward for being brave and obedient was a visit to what was effectively some kind of latrine. When we scan the Scriptures, we soon realize that following God is not always a bed of roses! Some calls are tough ones, yet we would be mistaken to think God has abandoned us, or that we have misheard him, when our plight leaves us stuck in the mud; it ain't necessarily so! God still loves, and still cares, but asks us to go through the mire for his sake. Will we?

THE FEELING'S MUTUAL

Be devoted to one another
(ROMANS 12:10 **NIV**)

The evening before I wrote this page, Heather and I went to the cinema with friends to watch a marvellous film, *Hunt for the Wilderpeople*. I shan't reveal the storyline, but suffice to say, it features a lovely Boxer called Tupac (named after the late American actor and rapper Tupac Shakur) being given as a birthday present to teenage runaway Ricky Baker. Ricky deeply loves his new friend from the word go, and the feeling is clearly mutual as the pair embark on a series of escapades and close shaves, never once thinking of deserting each other. Fair enough, some timely and sympathetic whimpering noises are dubbed onto the soundtrack whenever Ricky is in a spot of bother and Tupac the Boxer is standing by showing concern, but only ever to highlight their mutual devotion, never more poignantly illustrated than when Tupac is seen staggering from the wreckage of a car crash, bewildered but searching for Ricky ... however, if you want to know what that's all about, you'll need to buy the DVD!

Mutual devotion – the ideal for any relationship! What a staggering thought it is that God is entirely, unequivocally, completely, utterly, and unambiguously devoted to us. For our reflection today, I leave you with words from a hymn penned by the late Colonel Brindley Boon (1924–2009), one of The Salvation Army's finest musicians and writers:

Take thou my life, Lord,
In deep submission I pray,
My all to thee dedicating,
Accept my offering today.

WHAT WE MIGHT BECOME

The hope to which he has called you
(EPHESIANS 1:18 *ESV*)

Have you started your Christmas shopping yet? Forgive me, please, if you think it's too soon to be thinking all things seasonal, but this is just a gentle reminder that you have about a month to go! Should you be stuck for relatively inexpensive but perfectly acceptable gift ideas, allow me to suggest a set of coasters, perfect for protecting one's table or desk while enjoying a cuppa, enabling the recipient to savour their tea or coffee whilst thanking you for preserving their furniture. Even better, there are plenty of dog-themed coasters available, an example of which I saw on sale the morning before writing this. Featuring an appealingly cheeky chappie of a Terrier looking up towards its owner, the caption read, "Dear Lord, please make me the kind of person my dog thinks I am". The coaster artist has done a great job in capturing the Terrier's look of absolute trust, thereby emphasizing the prayer ...

... And what a prayer it is! Dogs see only the best in us, believing we love them as much as they love us. A dog would struggle to think otherwise, optimistically offering affection and loyalty in the conviction that that is our only intention too. Somehow, dogs are unable to register anything sinful or evil about us ... yet we know differently! The gospel truth is, we are flawed, and our Adamic DNA means that we aren't quite as perfect as our dogs seem to think! By the same token, though, the gospel truth is that we are loved, for all that, by a God who certainly does know all about our flaws. He, quite remarkably, was willing to pay the price for them, taking upon himself, in Christ, not to overlook our imperfections but to address them and offer us a route to forgiveness and improvement. God is not blind, but his awareness of our sinfulness only ever prompts him to make us the kind of people he thinks we can become.

GOD IN THREE PERSONS

The grace of the Lord Jesus Christ and the love of God and the fellowship of the Holy Spirit

(2 CORINTHIANS 13:14 *ESV*)

If, though, you prefer to buy a Christmas present for your dog, you could do worse than search the shops for some kind of dog mitt, a type of glove which I am told is designed in such a way as to work as a cleaning/grooming aid to be worn (by you) when you stroke your dog; it will, apparently, gently remove hair when your dog is malting, to prevent it lingering on your carpet, while at the same time applying a mild shampoo or cleansing agent. Sounds like a great idea – doggie collects plenty of strokes and attention, a lot less vacuuming has to be done, and your dog's coat retains an impressive sheen!

This mitt cleans, soothes, and polishes, all in one! Simple! Tell me, though, if you understand quite as quickly the work of another trinity; that of God the Father, God the Son, and God the Holy Spirit! I have no doubt about the existence of God as three-in-one, but I can't pretend to entirely understand the doctrine. I accept it – indeed, I love it – but it remains a glorious mystery. Should we reject that which we cannot comprehend, as some cults and teachers do? Not at all. Should we embrace and explore those mysterious elements of the Godhead that bear scrutiny but define explanation? Of course! Were God not an enigma, he would hardly be God. May this marvellous Trinity give us the grace and humility to accept his inscrutability whilst at the same time studying to appreciate the splendour of God as one-in-three.

HAVING YOUR CAKE AND EATING IT

Jesus … cleanses us from all sin
(1 JOHN 1:7 **ESV**)

A radio science programme was contacted by two listeners wanting to know why, when both their dogs had stolen and devoured massive cakes, only one of them, Poppy, a Labrador, had to visit the vet to have her stomach pumped, while Spay, a black Labrador, needed no such treatment. The answer was that Poppy had eaten a double chocolate sponge covered with chocolate icing and the entire contents of two boxes of chocolates (!) whereas Spay had munched his way through a relatively ordinary, though equally large, fruit cake. One of those cakes, it was explained, is considerably more harmful to dogs than the other, chocolate being potentially lethal to canines because it contains the chemical theobromine, which acts as a stimulant and a poison inside a dog's intestine. Furthermore, the chemical can have such an intense stimulative effect on a dog (especially when a complete birthday cake has been gobbled up in one go!) that it can induce cardiac arrest. It seems Poppy chose the wrong cake to steal! (Spay suffered no side-effects whatsoever!)

I am pleased to report that Poppy was perfectly alright and back to her normal (greedy) self. Her owners rushed her to the vet and the offending theobromine was flushed out of her system – not particularly pleasant, but efficacious! Let us, dear friends, rush to the feet of Jesus if and when we have plunged (once again?) into a wrong and potentially harmful decision, flirting with the toxicity of sin in one form or another, however sweet and attractive that sin seemed at the time. There is no other remedy, for no one else has the authority to forgive us and make us clean again, in thought, word, and deed. Jesus, though, is a wonderful Saviour; he not only understands and forgives (over and over), but he washes too, with the thoroughness we need. No one else can, but he will, and we are made well again. This is Jesus.

WEDDINGS AND WORSHIP

We have been made holy through the sacrifice of the body of Jesus Christ once for all
(HEBREWS 10:10 **NIV**)

Heather and I celebrate our wedding anniversary today! (No medal has yet appeared, but I think a large one should be struck for Heather as soon as possible!) We shall celebrate with a restaurant meal, as always, but I am aware of the trend that now exists whereby happy couples include their dog(s) in their nuptial celebrations or anniversary commemorations. We shan't go down that line, largely because we don't actually own a dog, but also because it's not really our thing, however should that be your preference, you may wish to consider the following before you dress your dog up in a tuxedo or a dress:

Your dog's personality. Will your pooch be comfortable as the centre of attention, surrounded (for a few hours) by guests – and lots of children, maybe – all keen to fuss the canine guest of honour? This could be overwhelming and stressful. *A dog-sitter/minder*, bearing in mind that you, its beloved owner(s), will be preoccupied but visible all day, which may confuse Bella to the point of distress. *Confirm beforehand that dogs are actually allowed in your ceremony venue, and that the officiating minister/celebrant is comfortable with this.* Don't opt for a vicar who is scared of dogs! (Likewise, the photographer, who may prefer not to be expected to cajole a dog into his snapshots, and guests who may have animal allergies.) *Health and safety.* As we have heard, some dogs are partial to chocolate cake, and there are better ways to spend your wedding day than at the vet's! Likewise, check the flowers, as some can be toxic to dogs.

God is in the detail – so goes the saying, anyway, expressing the importance of doing things thoroughly, checking for loopholes and potential problems, never more gloriously expressed than the attention God has paid to securing our eternal happiness. Note our text for today as an expression of divine thoroughness; nothing is left to chance, not one sin is excluded from the plan of redemption. We are completely saved and thoroughly redeemed. God is indeed in the detail! Hallelujah!

PUBS AND PARADISE

Jesus said ... "I am the resurrection and the life. The one who believes in me will live, even though they die"

(JOHN 11:25 **NIV**)

From time to time, I enter short story competitions (mainly for fun, which is just as well as I have only ever won once!), and I am always on the lookout for opportunities to submit entries. One magazine I check quite often featured a winning entry (not mine!) about a ghost dog, of all things; in a nutshell, a pub landlord had lost his beloved dog, Melville, but was convinced his deceased friend haunted the bar as he said he sometimes heard glasses rattling mysteriously and claimed to smell Melville's scent following him around. The landlord was comfortable with this, as his supposed awareness of Melville's ghostly presence helped him to cope with his loss, especially as Melville had been killed in an accident that was probably the landlord's fault; to believe his much-loved dog was still alive, and still wanting to be beside him, assuaged his grief (and guilt) somewhat. He took comfort in that.

I have no time for clairvoyance and I would never recommend a visit to a medium. I do, though, empathize with those who grieve, and I have enormous sympathy with anyone wanting to contact a dead relative or friend at a séance. Do I believe in ghosts and ghostly presences? I believe we all have eternal souls, in that no one actually ever dies. Our physical bodies give way, but we live on beyond that death, so in that sense – according to that definition – then, yes, I believe life goes on beyond the grave or crematorium. My hope – my belief, my faith – for eternal security and joy rests entirely, and only, on Jesus; on his death and resurrection. He has conquered death, and he will shepherd me safely over the great divide between this world and the next. I have no other argument. I want no other plea. Christ is all.

YOU'LL NEVER WALK ALONE

Walk humbly with your God
(MICAH 6:8 **NIV**)

The story of the landlord's departed dog comes to the attention of the local newspaper editor, who dispatches a reporter to check it out. The journalist sent to investigate, becomes aware of what she thinks might possibly be ghostly goings-on as she interviews the landlord. She chats to some regulars, who confirm her suspicions that the dog might still be present, but notes the fact their stories tend to become increasingly dramatic as the free drinks – on expenses – flow! Time comes for Megan to leave the pub and step into the pitch black outside, alone, when she thinks she sees, in the newly fallen snow, paw prints in a line, alongside her, that vanish as soon as they appear ... We are left wondering whether Megan did or did not see Melville's paw prints as she trudged through the snow, but I reproduce below a poem held as factual personal experience by many who follow Christ – Christ who is, incidentally, very much alive.

One night a man had a dream.
He dreamed he was walking along the beach with the Lord.
Across the sky flashed scenes from his life.
For each scene, he noticed two sets of footprints in the sand:
one belonging to him, and the other to the Lord.
When the last scene of his life flashed before him,
he looked back at the footprints in the sand.
He noticed that many times along the path of his life
there was only one set of footprints.
He also noticed that it happened at the very lowest and saddest times in his life.
This really bothered him and he questioned the Lord about it.
"Lord, You said that once I decided to follow you,
you'd walk with me all the way.
But I have noticed that during the most troublesome times in my life,
there is only one set of footprints.
I don't understand why, when I needed you most, you would leave me."
The Lord replied,
"My son, my precious child, I love you and I would
never leave you.
During your times of trial and
suffering, when you see only one set of footprints,
it was then that I carried you."
(Authorship disputed)

POSTER BOY

A good word makes him glad
(PROVERBS 12:25 **ESV**)

As celebrity dog owners go, David and Victoria Beckham are at the top of the A-list, with three pet pooches – a French Bulldog called Scarlet, an English Bulldog christened Coco, and Olive, their Cocker Spaniel; quite a hat-trick for the former England captain! No doubt, David Beckham is idolized by his trio of dogs, as indeed he has been, and is, by thousands of football fans worldwide. That wasn't always the case, though, as in 1998, Beckham became something of a hate figure when he received a red card in a World Cup game against Argentina and was (unfairly) blamed and vilified for England's exit from the tournament. Levels of abuse and hatred reached disgusting proportions, but one church took advantage of the furore by placing an enormous bright yellow poster outside their building, proclaiming "God Forgives Even David Beckham"! What a clever – and lovely – response. God bless that church for its initiative, and God bless the Beckhams and their dogs!

For today's devotion, let's have a bit of fun and imagine that same unmissable poster on prominent display outside whichever church we attend, but let's replace the words "David Beckham" with our own names … picture it the next time you walk into your church; a massive poster there for all to see: "God loves [insert your name here]"!

THE SAVIOUR SOUGHT AND FOUND ME

God bought you with a high price
(I CORINTHIANS 6:20 **NLT**)

Everyone loves a bargain! Occasionally, if I am at home over lunchtime, I take a break from the computer screen to watch a TV programme in which amateur antiques experts hunt for bargains at collector's fairs. The last time I tuned in, a lady spotted a beautiful silver brooch of an Airedale Terrier on sale for £35, and I was so hoping she would buy it – it looked for all the world like an actual Airedale in miniature, so fine was the detail. Sadly, the bargain-buyer opted for something else instead, but not before weighing up the pooch brooch in the palm of her hand and saying (reluctantly, I like to think, put off by the price), "Let's put him back into his kennel" (which was, actually, a glass display case). I can only hope another bargain hunter parted with their money and gave the Airedale a good home!

One of the attractions of such programmes is speculating on the history of the items on offer – who might have owned them, where were they stored, was something once a gift, that sort of thing. Some finds come with good provenance, but most have no traceable origin. I have a Bible like that, which I bought from the internet because it is almost identical to one I had as a child; I don't know where it has been since it was published in 1958, nor who has owned it but, now that it is mine, I treasure it. So it is when we come home to God, who parted with his all to purchase our souls, and who treasures us. All that we may not know or understand or comprehend about ourselves (including, in some cases, our ancestry) is quieted and calmed in his embrace – those great questions, the mysterious complexity of simply being human. God holds us – for eternity – in the palm of his hand, meeting our need with his presence. *He is where we belong.*

AN UNWANTED WORD

*They will turn away their ears from the truth and turn aside to myths. But ... do
the work of an evangelist, discharge all the duties of your ministry*

(2 TIMOTHY 4:4–5 ***NIV***)

Did you know that dog lovers are canophiles? Either that, or canophilists. That
is, "people with a fondness for dogs". For some reason, my computer refuses
to acknowledge either word, and insists on letting them appear on my screen
only on condition they remain underlined in angry red. I'm not sure why, as
they are both perfectly legitimate words, but (a bit like Skipper) my laptop
is refusing to play ball. Oh well, it can't be helped, and with a publishing
deadline looming, I can't afford the time or energy to investigate the matter or
go to war with technology. I know I'm a canophile and a canophilist, and so do
you! That will have to do!

The day before writing this devotion, I preached from 2 Timothy, using the text above, and
I was impressed by Paul's advice to his protégé, in which, effectively, he urged him to "carry
on regardless". Paul advised Timothy that there would come a day when people wouldn't be
interested in hearing the gospel, and that the good news would fall on ears as deaf as Skipper's.
That notwithstanding, Paul urges Timothy not to be discouraged, but to devote his energies to
the task in hand. I like that! We are called to be witnesses, but the results of our witnessing
are not up to us. People might refuse to accept the story of salvation as stubbornly as my
computer refuses to accept the words canophile and canophilists. No matter. We pray, we
press on, we preach, we persevere, and we leave the rest to providence.

THE CARES OF THIS WORLD

A happy heart makes the face cheerful
(PROVERBS 15:13 **NIV**)

Basset Hounds are wonderful, aren't they? With their doleful expression – the epitome of "hangdog" – they are instantly appealing and likeable. One in particular, though – Duke – was reported in the newspapers as having such an abundance of heavy skin on his forehead that it was falling and sagging in front of his eyes, effectively turning him blind. His concerned owners consulted a vet, who diagnosed entropion, a condition sometimes found in older Bassett Hounds whereby the eyelids begin to descend and fold inwards. A facelift was prescribed! The excess skin was removed and the skin on his face pulled upwards! Thanks to the skill of the veterinary surgeon, Duke is now able to see again, and no longer feels like falling asleep all the time. Doubtless, he still looks pensive, as Basset Hounds do, but no longer quite so wrinkled! His furrowed brow is impressively smooth again!

I guess they can't help it, but Basset Hounds do tend to look as though they have the cares of the world on their shoulders, as though they are miserable and world-weary. They probably aren't, but they sure do give that impression! Have you ever encountered a Christian like that, trudging into church Sunday after Sunday as though it were an ordeal? I'm not suggesting we all go about with fixed grins and false optimism oozing from every pore, but surely, we of all people can afford to be cheerful more often than not? We have our sins forgiven, we walk with a God to whom we can daily hand over our cares and woes, and our journey ends in Glory! Of course, sadness crosses our threshold sometimes but, by and large, should any believer permanently resemble a Basset Hound with a ministry of misery? (Just for fun, have a look around your congregation and see for yourself!)

RAIN STOPPED PLAY

All the days ordained for me
(PSALM 139:16 **NIV**)

The unusual weather patterns of recent years – global warming, climate change, call it what you will – have resulted in wetter summers than usual in Scotland. Yes, I know Scotland isn't renowned for its balmy climes, but even with that caveat in mind, it appears Scotland is struggling with bouts of incessant rain that weren't previously common in summer. A consequence of this is that grouse shooting programmes – popular on many Scottish estates – are either drastically reduced or cancelled altogether, as grouse chicks cannot survive the damp. Subsequently, dogs usually employed during grouse season – Retrievers, Labradors, and Spaniels, typically – are sitting by in many areas, unemployed and idle. I have just seen a great picture of a grouse beater looking out across hundreds of acres of spectacular moorland, with three rather bored dogs at his feet – a black Labrador and two Cocker Spaniels. The area, as majestic as it is, is entirely deserted; nothing is happening, and these three dogs, I have to say, look somewhat bemused, wondering what comes next.

Maybe we can pray today for those whose days are long and empty? Let us remember in prayer those who have no work to do, no job to go to, and those whose physical limitations impose conditions whereby the only voice they might hear between getting up and going back to bed comes from a radio or a TV. The grouse dogs are not intentionally inactive, and neither are many people; most would prefer to earn a living, or at least be able to socialize. Their boredom can be dreadfully oppressive, so too their loneliness. We pray for those without work and without company. Lord, have mercy and intervene. May what comes next be only good.

WILL YOU STILL NEED ME?

Honor the face of an old man
(LEVITICUS 19:32 **ESV**)

On this day in 1930, Ronald Balfour Corbett was born – that's Scottish comedy giant Ronnie Corbett to you and me! Best known as one half of the double act *The Two Ronnies*, which at one time had millions glued to their TV screens, Ronnie C, as he referred to himself (his on-screen partner, Ronnie Barker, being known as Ronnie B) was also hugely successful all by himself in any number of television and radio roles, not least the BBC radio sitcom *When the Dog Dies*. Wrapped up in the entertainment was the slightly sad tale of a chap called Sandy Hopper (Ronnie Corbett), whose children are keen for him to move into a retirement home as soon as possible, not because they are concerned for his welfare, but because they want to sell his house and get the money. The episodes revolve around plots to uproot Sandy, but he sticks to his line that he will only move out when his dog, Henry, dies! The onus then falls upon Ronnie Corbett to keep his dog alive as long as possible, and for Henry to cooperate, the logic being that it would be inhumane to expect Henry to relocate ... an excuse that wears thinner and thinner with each visit from his grasping offspring!

Friends of ours received a vision from the Lord encouraging them to develop a church for elderly people – the likes of Sandy Hopper. I witnessed the progress of their plans, and was so pleased to see great blessing upon their work, as it made a refreshing change to see grey hair being the focus of attention instead of, if I may say so, the seemingly overwhelming drive to put all our eggs in the basket of youth work, valid as that is. (You disagree? Have a look in any Christian magazine and compare the number of vacancies for Youth Workers to those for Outreach Workers to the Elderly.) Everyone matters, of course, but there needs to be a balance. Something to consider in your church, perhaps? Sandy (and Henry!) would appreciate that, I'm sure.

A BORROWED STRENGTH

Let the weak say, I am strong

(JOEL 3:10 **KJV**)

Debate rages, and has done for some time, regarding the question of Scottish independence from the United Kingdom. Arguments and points of view fly to and fro as the leader of the Scottish Nationalist Party, Nicola Sturgeon, campaigns to lead her country out of the UK. Let's be honest – anyone who is leader of the SNP has to be made of tough stuff! The job is not for the fainthearted, thin-skinned or easily offended, and Nicola Sturgeon appears to have what it takes to handle controversy as a political leader. Except, that is, when it comes to dogs, of which, it is reported, she is terrified. Hard to imagine her being scared of anything, but the phobia emerged when a cabaret artist took his dog, Lala (a beautiful all-black Whippet cross, I think), to meet the politician backstage, after a show, and Sturgeon's fears were explained. That's no fun, but there is a happy ending, in that Lala, a calm and soothing dog, was able to reduce some of Nicola Sturgeon's anxiety, and is said to be the first dog the SNP boss ever felt safe with. Well done, Lala! (I think she got Nicola's vote!)

Some of Nicola Sturgeon's political opponents would undoubtedly ascribe Terrier-like qualities to her style of leadership, and would do so in a complimentary way. She is tenacious and can be aggressive in debate, as indeed her job requires her to be. It is somewhat surprising, then, to learn that she has an Achilles heel, a weak spot, an area of vulnerability. In a way, that comes as a relief, and many of us will say, "Welcome to the club, Nicola!" There is no particular virtue in weakness, but there is every virtue in having the wisdom and humility to admit that none of us is Superman or Superwoman, especially when acknowledging that leads us towards Christ as our friend and Saviour. He knows our every imperfection, and stands ready to help, protect, and support. This is our God.

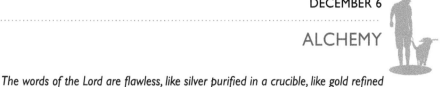

ALCHEMY

The words of the Lord are flawless, like silver purified in a crucible, like gold refined seven times

(PSALM 12:6 **NIV**)

I like art, and I am fascinated by an art form known as metalpoint, where a thin stylus of a soft metal such as silver or gold is scored onto a surface that has been prepared with some kind of brushed-on ground made of pulverized animal bones mixed with glue. The tip of a soft stylus on ordinary paper leaves behind nothing but colourless grooves, whereas the roughness of the bone mixture causes a minute trace of the silver or gold to remain and leave a mark. If you have access to the internet, or can look it up in a book, you might want to search for a copy of Albrecht Dürer's *Dog Resting* (c. 1520), a superb example of this skill. Using only these materials, the artist has sketched a beautifully detailed picture of what is almost certainly a Hungarian Agar Hound. One of these days, I might give metalpoint a go, but for now, I would encourage you to study Dürer's marvellous attention to detail; his *Dog Resting* will, I hope, fascinate you as much as it does me.

I suppose the principle is already clear – that of allowing a degree of friction to produce something beautiful; that which rubs us up the wrong way and costs us something of ourselves. What do we leave behind at such (inevitable) times? Traces of gold and silver, so to speak? Fragments of Christ? When the rough ground of life takes all we have to give, do we regard it as theft, or an opportunity to offer something precious? In the nitty-gritty times, may the Lord help us to make good and lasting impressions that he will then turn into mementoes of beauty – his beauty rubbing off on others, making a mark.

HIS WONDERS TO PERFORM

"My thoughts are nothing like your thoughts," says the Lord. "And my ways are far beyond anything you could imagine"
(ISAIAH 55:8 **NLT**)

Albrecht Dürer was well known for including dogs in his metalpoint works. All kinds appeared, some prominent and obvious, others hidden and more difficult to spot. Undoubtedly, he included some simply because of his love of dogs, especially hunting hounds, an integral part of medieval society, but speculation persists about political messages his artwork may contain – for example, his inclusion of Hungarian Agars and Vizslas, sometimes regarded as symbols of nobility; did Albrecht the artist feature them in his metalpoint as tacit support of the nobility of the day? Or was the explanation more mundane and only a clever reference to his Hungarian heritage? Dürer's *The Martyrdom of St John the Evangelist* features a Portuguese Water Dog (an ancestor of the Poodle, incidentally), almost certainly significant because this breed was noted for its exceptional loyalty to a master (for which read John in his relationship to Christ) and was favoured by sailors for its brave (martyr-like) willingness to dive into deep waters and retrieve seafarers who might otherwise drown at sea. Numerous other examples abound of dogs appearing bearing secret, coded messages – check out Dürer's work for yourself!

The Bible is laced with symbolism. I wish I understood every subtle prophetic nuance but I'm afraid I don't – sorry! Much of Daniel's work, for example, is shrouded in mystery; likewise, John's Revelations. To be honest, some Old Testament prophecies leave me baffled, and it is painfully obvious I need to study more in order to dig out the hidden meanings. To that end, we give thanks to God for gifted teachers, interpreters, lecturers, and prophets who use their intellects and visionary insights to help the likes of me glimpse a little more of God's mysterious ways. Theirs is not an enviable task, but we are indebted to them!

FAITH, FADS AND FASHIONS

Jesus Christ is the same yesterday and today and forever
(HEBREWS 13:8 **ESV**)

I have been offered a free cape! I think, but I'm not sure, this freebie is meant for my dog to wear (or would be, if I had one), not me – at least I hope that's the case. I can't honestly see myself wearing a cape, but the free gift is offered as an incentive for anyone wanting to join in a sponsored walk in aid of Guide Dogs. Fair enough – a great cause – but my confusion arises because the publicity shot features five enthusiastic dogs – a Terrier, three Irish Wolfhounds, and a Labradoodle – none of whom are wearing capes, and six human beings, one of whom is actually caped! Having said that, the Labradoodle is wearing what look to me very much like pyjama trousers, so it's all a bit confusing. I think I'd need the sponsored walk just to clear my head in the fresh air!

When I received my cape offer, I couldn't help but think of the capes worn by female Salvationists in the 1970s, as part of their uniform. Quite why capes were phased out for Army lasses is beyond me, as I always thought they looked impressive, but such, I guess, are the whims of fashion. Clothing fads are one thing and don't matter much in the long run, but I long for a Church that holds fast to established truths, when I sometimes sense a rush to modernity and relevance that is not always appropriate. Of course we must be modern and relevant, but not at the expense of non-negotiables; the fact that Jesus is Lord, for example, and not merely one of many routes to God, and so on. Capes came and went, whereas Christ is eternal, and our duty to proclaim him as a unique Saviour remains permanently in vogue.

BLUE LIGHTS AND RED SEAS

The Lord their God will intervene

(ZEPHANIAH 2:7 **NET**)

A lovely, heart-warming story emerges, of Sophie, a ten-year-old Jack Russell/ Patterdale cross who saved her master's life when he suffered a stroke while they were out walking together. Sophie was strolling along when her owner collapsed in need of urgent medical help, and ran to a nearby football field where she started barking and running backwards and forwards near to where some footballers were playing. Thankfully, two football coaches realized Sophie was trying to alert them to something, and followed her to where her owner was lying unconscious in a wooded area. To cut the story short – with respect to Sophie's heroics! – an ambulance was called and the stroke victim was rushed to a neurosurgery unit, where medics confirmed it was unlikely he would have survived without such intervention. God bless Sophie and God bless her owner!

Quite a miracle, really! Scripture is full of examples of God's interventions; the miraculous deliverance of Moses the baby, for example, when his mum placed him in a basket in the crocodile-infested Nile in order to escape the cull of little boys, the dramatic Red Sea escape made by the Israelites (led by Moses the man) when God rescued them from bloodthirsty Egyptians, Daniel's rescue from the furnace and the lions' den, and so on, and so forth ... the list is a long one! One of God's names is "Lord of the breakthrough" (Baal-perazim), and I pray for you as I write, that God will intervene in your circumstances if you need him to; that your breakthrough will appear. The God of Moses and miracles is our God, today, not a God consigned to ancient history. Go with my prayers. God bless you.

THAT WHICH GOD HATH JOINED

"I hate divorce!" says the Lord
(MALACHI 2:16 **NLT**)

Not for the bashful, this one! A vet tells the story of a vomiting West Highland Terrier brought to him for treatment by an anxious couple. So far, so good – all in a day's work, and he treated the Westie with a drug that would make it so sick that everything – everything, bear that in mind – would be brought up. The drug worked but what happened next hadn't been anticipated, as the Terrier vomited up ... a bright red suspender belt! Cue an angry outburst from the female half of the couple, who had never seen the offending article before, and the rapid draining of blood from her husband's face. Their private life is their private life, and we'll leave it at that, but suffice to say, she made an appointment to see a divorce solicitor exactly one week after she had made that fateful appointment to see the vet ...

Oh dear! I wouldn't have liked to be that vet! (I wonder what happened to the West Highland Terrier once this couple divorced.) There is a funny side to this, insofar as the scenario has all the ingredients of a comedy film or a stage farce, but in reality, it is not funny at all; it is about the sad breakdown of a serious relationship. I wouldn't dream of taking sides, as divorce is painful, personal, and complex, and in any case it's not mine to judge, but we know it breaks God's heart. Various strands of theological opinion exist around divorce (and remarriage) amongst Christians, but I would like to think compassion would be our first port of call because the point is, God hates divorce, but he loves divorcees with a passion. Whatever the ifs, buts, and maybes of broken marriages, perhaps today we can pray for those experiencing that pain and distress. Lord, have mercy.

FLEAS AND FAITH

The king of Israel has come out to look for a flea

(1 SAMUEL 26:20 **NIV**)

Well, well – you live and learn! I am reliably advised that rising temperatures (climate change, etc.) are accountable for an increase in domestic flea infestations. Fleas, apparently – dog ones – prefer being warm to chilly, and warmer climes suit them just fine, in much the same way as we humans tend to search out the sunshine for a holiday. What I didn't realize is that when such infestations strike (when one's dog has brought home a family of fleas for their vacation), only 5 per cent of those fleas will choose to stay tucked up in dog hair (staycation). The rest, an astonishing 95 per cent, will invade your house, treating it like their own private hotel. Thankfully, help is at hand in the form of any number of treatments but, should you notice your dog beginning to scratch itself more than normal, take action, lest you be overrun with tiny guests!

It is not unreasonable to wonder why God allowed fleas and their like to survive the great flood, when they could easily have been wiped out and perfectly innocent dogs saved an awful lot of irritation and scratching! That, though, is too simplistic a question, as even I know this marvellously complex ecosystem in which we live depends heavily upon fragile interactions between different species. Quite what purpose a flea serves in that plan is beyond me, but what little I know about the interdependencies of the natural world persuades me that even fleas have a role to play. Granted, I would rather they didn't play that role on my dog or in my house, but if I acknowledge God as Creator, then it behoves me to also acknowledge the fact that I don't know much at all, whereas he does!

SUPER BOWL COMES TO ENGLAND!

Ponds of water

(ECCLESIASTES 2:6 **NASB**)

From the tiny to the enormous – the world's largest dog bowl has made an appearance in London. Standing 1 metre tall and stretching 4.5 metres in diameter, the British version of Super Bowl can hold a remarkable maximum of 2,000 litres of water! Touring the country, the giant receptacle will be on display in a bid to educate dog owners about keepings dogs hydrated; did you know, for example (I didn't!) that over 80 per cent of a dog's weight comes from water? Generally speaking, the average dog (Skipper was a relentless drinker at times, especially when he was ill) should drink between twenty and seventy millilitres of water daily for every kilogram they weigh, but don't worry about weighing your dog and measuring out appropriately measured quantities of water! Just leave plenty of water available (at all times, not only with meals), and your dog will figure out the rest – bearing in mind, of course, that dramatic increases in fluid intake usually indicate some kind of health problem.

I took my mum and her friend out for dinner, and Mum and I were pleasantly surprised at the enthusiasm shown by Mum's friend for a simple glass of water! To be honest, I hadn't noticed my drink much as I was focusing on my meal, but this lady waxed lyrical about the multiple health benefits of such a plain and commonplace drink! She was right, of course, as any doctor will tell you, but what struck me was my daily tendency to take such a thing as a jug of water for granted, when God has created such a wonderful, life-sustaining liquid. May God forgive my ingratitude and, by the same token, help those who are confronted with the nightmare of drought and/or an absence of clean drinking water. Lord, have mercy.

CHECK IT OUT

Whoever drinks the water I give them will never thirst
(JOHN 4:14 **NIV**)

While I'm on the subject, it might be worth my while outlining classic signs of dehydration in a dog, as well as the excessive consumption of water I have already mentioned. One problem is that doggie dehydration is not always easy to spot, but the following pointers may be useful, and might even prevent illness developing. Signs to keep an eye out for include:

- Sunken eyes
- Dry gums
- Lethargy
- Loss of skin elasticity
- Weakness
- Collapsing

Dramatic as some of these signs sound (and they may indicate something other than dehydration), they are recognized indicators of a dog failing to drink sufficient water, and most vets recommend a brief monthly check-up at home, just to err on the side of caution.

It would be interesting to come up with a list that would diagnose problems of spiritual well-being. Speaking personally, when I am out of sorts spiritually, my gums remain much the same and my skin loses none of its elasticity, but I would recognize other symptoms, and I would know I needed to return to prayer and fellowship with God. Perhaps, to that end, I should consider asking a mentor or spiritual guide to help me, to meet with me from time to time (monthly?) in order to keep an eye on the health of my devotional life? What do you think? If prevention is better than cure, then it might be a good idea …

LETTING OFF STEAM

Do not let the sun go down while you are still angry
(EPHESIANS 4:26 **NIV**)

The day before writing this page, I was on the receiving end of a telephone call from a Christian friend who was hot under the dog collar about a particular issue. The details don't belong here, but I could almost feel the temperature of my earpiece rising as the call continued! (I thought it might melt at one point!) Honesty compels me to say the call generated more heat than light, but these things happen, and no lasting harm was done. I am, though, amused to have seen, since, an advertisement for a pad that will cool your dog as soon as it sits on it, and which refreshes itself as soon as your dog steps off again. (My friend could have used one during that telephone exchange!) The idea is that Rover uses the pad to lower his temperature on a hot day, or if he has worked up a sweat running around, and is ideal for, say, a car journey if the sun is shining. Cool!

Let's face it – tempers fray, and even the saints feel their blood boiling sometimes! That's life, and very few people manage to stay placid all the time, however devout and determined they are. If we accept that as part and parcel of living in a fallen world, then our text for today comes into its own. Given that there is a certain inevitability about disagreements – heated or otherwise – we might just have to settle for damage limitation involving apologies, explanations, and helpings of humble pie in order to get a good night's sleep; time out with God on the cool pad, perhaps! Please don't beat yourself – or anyone else! – up if this is you today; God understands, and is only too willing to apply a cooling balm. God too is remarkably cool!

FOXY ROXY

Bear one another's burdens

(GALATIANS 6:2 **ESV**)

Roxy is a Dog (male) Fox who was rescued by an animal welfare centre and, at the grand old age of fifteen, can't now be released, as he wouldn't survive in the wild; he needs to be kept in captivity for the rest of his life. He will be well cared for, but Roxy is, effectively, a prisoner – which I mention because the centre in question runs a scheme whereby prison inmates (human ones!) visit to look after the animals, as part of their rehabilitation. This is a beautiful idea; the scheme teaches the prisoners the therapeutic benefits of animal interaction, the centre staff appreciate a helping hand, and who knows what difference this may make in the life of someone whose life hasn't gone according to plan.

Here's a poem I wrote for a friend whose life seemed to be crumbling into disarray – somewhat like the prisoners in our story, maybe. It is also a prayer ...

My friend, worry not that I shall judge you, for I shan't.
Worry not that you may need to face my anger, for you shan't.
Though your wounds be self-inflicted, you shall not lose my friendship,
Nor, for that matter, any of my respect;
Let not any of these concerns add to your woes, for your burdens are
heavy already.
Worry not that I may shun you, or be ashamed to share a pavement with you,
Or even reluctant. For I shan't. Nor shall I write you off.
Nor shall I behave imperiously, as though your deeds make me superior;
They do not; nor you, inferior. You are still my friend.
Nor shall I close doors, or cease contact, though you are guilty.
For who am I to judge? Or tolerate gossip? Or speculation?
Who am I to condemn, and not to love?
Especially now, when you will need friendship more than ever?
No. As the bricks and rocks upon which you have built your life begin to
crumble,
Perhaps you would allow me the privilege of kneeling at your feet,
collecting them,
Carrying them for you, so that we can, one day, build a better tomorrow?
For this too will pass, and while it passes, we are friends.

A TEXT WITHOUT A CONTEXT IS A PRETEXT!

*Study to shew thyself approved unto God, a workman that needeth not to be
ashamed, rightly dividing the word of truth*
(2 TIMOTHY 2:15 *KJV*)

It's a few years since I studied at any formal level, but I am interested to learn of an education and training course offering the opportunity of studying dogs. The course offers units in Canine Behaviour, Canine Aggression, Canine Anatomy and Physiology, Canine Care, Canine Nutrition, Canine Communication, Canine First Aid, Dogs and the Law, Dog Behaviour Problems, Puppy Training, and even Wolf Studies and Conservation. Aimed at dog owners, vets, dog wardens, and kennel operators in particular, the studies are designed to ensure that those handling dogs on a regular basis, domestically or professionally, get things right, with the aid of better understanding. Certificates are also available!

To a certain extent, studying God is pointless, in that he can never be fully understood. Even our greatest achievements in theology represent but a drop in the ocean, such is the incomprehensible nature of his majesty. Nevertheless, we are encouraged to explore and excavate his word – the Bible – in order to appreciate context, nuance, chronology, authorship, and all those points that surround familiar texts, so as to navigate ourselves towards the truest and richest meanings of well-loved Scripture verses. A jewel is a jewel, but we appreciate it more when it is set against a fitting background; likewise, God's word is God's word, but we deprive ourselves of a host of insights if we fail to notice (or investigate) the original backdrop of cherished lines, when we can, for want of a little diligence, treasure words of Scripture all the more because we glance them in their most accurate and authentic setting. Certificates might not necessarily be available, but great blessings are!

HAIR OF THE DOG

They shall surely trim the hair of their heads
(EZEKIEL 44:20 **ESV**)

Meg and Skipper were enthusiastic malters – so much so, my wife gave up on the idea of a rug in our living room and settled for wooden flooring instead, all the better for sweeping and vacuuming! I have to say, though, for all Skipper and Meg left quite a bit of hair around the place, I am grateful Heather didn't resort to an idea practised by a Chinese lady who took to eating the hairballs produced whenever she brushed her Poodle, and who has now swallowed over 1,000 of them (hairballs, not Poodles)! Originally, she began eating Poodle hair simply out of curiosity, but grew to like the taste and texture before discovering it served her well as a stress-relieving technique, almost a pastime. Poodle hairballs are now her snack of choice.

It would be easy to read about this lady and wonder whatever possessed her to take up such a hobby, but the Old Testament gives examples of behaviour which definitely challenge hers for individuality! Isaiah walked around in the nude (Isaiah 20), Jeremiah hid his underpants (Jeremiah 13), then attached himself to a cattle yoke (27 and 28), Hosea named his daughter Lo-ruhama, which means "unloved" (Hosea 1), Ezekiel swallowed a scroll, then took to lying on one side for 390 days (Ezekiel 3 and 4), and Jonah managed to doggie paddle directly into the mouth of an oncoming giant fish. (Jonah 1) One crucial detail is that these prophets were commanded by God, which means we cannot dismiss their behaviour, but maybe another moral of the story is that we should pause before passing judgment on those whose actions initially strike us as a bit weird; better that we try to understand. Differences in norms can be shocking, but kindness needs to have the upper hand, always.

GIVEN THE BRUSH-OFF

Naaman, the commander of the Syrian army, was highly respected and esteemed by the king of Syria … but he suffered from a dreaded skin disease
(2 KINGS 5:1 **GNT**)

We were on holiday in Northumberland when we noticed a scabbing/dandruff in Meg's thick coat. Hundreds of orange flakes seemed to have taken over her skin, so, as we were out for the day, we found a pet shop and invested in a sturdy brush, hoping to rid her of the offending flakes, if not solve the underlying problem. Heather and Jasmine then went into a supermarket, while Alistair and I sat on a bench outside, where we commenced Operation Brush. We weren't creating any trouble at all, but one lady took great, loud, and angry exception to our efforts. She really did fly off the handle, expressing her unambiguous opposition to the clean-up. It was a tad embarrassing, but reached a slightly more alarming level when she informed us that her dog would fight ours. Given that Meg was an arthritic octogenarian with a skin complaint and fading eyesight, that was no great boast, but we took the hint and, when Heather and Jasmine emerged again from the aisles, walked quietly away. To this day, we aren't entirely certain what her problem might have been, but Meg's, we discovered, was some kind of psoriasis, soon sorted out with medicated shampoo.

Naaman the warrior, conqueror of countries, defender of kings, and national hero, met his match not on a battlefield, but in the form of a dreaded skin disease (possibly leprosy). The mighty man hardly batted an eyelid at the thought of war, yet was forced to seek help from an enemy nation when his skin began to flake, sending word to Elisha and pleading for healing. How do we view this? Given that one element of the cleansing miracle that took place was Naaman's consideration of Elisha's God, might we therefore contend that God sometimes allows illness to enter our lives in order to grab our attention (when we have previously ignored him)? It's a controversial line, but I see no reason to airbrush Scripture, for if God is love, and if health concerns bring us to our knees, then it might possibly be that such love will reach out to our eternal souls via physical distress. I don't know for sure, but our spiritual healing – our recovery from the illness we call sin – is, arguably, more important to God than our temporary physical restoration. What do you feel?

ON A WING AND A PRAYER

Who are these that fly?

(ISAIAH 60:8 *NIV*)

Callie, a chocolate Labrador from Leighton Buzzard, Bedfordshire, England, is the only dog to have been awarded an Air Crew Member card by the Aircraft Owners and Pilots Association! She has earned it, having clocked up over 50,000 air miles on flights from Bedfordshire to places as far away as Barra in the Outer Hebrides, Scotland. By all accounts, Callie loves flying – well, she likes the taking off and landing bits, but sleeps while she is airborne! (She is also rather fond of the sausage she is given at the conclusion of each flight!) Good for Callie! She flies all over the UK with her owner – from Leighton Buzzard to Wales and Cornwall – but Barra is her favourite destination because the landing strip is actually on the beach, so she can just step out of the plane and enjoy a good run as soon as she lands!

A lady in my church is (quite rightly) extraordinarily proud of the fact that one of her sons is something or other to do with Mission Aviation Fellowship (she knows what he does, it's my memory that's lacking, not hers!). To that end, out of respect to her and her son, and with a nod to Callie, the flying Labrador, I would ask today that we say a prayer for MAF. I've looked at their website, and theirs is an impressive ministry, reaching the isolated with practical (medical) care and sharing the gospel in far-flung outposts as far apart as Ecuador and Papua New Guinea. Interested?

Mission Aviation Fellowship,
Castle House, Castle Hill Avenue,
Folkestone, Kent CT20 2TQ
United Kingdom

Telephone: (01303) 852819
www.maf-uk.org/contact-us

COPS AND ROBBERS

I will lead you to a land flowing with milk and honey
(EXODUS 3:17 **NLT**)

A friend of ours spent some of her childhood in a Salvation Army children's home, where her parents were the officers in charge. Their dog lived with them, with the unofficial role of guard dog, except it didn't really take its guarding duties too seriously, and was more interested in being made a fuss of. Thus it was, one night, that our friend's parents heard some suspicious noises in the wee small hours, including what sounded like frantic breathing. Wondering if a) They had burglars or b) One of the children was ill and struggling to breathe, they investigated, only to discover a would-be burglar standing by their fridge, panting for breath. In his efforts to deprive The Salvation Army of what was rightfully theirs, this hapless thief had stolen a small bottle of tabasco sauce from the kitchen and, in the dark, thinking it was an alcoholic beverage – a miniature – swallowed the lot in one go, half-burning his throat! The police were called, but not without an amount of laughter, though these good people did also offer plenty of cold milk to drink. Meanwhile, their "guard dog", who could have prevented the whole thing with a well-timed bark or two, or even some alerting interest in the burglary, padded about entirely oblivious to his non-role in the whole affair, wondering what the commotion was all about!

Friends, let us be careful about taking every word of Scripture literally, as some would have us do. A land flowing with milk and honey, for example, might have been just what that unfortunate thief with his burning need would have welcomed, but if there really were any such place, in a literal definition, living there would just be sticky and wet, and not particularly pleasant! I do not preach a gospel of scepticism when it comes to the gospel, just one of common sense where credibility is at stake. Literalism isn't always intended, and we should not be afraid simply to enjoy the descriptive – but allusory – word-pictures often painted by Bible writers.

DECEMBER 21

IN OR OUT?

Whoever is not with me is against me
(MATTHEW 12:30 **NIV**)

The morning of putting this page together, I created a problem for Oxfam – not deliberately (I like Oxfam), but just because this sort of thing seems to happen whenever I am allowed out on my own. I had wandered into the Oxfam shop in town, and was wandering out again when I noticed three children outside, clamouring to come in. Their parents were browsing around inside, while the children were waiting by the door – not because Mum and Dad were unkind, but because the youngsters had been detailed to look after a Yorkshire Terrier, and dogs are not allowed on the premises. Furthermore, one of the kids was eating noodles from a tinfoil container, and food is also barred from Oxfam shops. None of this, strictly speaking, was any of my business, except that when I went to leave, the children spotted the door opening and tried to make/ barge their way in; tinfoil, noodles, Yorkshire Terrier, and all. Oh dear! I was faced with the unenviable task of having to point out to someone else's children that they couldn't actually enter, while Mum and Dad did precisely nothing to ease my dilemma. In the end, I'm afraid I abdicated any responsibility that anyone might have considered mine (I can't honestly see how it was in the first place, except it was me who opened the door), and in came the trio, the dog, and the foodstuffs, much to the consternation of the Oxfam staff, who I could tell by the looks being shot in my direction, held me entirely responsible ...

They say, don't they, that it is inadvisable to work with children and animals! The truth is, I just walked away, a little embarrassed, somewhat flustered, and slightly annoyed (by the inactive parents). I had failed to take decisive door-keeping action and a bit of a mishmash of confusion was the net result, with a mixture of culprits and suspects. That's neither here nor there, really, but can I afford to dither like that when it comes to the gospel? Hardly! I must take a clear stand for Jesus, pretty much regardless of what anyone else thinks or any looks I may receive; regardless, too, of what anyone else does. I'll stand for Christ. I'll not dither. Will you join me? The door to the Kingdom is open wide, and there is always room for more!

CAN I COME IN?

I am the gate; whoever enters through me will be saved
(JOHN 10:9 **NIV**)

Popping in to the newsagents one dark December evening, I tied Meg to a tall wrought-iron gate next door, and was standing in the queue, waiting to pay, when a lady came in and asked me if the dog outside was mine. Thinking she too was a queuing customer, and that she was making polite small talk, I gladly admitted ownership of such a fine and docile beast, and proceeded to smilingly extol Meg's many virtues and parts of her fascinating life history. Well, it would pass the time, I thought. It wasn't until a few minutes had passed that I noticed her initial cordiality turning to mild agitation, at which point I began to sense something might be wrong. It was! She wasn't a customer, she wasn't queuing, and she wasn't waiting to pay for anything – the iron gate, she explained (somewhat tersely), led to the pathway that led to her house. In the darkness, I hadn't noticed either, but here she was, anxious to get indoors on a cold evening after a long day at work, but unable to access her home because someone had parked their big old dog there ...

Not too much harm was done, though I did feel a bit rotten about the misunderstanding. I untied Meg and the lady was able to anticipate a relaxing evening in the warm (though I did note she didn't offer much more by way of conversation). If only she had realized, Meg wouldn't have bitten her, or snarled at her, or even minded at all, had she marched right up to the gate and let herself in. Do you think that might be the same with the gate to Heaven, Jesus? He has no intention of harming anyone, yet he is all too often treated with fear, suspicion, scepticism, and, therefore, avoided, not mentioned in polite company. Here is Jesus, the beautiful gate to eternal life, yet many cross the road in order to avoid him, rather than speak to him about access. Might that form the focus of our prayers today?

SERVANTS OF THE SERVANT KING

I heard the voice of the Lord saying, "Whom shall I send? And who will go for us?"
And I said, "Here am I. Send me!"

(ISAIAH 6:8 *NIV*)

In the days when Heather and I both worked for The Salvation Army in London, it was necessary for us to employ a dog walker for Meg. We found a lovely lady and Meg was perfectly happy to join her on lengthy midday excursions. One bonus was that this lady brought her own dog with her, an idea that would never have worked with Skipper (!), but was good for Meg as the other dog was also aged and arthritic, which meant the walking pace suited our old girl who, towards the end of her days, would sometimes need to take a breather and/or be cajoled back to her feet again after falling down (despite which, she was always keen to go walkies!). We took great comfort in knowing that while we were locked up in our London offices, Meg was being visited, fussed, and walked in excellent company. I can only hope all dog walkers are as kind and sympathetic as ours was. She really was a Godsend.

No doubt you have heard similar testimonies, but I was chatting to a Salvation Army officer once, who related the story of how he suddenly felt an urgent need to visit one of his congregation, for no apparent reason; he simply felt the Holy Spirit telling him to get there quickly, immediately, though he had absolutely no idea why. Dropping his plans, he obeyed and visited, only to find that member of his congregation on the very brink of suicide. His arrival was instrumental in a life being saved. That sort of scenario is of course – thankfully – the exception, but my point is that every one of us, albeit in more mundane ways, can serve the Lord as good neighbours. All would hear the Holy Spirit, if they listen to his voice, and who knows what avenues of service might open up!

HOME FROM HOME

The Lord will take me in
(PSALM 27:10 **ESV**)

On average, dogs taken in by the marvellous Battersea Dogs' Home live there for a month or so before being rehomed. One exception, though, was Bud, who was looked after by staff at Battersea for a staggering 1,000 days before anyone came to claim him, during which time 5,000 other dogs were adopted! Poor Bud! As much as the care he would have received was excellent, the fact is, he spent three years in a rescue centre – not great for any dog. He is a Greyhound cross and was consistently rebuffed because he is big, boisterous, and very lively – something of a handful for prospective owners, many of whom felt unable to manage him. His speciality, apparently, is involving himself in whatever is going on! Bud is no idle bystander! The good news is, he is now doing marvellously well with a family who love him. Britain's loneliest dog will be home for Christmas!

On Christmas Eve, our thoughts turn to those who would love to be, like Bud, home for Christmas, but aren't; service personnel who will spend today under canvas and possibly under fire too, emergency services personnel whose shifts mean they can't spend much of the Christmas season with loved ones, clergy, for whom this is a busy and demanding time of year – not forgetting, of course, those who find themselves in hostels for the homeless (and those who staff such havens), or sleeping on a rock-hard pavement. We give heartfelt thanks for those whose time is devoted to others, and we pray God's blessing on those in need of temporary shelter, that their stories too may include a happy ending. Lord, have mercy.

SEASONAL SPECULATION

A Saviour has been born to you; he is the Messiah, the Lord. This will be a sign to you: You will find a baby wrapped in cloths and lying in a manger

(LUKE 2:11–12 **NIV**)

Was there a dog in stable stark and bare?
Was there a dog when Jesus Christ was there?
Who's to say no! Who knows who gathered then?
Was there a dog in Bethlehem's cattle pen?

Was there a dog who came to sniff the baby?
Do you know? No, me neither! A dog with God? Well, maybe.
A dog in straw? Or at the door? A dog asleep on barnyard floor?
Was there a dog in stable stark and bare?

I can't think why, on that first Christmas Day,
A curious dog would have to go away,
If sheep and cows were all allowed to stay,
And horses too, all clip-clop, wind and neigh;
A dog would bark his homage, wag hooray!

I hope a dog was present at the stall
To visit Jesus, infant King of all.
I hope a canine presence came
To woof a welcome and the Lord proclaim.

MORE OF THE SAME!

The Lord … will not grow tired or weary
(ISAIAH 40:28 **NIV**)

Our neighbours own a lovely old dog, Phoebe. Well, I say old – ancient would be nearer the truth. Phoebe is an adorable Golden Retriever, but it would be incorrect to describe her as energetic. I love Phoebe, but I have come to realize she is an affection junkie! If I bump into her owner when he is strolling along with Phoebe, and stop for a chat, Phoebe snuggles into my legs, nudging my knees with her head and asking to be stroked. Fair enough, but the problem comes when I need to conclude the conversation and move on! Phoebe nudges closer, and I am now convinced she would be perfectly content for me to stand there all day, stroking her head and tickling her under her chin … her appetite for tactile devotion knows no bounds!

I offer you, for our devotion today, the words of an old hymn. These speak for themselves, and I pray the blessing of our inexhaustible God on you as you read:

He giveth more grace as our burdens grow greater,
He sendeth more strength when our labours increase;
To added afflictions He addeth His mercy,
To multiplied trials, He multiplies peace.

When we have exhausted our store of endurance,
When our strength has failed ere the day is half done,
When we reach the end of our hoarded resources
Our Father's full giving is only begun.

Fear not that thy need shall exceed His provision,
Our God ever yearns His resources to share;
Lean hard on the arm everlasting, availing;
The Father both thee and thy load will upbear.

His love has no limits, His grace has no measure,
His power no boundary known unto men;
For out of His infinite riches in Jesus
He giveth, and giveth, and giveth again

(Annie J. Flint, 1866–1932)

COLLARED FOR CHRIST

Make holy garments for Aaron your brother and his sons, that he may minister as priest to Me

(EXODUS 28:4 **NASB**)

Does your minister wear a clerical collar? (If so, do you approve? If not, do you disapprove?) Also referred to as a "dog collar", the modern version of the essential fashion item for clergy was invented by the Reverend Donald McLeod, a Church of Scotland minister, as a practical variation on a theme dating back centuries, more suitable as "street dress" than other options. It has survived various abolition attempts, and (I think) serves a useful purpose in visibly distinguishing the wearer as a man or woman of God in a secular society. Each to their own, but I am sorry to learn that dog collars might now be under threat because of the increasing risk of violent attacks aimed at people easily identified as clergy. Indeed, discussions have taken place at Lambeth Palace, home of the Archbishop of Canterbury, as to whether or not Church of England priests should continue wearing collars in public (as opposed to in church, for services). Such instant identification is, in the mad world we now inhabit, risky, and might be phased out, for the sake of clergy safety, in favour of considered alternatives.

It's a fine line, isn't it? There is no particular logic in ministers and vicars unnecessarily putting their lives at risk, but a certain personal disappointment would accompany the abandonment of dog collars. I have to be careful, though, not to take a misty-eyed view of such matters, lest I forget what is really at stake. Am I perhaps hankering after nostalgic thoughts of what is actually a bygone England, where parsons cycle to church and films are still made in black and white? Could that account for my reluctance to see clerical collars disappear? If so, forasmuch as I would always bemoan any demise of the Church Visible, I must remind myself that such matters as ministerial apparel are hardly the point; it is my personal witness that counts, and if people see the marks of Jesus in me, then the rest is secondary. No dog collar need not equate to no secular awareness of a vibrant – though collarless – Church! Bottom line is, if my God is dependent on neckwear, then maybe I need to find another God!

MAÑANA

Renew a steadfast spirit within me
(PSALM 51:10 ***NIV***)

So, you've opened your Christmas present(s), you've been to church, you've watched one or two seasonal films, you've overdone the Christmas pudding/turkey/mince pies/Brussels sprouts, the relatives have been and gone/the relatives are still with you, and that yearning for a bit of fresh air is slowly dragging you away from the sofa ... Does any of that sound familiar? If so, may I gently encourage you to wrap up warm and take Fifi for a long walk? You'll thank me for it! It is commonly accepted that dog walking – even after holiday indulgences! – has umpteen health benefits; even a twenty-minute walk, five times a week, improves cardiovascular efficiency, lowers blood pressure, builds stronger bones and muscles, and decreases stress (handy, that last one, if your relatives are still *in situ*!). As if that isn't enough, allow me to offer a dollop of smugness to go with those dollops of cream that have been consumed – evidence shows that people who regularly walk dogs are 25 per cent less likely to be overweight than people without dogs! How about it? Hat, scarf, gloves, coat, leash, dog – off you go!

It's the getting going, isn't it! The resolve, the resolution, the starting, much more than it is the actual doing or the keeping going. What holds you back? The settee? The blank sheet of paper? The warm duvet? Procrastination appears in all shapes and forms; that human tendency to put things off until tomorrow. We all do it! God understands, but he won't get off our case! He knows how we are made, but he also believes in our potential, and it just so happens that he is the best Life Coach/Personal Motivator/Personal Trainer in the business! How about an End-of-Year Spiritual Resolution/Ambition/Target List? I'll do one if you will!

WATCH DOG

As Jesus was sitting on the Mount of Olives, the disciples came to him privately. "Tell us," they said, "when will this happen, and what will be the sign of your coming and of the end of the age?"

(MATTHEW 24:3 **NIV**)

Speaking of walkies, can your dog tell the time? Skipper could, so it seemed, almost to the minute, and I never did figure out how! For example, he would start to agitate (well, agitate more than usual!) whenever Alistair was due home from school at around 4 p.m. He would start "telling" me that Alistair would be home soon, even though I was already perfectly aware of that fact, then he would start to move towards the front door. He was unerringly right. Likewise, Skipper would unfailingly advise me – sometimes so energetically and annoyingly that I would need to put him out in the garden while I was putting my coat and shoes on! – when it was time for him to be taken for a walk. My memory might be playing tricks, but I don't honestly recall him ever being much more than a few minutes out. How do they do that? If Skipper was anything to go by, dogs appear to have some kind of inbuilt clock!

I read somewhere once about an old saint who said something like, "Lock me in a cell with just a candle and a Bible, and I will tell you everything that is taking place in the world outside." My apologies for not being able to remember the exact quote, or who said it, but you'll understand the point being made. Somehow, Skipper knew what time of day it was, despite only being a dog, and there is a similar knowledge to be had from reading the Bible, when it comes to discerning the times in which we live. It is not really necessary to watch the news on television or listen to radio bulletins, or read newspaper reports. They do, of course, provide specific details and fill in the blanks, but in general terms, the Bible has it covered, from beginning to end; ours is to read the script therein and correctly apply eternal truths to world events.

GIVING TO GOD

People and animals are in your care
(PSALM 36:6 **GNT**)

Rudyard Kipling was born on this day in 1865 (the same year, incidentally, in which The Salvation Army came into being!), so in honour of that great soul, I share one of his poems; which, as is often the case with Kipling's works, might also double as a prayer; bordering on the mawkish, perhaps, but this might be for you, today:

I wish someone had given Jesus a dog
As loyal and loving as mine
To sleep by His manger and gaze in His eyes
And adore Him for being divine.
As our Lord grew to manhood His faithful dog
Would have followed Him all through the day
While He preached to the crowds and made the sick well
And knelt in the garden to pray.
It is sad to remember that Christ went away
To face death alone and apart
With no tender dog following close behind
To comfort its Master's Heart.
And when Jesus rose on that Easter morn
How happy He would have been
As His dog kissed His hands and barked its delight
For The One who died for all men.
Well, the Lord has a dog now, I just sent Him mine
The old pal so dear to me
And I smile through my tears on this first day alone
Knowing they're in eternity.
Day after day, the whole day through
Wherever my road inclined
Four feet said, "I am coming with you!" And trotted along behind.[1]

---

1   www.pinterest.com (Attributed to Kipling, but he may not have written it.)

YEAR'S END

The Lord bless you and keep you; the Lord make his face shine on you and be gracious to you; the Lord turn his face towards you and give you peace

(NUMBERS 6:24–26 **NIV**)

Well, my friends, it has been an immense pleasure and a tremendous privilege to spend this year in your company. Thank you, very much, for allowing me to do so. I hope – and pray – that something you have read throughout these 365 days together will have spoken to you; words of blessing, perhaps, or comfort, or guidance, maybe even challenge. Doubtless, we shall disagree on some points, but that's OK, because overarching all of that is the love of God. Together, we will have made a few stabs at truths so deep and so rich that we shan't ever appreciate them until we meet in Heaven. Likewise, the stunning grace of a God who was dying to love us. I don't know much about God, about that vast ocean of mercy – or dogs, for that matter! – but I do know that Jesus (the God-man) died for me, and if he died for me, then he died for you too. May the lovely presence of God the Holy Spirit accompany you as you continue on your way. God bless you, and those you love and care for – and please, give your dog a treat and a stroke from me! S. J. P.

NOTES

NOTES

NOTES

NOTES

THROUGH THE YEAR WITH

Catherine Booth

365 daily readings from Catherine Booth,
founder of The Salvation Army

Catherine was both a woman and a fine preacher, a magnetic combination that attracted large numbers to hear her. This book of daily readings introduces us to Catherine's heart and convictions. Here we find the passion, urgency, thought and humanity which drove her on. Each devotional will take one page of the format above. Catherine's succinct, direct style is ideally suited to this form.

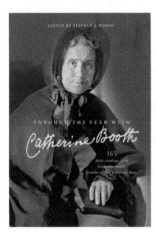

"Whatever one might think about her convictions there is no doubt whatsoever that both she and William were a formidable team in the fight against some of the evils present in this world. This book reveals something of her faith and belief. It would, I am sure, be her hope that as she was inspired by the teaching and life of Christ so others might also be encouraged in their pilgrimage."

–Terry Waite CBE

"If I could choose a person from history to ask about the essentials of life and ministry, I would choose Catherine Booth. A woman far ahead of her time, she blazed a trail and used her gifts in a way that still makes me wide eyed with wonder."

– Major Danielle Strickland

"I hope that, through this insightful book by Stephen Poxon, some may find inspiration from the life of this remarkable lady."

– Lord Foster of Bishop Auckland DL DCL

Hardback ISBN 978 0 85721 739 4 | Paperback ISBN 978 0 85721 889 6
e-ISBN 978 0 85721 740 0

THROUGH THE YEAR WITH

William Booth

365 daily readings from William Booth,
founder of The Salvation Army

*"Some talk of changing the world. Others actually do it. If there is a voice for our
day and our time, bringing social reform and spiritual passion together, it's William
Booth."*

– Major Danielle Strickland

William Booth – pawnbroker's assistant, firebrand
preacher, advocate of women's rights, friend of the poor,
confidant of statesmen, politicians and royalty, father
of eight children, champion of the marginalised, and
founder and first General of The Salvation Army. General
Booth's courage, oratory, and passion changed Victorian
Britain. He resolutely ignored his critics – including those
who decried him as the Anti-Christ – and reached out
to those who considered themselves well outside the
concern of Almighty God. Prayer and practicality were
his hallmarks: he ridiculed the idea of preaching to a
beggar while that beggar was cold and hungry. William
Booth worked tirelessly, campaigning, researching,
negotiating, adapting music-hall songs – and writing. This book introduces us to his heart
and convictions. Here we find the urgency, thought, and humanity which drove him on.

*"A glorious treasure trove of daily readings from the pen of William Booth ...
a superb anthology of devotional gems."*

– Jonathan Aitken

*"William Booth was first of all a preacher and a student of the Bible. Stephen Poxon
has quite brilliantly linked William's words to Scripture."*

– Colonel Bramwell Booth

Hardback ISBN 978 0 85721 614 4 | Paperback ISBN 978 085721 890 2
eISBN 978 0 85721 615 1

Lightning Source UK Ltd.
Milton Keynes UK
UKHW02n1016190718
325963UK00003B/24/P